MEMOIRS OF INDIA

MEMOIRS OF INDIA:

COMPRISING
A BRIEF GEOGRAPHICAL ACCOUNT
OF

THE EAST INDIES;

A
SUCCINCT HISTORY OF HINDOSTAN,
FROM THE MOST EARLY AGES,
TO THE END OF
THE MARQUIS OF HASTINGS' ADMINISTRATION
IN 1823.
DESIGNED FOR
THE USE OF YOUNG MEN GOING OUT TO INDIA.

R. G. WALLACE, ESQ.

GYAN

Published by

GYAN

Gyan Publishing House
5, Ansari Road
Daryaganj, New Delhi-110002
Phone: 011-47034999, 9811692060
E-mail: books@gyanbooks.com

Distribution Network
gyanbooks.com
India, USA, Canada, UK, Australia, France

ISBN: 978-81-212-8362-5 (PB)
First Published, 1824

2nd Impression 2023

Printed at: Gyan Press, Delhi.

MEMOIRS OF INDIA
Author: R. G. WALLACE

MEMOIRS OF INDIA:

COMPRISING

A BRIEF GEOGRAPHICAL ACCOUNT

OF

The East Indies;

A

SUCCINCT HISTORY OF HINDOSTAN,

FROM THE MOST EARLY AGES,

TO THE END OF

THE MARQUIS OF HASTINGS' ADMINISTRATION IN 1823.

DESIGNED FOR

THE USE OF YOUNG MEN GOING OUT TO INDIA.

By R. G. WALLACE, Esq.

AUTHOR OF "FIFTEEN YEARS IN INDIA."

Forsan hæc olim meminisse juvabit. VIRGIL.

LONDON:

PRINTED FOR

LONGMAN, HURST, REES, ORME, BROWN, AND GREEN,

PATERNOSTER-ROW.

1824.

TO

THE MOST NOBLE

THE MARQUIS OF HASTINGS,

&c. &c. &c.

AS A SMALL TOKEN OF SINCERE GRATITUDE

AND ADMIRATION,

THIS EFFORT OF MY PEN

IS INSCRIBED,

WITH

THE GREATEST RESPECT.

PREFACE.

THE Author of this work spent a great part of his life in India. In the year 1805 he had opportunities of seeing Madras and part of the Carnatic. He served a few years in Mysore and Malabar. From 1810 till 1813 he was in Bengal, &c. In the beginning of 1814 he was at Bombay; soon after he marched with the 65th regiment for Guzerat, and spent some time on the frontiers of Scindea's dominions. The force to which he belonged invaded Cutch-Booge in 1816, and attacked the pirates in Okamundel. In 1817 he was in the Deccan, where he served till the termination of the last Mahratta war. For several years he held a staff situation, which increased his opportunities of personal observation.

He had often to regret the want of such a work as he now presents to the public. On every favourable occasion he laid up materials for this undertaking; and since his return home, he has been engaged in digesting the whole into the contents of this volume. A considerable part of his labour, however, does not appear. This consisted in a pair of maps, and a set of drawings, intended to illustrate his book; but finding that their publication would enhance the price too much, he has consigned them to oblivion. In revising his manuscript, he threw into an Appendix some Notes, which he thinks will be useful to the reader; and in going over the whole again with care, he has given in an Addenda such matter as he further conceived to be interesting. He is, therefore, conscious of having bestowed much pains on this production of his pen.

Some authors have complained of a want of public interest respecting the affairs of India; or rather that their books were unfortunate in not passing rapidly from the shelves of their publishers to those of our numerous libraries and reading societies. He hopes, however, that there is a great increase of curiosity respecting India.

Hindostan in ancient and modern times presents an interesting spectacle to both the Christian and philosopher. If memory recurs to those pages of history which describe commerce, it will be found that struggles between rival states for the spices, gems, and silks of the East, occasioned the discovery of America, and the expansion of civilisation in Europe, after barbarism and priestcraft had sunk the noble remains of liberty and science in darkness. Let observation be directed to the modern state of that extensive region of Asia, and it will occur to the contemplative mind, that there must be something extraordinary in institutions which have withstood the sword of conquest and the persuasive force of Christianity, while their enfeebling effect has been so great upon the inhabitants, that from the fabulous invasion of Bacchus to the real possession of Hindostan by an English company of merchants, every invader has found the natives unable to oppose vigorous encroachment.

In short, a spirited individual *, only a few years ago, deemed the pursuit of research so important, as to merit the devotion of a considerable sum from his moderate fortune, which he offered as a reward for the best essays on the most likely means of civilising the natives, and of diffusing the light of the Christian religion through the Eastern world.

Whatever an author's motive for writing may be, he should aim at promoting the interests of morality and religion; so that public utility may be obviously paramount to all other objects. Such is the sentiment of the writer of the following pages. What he has attempted to accomplish may be described in a single sentence.

He has endeavoured to abridge much that has been written on India; and to speak of what he himself saw, felt, and thought whilst in that country,

* The Rev. Dr. Buchanan.

as a plain soldier and an unprejudiced gentleman, anxious for the interest of truth and the welfare of his native land.

To assume that he has successfully executed his task would be presumptuous; but he has assiduously laboured not to mislead. To the justice and judgment of a discerning public he submits his work with respectful deference, humbly saying to all in the beautiful language of the Roman poet—

> Vive, vale: si quid novisti rectius istis,
> Candidus imperti; si non, his utere mecum.
>
> *Horace*, lib. i. epist. 6.

This work will be found divided into three books, of a geographical, historical, and miscellaneous description; and each book, into chapters, or subjects, according to the natural sections which the matter suggests; followed by a copious Index.

ADVERTISEMENT.

It was intended that a map should accompany this work, containing the name of every place mentioned in it. In attempting, however, to make one upon a scale suitable to an octavo volume, the Author found it would be too crowded for easy reference. The best map he could give would be more ornamental to the book than useful to the reader; and the expense of this work would be so much increased by a geographical sketch of the extensive regions he describes, that in abandoning the idea of adding a map, he is confident he has consulted the best interest of the public. Arrowsmith's new map of Hindostan is now in general circulation; to it he refers the reader for the interior of India; and reference to any of the common geographical delineations of the globe will be sufficient in all other respects.

CONTENTS.

BOOK I.

MEMOIRS OF INDIA.

BOOK I.

India is divided into three distinct parts by the hand of nature. Hindostan Proper extends from the Himalaya, or region of eternal snow, to the river Nerbudda, which falls into the Gulf of Cambay, nearly in a latitudinal line with the mouths of the Ganges. The Deccan is all that space from the Nerbudda to the river Krishna, which springs not far from the western shore and flows into the Bay of Bengal. All the rest of India thence to the island of Ceylon is called the Peninsula; whose table land is propped up by that amazing wall of granite the ghauts, which, on the south-western quarter, rise so high above the clouds, that while storm howls on one side, zephyr reposes in perfect security on the other.

There is hardly a place in this vast region that bears the name it did in the days of Alexander the Great. Many of those cities, which were then objects of wonder, have passed away under the mouldering pressure of time. Others of more modern structure are now in heaps of ruins. They serve but as fleeting monuments to instruct mankind respecting the instability of human grandeur. Such questions, therefore, as whether Palibothra were the modern Allahabad or Patna; or whether the island described under the name of Taprobana be Ceylon or Sumatra, seem of little use in the present age. The discrepancy proves that the ancients had a very confused knowledge of Hindostan; and it must be confessed that its geography is as yet very imperfect. Those parts which have been accurately surveyed are laid down in Arrowsmith's four sheet map tolerably well. But many others are only approximations from the reports made by native observers.

The inhabitants of all those countries known by the names of Baloochistan, Afghanistan, Cabul, &c., which lie westward of the river Indus, may be called with propriety Indo-Persians; and all those who occupy the regions east of the Tiperah wilds, which bound Bengal, under the names of Arracan, Assam, Ava, the Birman Empire, Siam, Pegu, Tunquin, Cambodia, Laos, &c., may with equal correctness be called Indo-Chinese. Northward of the great mountains called the Himalaya range, which are covered with eternal snow, the inhabitants are of the Tartar race; and in the islands of Ceylon, Sumatra, Java, the Sunda Chain, Bornes, Celebes, the Moluccas, the Philippines, &c., which gem the Indian Ocean, the natives are a mixed people, assimilating to the aborigines of the continents near them.

In order to systematise as much as possible this brief geographical description of India, it is intended in the first place to travel round the outline of our sketch.

CHAPTER I.

GEOGRAPHICAL OUTLINE OF INDIA.

LITTLE was known respecting those countries which lie between the river Indus and Persia, till Captain Christie and Mr. Pottinger undertook to travel through Baloochistan, disguised as Mussulman horse-dealers. After a journey of fifteen hundred miles from the mouth of that great river, they joined Sir John Malcolm, at the Persian court.

In all their course they found Hindoos, and monuments of the Brahmanical institutions; but the mass of the inhabitants are Moslems of the same origin perhaps as the Afghans and Sinds, and probably descendants from the Tartars, who, according to Chinese historians, invaded the kingdom of Bactria, so long subject to the successors of Alexander. The Baloochees are governed by petty chiefs; some of whom live by plunder.

The king of Cabul claims their obedience as sovereign; but, owing to the distracted state of that kingdom, every chieftain now acknowledges no power but that of the sword. These chiefs are at eternal war with each other. We accordingly find, that the high feelings generated by feuds prevail among them. Like the Highlanders of Scotland, they are proud, hospitable, and brave; but much addicted to debauch, and depraved in their morals. They swear by their beards, constantly go armed, and resent personal affronts with great spirit.

Baloochistan is by nature a strong rugged country; exceedingly cold in winter, but so intensely hot in summer, that the most burning wind known in the world is generated in it, under the name of Badé Sumoom. Its approaches are indicated to the natives by an unusual closeness of the atmosphere. Its dangerous effects, however, may be shunned by covering the body with even a very thin cloth, and lying prostrate till the fiery fluid passes; but should this precaution not be taken, says Mr. Pottinger, "the muscles of the unhappy sufferer become rigid and contracted, the skin shrivels, an agonizing sensation, as if the flesh was on fire, pervades the whole frame, and in the last stage it cracks into deep gashes, producing hemorrhage, that quickly ends this misery." Deserts and barren sands abound; but the fertile parts produce wheat, rice and pulses in abundance, together with sugar and several drugs for exportation. In traversing some of the wilds, Mr. Pottinger has described distress from thirst with much strength of feeling. "The shrab, or water of the desert," says he, "floated around us, as though it were mocking our distress, by its delusive representation of what we so eagerly thirsted for, the absence of which, I can affirm with perfect confidence, from my individual experience, to be the most insupportable of all the wants of what are termed the absolute necessaries of life. A person may endure, with patience and hope, the pressure of fatigue or hunger, heat or cold, and even a total deprivation of natural rest for a considerable length of time; but to be scorched under a burning sun, to feel your throat so parched and dry that you respire with difficulty, to dread moving your tongue in your mouth from the apprehension of suffocation which it causes, and not to have the means of allaying those dreadful sensations, are, in my ideas, the extreme pitch of a traveller's calamities."

Both banks of the Indus for a considerable way are inhabited by Sinds, under the government of two chiefs called Meers, who, though tributaries to the king of Cabul, now hardly acknowledge any subjection. The Sinds are distinguished from the Baloochees, who wear turbans, gowns, and trowsers, in little but their head-dress, which is a cap something like the crown of our hat fancifully embroidered round the lower edge. A similar cap is worn by the females; some of whom are very beautiful. At Hyderabad, which is the capital, the artificers are very skilful in working iron and gold; and in many parts of the country there are monuments, which indicate the superior prosperity of the whole at some remote period. The small province of Tatta, now part of this region, is the Delta of the Indus. It is in many parts susceptible of the highest state of cultivation. A great deal of it is now a desert, which in former times was a perfect garden. Near the capital, which is named from the province, there are prodigious numbers of graves and mausoleums; one of which over the tomb of Mirza Eesau is uncommonly magnificent. Tatta is built upon the ruins of the ancient Brahmanabad, which in old times was called Pattala by the Greeks; but there is scarcely a trace now of the 1400 bastions, which Abul Fazel described it to have had.

The river Indus, in a fine course of more than 1350 miles, fertilizes the whole country, and produces the same effects as the Nile. Some of the tributary branches of the Indus are equal to the largest rivers in Europe. The Hydaspes, Hydraotes and Hysudrus are as large as the Rhone. The Hyphases, forty miles longer than the Elbe, and nearly all the inferior branches as noble as the Thames.*

* Vide Mr. Elphinstone's account of Cabul.

Throughout Afghanistan, Hindoos are numerous. They are in fact found in considerable numbers as far as Astracan, and even in Arabia and the northern parts of Persia; where the love of gain induces them to reside, though held in a state of degradation, and only tolerated on account of the increase of revenue which their industry and taxation produce. The Afghans enjoy a considerable share of liberty, and have a sort of political constitution, that inspires an ardent thirst for glory and independence. Love is cultivated among this gallant race of men with much refinement; and the power the fair sex has, is so great, that, if a lady of rank sends a chief her veil, he feels himself bound by honour to espouse her quarrel, though the destruction of him and his tribe should follow. Ghizni, the ancient celebrated capital of this country, was situated on a hill in the province of Cabul. Its magnificent structures have scarcely left a wreck behind, to mark their passage down the flood of time; but pilgrimages are still made to the tombs of saints buried near it, of such sanctity that the Mohammedans call Ghizni the second Medina. For four centuries this was the seat of a mighty empire. Sultan Mahmood, the conqueror of India, ornamented it with noble edifices, the shapeless masses of whose ruins can now scarcely be traced. In A. D. 1171, the Ghizni empire ceased, having been conquered and subverted by Mahomed Ghori.

Cabul may be said to extend to the great northern mountains*; the lower ranges of which are inhabited by a wild race of men, who occupy all the valleys of Caffristan, from its western border to Cashmere, so justly celebrated for its manufacture of beautiful shawls. The wool, of which these shawls are made, is brought from Tibet. It is the inside coat or down of sheep peculiar to that mountainous region. The wool is at first of a dark grey colour, but being bleached, it becomes a beautiful white, and takes the various dyes readily when spun. It is a curious fact, that the borders are attached to the shawls after fabrication, so delicately, that no eye can detect the place of junction. To make a shawl of a fine description is very tedious.† The coarsest ones from the loom fetch about a pound sterling, but the finest sometimes sell for 100*l.* each. Lambs' skins, of the Tibet sheep, are so highly esteemed, that the dams are often killed before yeaning, on purpose to have the skin of a more delicate texture than after its exposure to the air. The valley of Cashmere‡ has been celebrated from the most early times for its beauty. Nothing can exceed its romantic advantages from nature, of which Bernier has given a fine description. It is all holy ground to the Hindoos, every part of it being dedicated to some god. In the centre of a

* Vide Addenda, No. I.

† Vide Addenda, No. II.

‡ Vide Addenda, No. III.

plain near the lake of Cashmere, studded with little isles, were the gardens and pavilions of the Mogul emperors, called, after those of Delhi, Shalimar. Thither the nobles made annual visits, to feast on the charms of this lovely valley, and to choose wives from among the beautiful girls of Cashmere; whose delicacy of complexion and symmetry of form were only surpassed by the elegant turn of their minds, the liveliness of their dispositions, and the sweetness of their tempers. Abul Fazel says there were no fewer than twenty-six roads out of this province into Hindostan.

The exports of Cabul consist of horses, poneys, furs, shawls, Mooltan chintzes, madder, assafœtida, tobacco, almonds, pistachio nuts, hazel nuts, and fruit; among which are many of those common to Europe; for the climate about Perishwar is almost like that of England, and in winter very bracing, though it seldom freezes hard below the Himalaya range. Their imports from India consist of cotton, muslins, silks, and brocade, indigo, ivory, chalk, bamboo, wax, tin, sandal wood, sugar, broad cloth, musk, coral, and drugs and spices of all kinds. The king of Cabul is not now very powerful, for his authority has for a long time been feebly supported; but one of his ancestors, Ahmid Shah Abdalli, was so much so, that he decided the fate of India, which was upon the point of being at the disposal of the Mahrattas. Abdalli entered Hindostan with about 80,000 fighting men, and eighty pieces of cannon, in the year 1760, and on the 7th of January following the famous battle of Panniput took place. The Mahrattas had a camp, it is said, of 500,000 men, and 200 pieces of cannon; all of which were taken, and the greatest part of their army put to the sword, on the same spot where Sultan Baber had destroyed the power of the emperor Ibrahim Lodi in 1525. Mooltan, Lahore, and a great part of the Punjab, belonged to Cabul in its flourishing state, but upon its decline the Seiks rose, and they now possess nearly all those provinces.

Perhaps in no part of the world is there a grander display of the sublime than along the Himalaya. The higher ridges of the mountains are seen in the distance clothed up to the snowy regions, with fir and oak; and the cataracts formed by the flow of water from melted snow, give an indescribable grandeur to the scene. The valleys, in the lowest ridges, are inhabited by a rude and savage race, clothed in the skins of wild beasts, and a coarse stuff manufactured from the long hair of their goats. They have but imperfect notions of God, and drink to excess of an intoxicating liquor produced from grain.

Beyond these mountains lie the extensive and dreary regions of Tibet, extending from the sources of the Indus and Ganges to the confines of China, 1600 miles in length, and in breadth from Hindostan to the great desert of Cobi. The elevation of this country is such, that the cold is almost insupportable, and under its influence, vegetation is parched, as if by extreme heat. Many of the great rivers of China and India have their sources in the Himalaya mountains, whose altitude, above the plains of Bengal, is in some places more than four English miles. The ways of Providence are wonderful. In this region, which one would suppose unfriendly to animal life, it abounds to an amazing degree. The whole atmosphere swarms with wild fowl and game, while the woods are filled with beasts, and the plains covered with herds and flocks innumerable. Among these are the yak or bushy-tailed cow, covered all over with very long hair, the musk deer, resembling a hog, and the shawl goat. The latter is very small, with straight horns, and covered with coarse long hair, under which is found the glossy substance manufactured into shawls in Cashmere. Gold is found here in great quantities, and very pure, with which the natives, who are numerous, purchase warm clothing, and buy up English broad cloth with great eagerness. The higher classes dress in rich furs, and the poorer sort in the skins of beasts and coarse woollens; but they all wear a prodigious weight of clothing, and very thick boots. At one time, the Brahmanical institutions prevailed all over this country, but the inhabitants are now Budhists, acknowledging an incarnation in the person of their high priest; but they make pilgrimages to Juggernaut *, and hold Benares in the greatest reverence, as the original seat of the arts and sciences. The most remarkable custom here, is, that the women have several husbands, there being seldom more than one wife to a whole family of brothers; the eldest of whom has the privilege of choosing; but immediately after she becomes the joint property of the whole, and confers her favours upon them by turns. Something like this is practised among the Nairs of Malabar, which shall be noticed in its proper place. All civil power in Tibet is derived from the great Lama, and he has several populous towns and strong forts.

It is now well ascertained that the Ganges flows from under an eternally hard mass of snow, a few miles beyond the village of Gangotra, where fancy has given to its source the shape of a cow's mouth; but it is, in fact, an aperture in the ice. To this sacred spot Hindoo pilgrims repair from all parts of India; and it is considered such an exertion of love to God, that its performance is believed to redeem from troubles in this world and the next. Indeed, this trial of Hindoo faith is almost superhuman; for the way to Gangotra lies for several days' journey over mountains almost perpendicular, the footpath winding along their sides with a precipice of two thousand feet immediately below,

* Vide Appendix, note 1.

and projecting rocks directly in many places over head, with hardly a resting place for the foot, so that a false step is certain destruction. But this is not all; they have to cross swinging bridges of rope or cane, over frightful torrents; and a shivering creature from the island of Ceylon, almost under the line, clothed in a thin cotton robe, has to encounter transitions of climate in the same day, which a Russian could scarcely endure. Hundreds, nay, perhaps thousands of them, perish every year in this enterprize, and the bottoms of the precipices are white with their bones. In short, some idea may be entertained of the almost insurmountable obstacles on the near approach to Gangotra by the reader, when he recollects that Captain Raper and Lieutenant Webb, sent by Government to explore the sources of the Ganges, found the difficulties so unconquerable on getting near that place, that they were obliged to abandon their purpose, though provided with every requisite that unlimited expenditure could procure. *

The greatest fair in all India is held at Hurdwarra, where the Ganges enters the plains of Bengal. Here the pilgrims to the five sacred junctions, mentioned in the Sastras, assemble; and as they combine commercial speculations with devotion, every one brings or takes something. Two

* Vide Asiatic Researches, vol. xi. where Captain Raper's Journal will be found.

millions of souls annually congregate at this place for purposes of traffic, pilgrimage, and profit. Here are exposed for sale, horses, mules, camels, tobacco, antimony, assafœtida, dried fruits; such as apricots, figs, apples, pears, prunes, raisins, almonds, nuts, and pomegranates; shawls, stuffs, blankets, turbans, looking-glasses, and toys in ivory and brass; shields, bows and arrows, rock salt, piece-goods, English broad cloth, muslins, sarcenets, cocoa-nuts; with slaves brought down from the hills, many hundreds of whom are sold, from three to thirty years of age, at the rate of from 1*l.* 5*s.* to 18*l.* 2*s.** each.

This prodigious mass, collected from various parts of Asia, and speaking different tongues, would be in the situation of the children of Noah at the tower of Babel, were it not that there is a general language of the fingers known and studied throughout Hindostan; which enables the seller and the buyer perfectly to understand each other. This mode of making bargains is common at every fair in the country. A purchaser goes up to a seller, and narrowly examines a camel, or whatever he wants. The person to whom it belongs makes him an enquiring nod, which is answered by a positive shrug, and they join their right hands, over which a part of their muslin robe or cotton dress is thrown, to conceal their operations from inquisitive eyes.

* Vide Captain Raper's Journal.

Then follows a most animated scene of gesticulation, which is conducted with patience and gravity; but when two experienced men meet, a bargain is concluded in a few seconds, and the price, fixed by the fingers and eyes, in general so perfectly intelligible, that disputes seldom occur.

Numbers of Fakiers, or rather Sanyassees, for the former word signifies a devotee of the Mohammedan creed, and the latter, one of the Brahmanical, assemble at this fair, to extort money under various pretences; some by torturing their bodies, and others by displays of buffoonery. There are four principal sects — Gosains, Bairagis, Jogis, and Udasis. The Gosains worship Seeva, and generally go naked, with a string of beads round the neck, their bodies frightfully painted, and armed often with sharp two-edged swords. Vishnu receives the adoration of the Bairagis, who are distinguished by peculiar stripes of yellow ochre *, or sandal wood ashes, on the forehead. The Jogis are followers of Seeva, but differ in some things from the Gosains, and are known by large slits in their ears, to which they hang various substances. They and the Gosains bury their dead, which is a custom very extraordinary in Hindostan, where burning is the general mode. Nanac, the founder of the Seiks, is the great object of respect with the

* For these distinctions, vide Asiatic Researches, vol. xi. Raper's Journal.

Udasis, who are easily distinguished, by wearing a conical cap, with a fringe. These four sects consider each other heterodox, and sometimes have sanguinary battles. In an engagement once at this fair between the Gosains and Bairagis, the latter left 18,000 dead on the field, and the former, who were victorious, nearly as many, having fought hand to hand, and foot to foot, with the broad-sword and target, for a whole day. *

From Hurdwarra to the sources of the Ganges, are temples of great antiquity, one of which, called Raghunaut, is said by the Brahmans to have existed 10,000 years. At some of these, the most disgusting scenes of moral depravity are practised, almost in open day. Captain Raper says, in speaking of the village of Rami Haut, "It is inhabited by dancing women; and the ceremony of initiation to this society consists in anointing the head with oil, taken from the lamp placed before the altar; by which act they make a formal abjuration of their parents and kindred, devoting their future lives to prostitution. A short distance beyond it, is a math or fane of 'the god of love.' The high-priest of Badrinaut was in a miserable state from the wounds of the deity, although he and all his Brahmans had taken a vow of eternal chastity. When he applied for relief, he significantly attributed his state to a certain something

* Vide Appendix, note 2.

which he did not pretend properly to understand, called by him "*a rarefaction of the atmosphere.*" His dress was a quilted vest, of green satin, with white shawl girdle, red turban, party-coloured socks, and gold earrings, with pearl pendants; triple rows of pearls formed his necklace, bracelets of precious stones ornamented his arms, and rings, sparkling with gems, glittered on his fingers. The great idol of the temple, during the season of pilgrimage, has a superb table laid at two o'clock, and his velvet couch is spread every night; but in the inclement part of the year he is shut up, and left to starve, while the high priest and his sensual Brahmans retire to a more congenial climate, to enjoy their dancing girls.

The surrounding mountains contain many natural curiosities; hot and cold springs; water-falls from projecting ledges of snowy hills, rolling in shower baths over precipices; lead and copper mines; and such frequent earthquakes occur, that nearly all the temples have been shattered. Some of the shrubs, plants, and trees of Europe are seen here; the hazel and briar, the fir and oak, and the strawberry, bloom in the valleys, and climb up the hills till lost in snow. But a custom prevails among the inhabitants not less interesting than many other things, and this is the human sacrifice they offer to the offended spirit of the great mountain after a bad harvest, by hurling a man from the top of a precipice, nearly a mile high, down a rope made fast above and below. If he have the dexterity to balance himself so as to reach the bottom unhurt, a great reward awaits him; but should he fall, and any life remain in him, his head is immediately severed from his body. *

Nepaul lies in the north-east of Hindostan. It may be said to occupy the whole of that quarter from the river Sutleje to Bootan, being a distance of about 700 miles, but its average breadth does not exceed 100, and it all lies between the latitudes 27° and 32°. It is one of the most mountainous regions in the world; the lower hills and valleys only being inhabited; so that by calculation its cultivated area does not exceed ten millions of acres, and its population may be estimated at two millions of souls. The district properly called Nepaul, is of small extent: it in fact consists of little more than a beautiful oval valley twelve miles long, and nine broad, watered by the Bhagmutty and Bishenmutty rivers. On one side of the Bishenmutty stands the capital called Catmandoo, and on the other the ancient city of Pattan. For several centuries this lovely spot was governed by its own rajahs, but in the year 1768 it was invaded and conquered by Parthi Narrain, the rajah of Goorca, who afterwards removed the seat of his government to Catmandoo, which is now the

* This is given on the authority of Captain Raper and Lieutenant Webb, who witnessed the ceremony. Vide Asiatic Researches, vol. xi.

metropolis of the whole Nepaulese territories. For a considerable time before, the Goorcas had been famous as warriors, belonging in general to the Khetri sect. Their rajah claims descent from the same origin as Sevagee, whose family is allowed to be very ancient. This warlike people soon conquered all the neighbouring provinces, seventeen in number, and forced the numerous rajahs to become tributary to theirs, who is now despotic sovereign of this extensive region.

Being forsaken by the principal families, who followed their rajah to Catmandoo, Goorca is now in a state of decay. It is famous for rock crystal, of which there is a great abundance near it. Many of the small provinces that compose the kingdom of Nepaul deserve but little notice. Mocwanpore is remarkable for containing a very strong fort, situated on the summit of a mountain, to which, when sore pressed by an enemy, the Goorcas send their families and treasure. This was the case when Nepaul was invaded by the Chinese Tartars. It is so very strong that Cossim Aly's Armenian general, Goorgeen Khan, besieged it during nearly the whole of the year 1762, in vain. Kemaoon is one of the most fertile provinces, containing several fine valleys. Almora is also a productive district. The tree called phulwarah, the nuts of which contain a vast quantity of fat, is found on its hills. This province is watered by the river Causila, which is deep and broad; and there being no bridge, it is crossed in a curious manner by means of large gourds, several of which are made fast to the waist of an excellent swimmer, many of whom attend at proper stations. The passenger has only to hold fast by his guide's girdle, and he is ferried over with safety. Almora, the capital of this district, is seated on the top of a mountain. Serinagur is another large province intersected by extraordinary chains of hills, and covered with forests of oak, holly, horse-chesnut, and fir: it has a very strong hill fort called Sangur, which resisted the Nepaulese, who besieged it for twelve months, about the year 1791. This was their first attempt to conquer the country, but it was not effected till 1803. An army of 10,000 men then entered it; and a furious battle was fought near Gurudwarra, where the Serinagur rajah was slain by a musket ball, his forces routed, and his country became the prey of the victor. The valley, in the centre of which Serinagur stands, is three miles in diameter, watered by the Alcananda, a fine broad river, which is crossed near the town by a bridge of rope thrown across a narrow part, eighty feet wide, where the rush of water has cut a passage for itself through a mountain. Here the houses are well built of stone, two stories high, and slated; but the streets are narrow; and with the exception of several curious pagodas, the rajah's house is the only remarkable edifice, being built of coarse granite to the height of four stories.

These mountainous regions are covered with deep forests in many places of Saul or Sissoo; in others they are barren: the elephant abounds, but he is here of a small breed; peacocks and pheasants are in great numbers; mines of copper, iron, and lead, are here in inexhaustible plenty, as well as fine marble; and the sand of the rivers, when washed, yields a considerable quantity of gold. The principal food of the inhabitants is wheaten bread, peas, rice, pulses, and vegetables, with such seasoning of animal food and curries as are permitted by the rules of their castes. All the country is subject to a sort of military government. The power of the Goorcas is absolute, the subject having no protection but that of the great council of state, called Punjunni, which consists of the ministers and such chiefs as the rajah nominates. By the decree of this tribunal, any subject may be deprived of life and land; but except on particular occasions the administration of criminal and civil laws is according to the Dharma Sastra, which is an ancient code founded in equity. In some cases, however, the mode of punishment is by levying a fine on the district where the offence has been committed, and in default of payment, the offender and family are seized. Nepaul has to its north the lofty Himalaya, covered with eternal snow. Though this range of mountains be forty miles from Catmandoo, yet its immense height (peaks of it being more than 22,000 feet above the sea) causes it to appear as if hanging over the town, to a spectator who stands at a little distance south of the city. Eastward the mountains are inhabited by barbarous tribes called Kyrauts, Hawoos, and Limbooas. The Company's territories nearly embrace it on the other sides. Its chief towns are, besides Catmandoo and Pattan, Goorca, Bhatgong, Jemlah, Olmira, and Serinagur. The capital is said to contain 50,000 souls, and with its suburbs, or immediate dependencies, a population of 168,000. Bhatgong is situated eight miles from Catmandoo: it is embellished with some fine pagodas, excellent houses built of bricks, and it has a palace which was once a magnificent pile. It is the Benares of the Goorcas, and great numbers of Brahmans reside here, who say the town resembles the guitar of Mahadeva for its beauty and harmony. The Bhagmutty and Bishenmutty rivers, by which this fine valley is watered, have their source in the gigantic mountain of Sivapuri. From a high hill called Chandiaghiri, the valley, said to contain half a million of souls, looks lovely; being thickly studded with villages, and laid out in fine plantations of sugar cane, and irrigated by numerous silver streams. The Brahmans say that this valley was once a lake. Its climate is that of the south of Europe, which is given by its elevation of about 4000 feet above the sea. The seasons are nearly the same as in other parts of India, but it has the monsoon earlier, and frequent showers. In three or four days' journey up the mountains, a man may here change the heat of Bengal for the cold of Russia; and our officers and soldiers are as much benefited, when invalids from relaxation, by being sent up above the clouds of Nepaul, as they would by being sent to the north of Europe. The soil is cultivated by the Newars, who live in the valleys. The people of the hills are called Parbutties; the other classes are Brahmans, Khetris, and Rajpoots. There are not many Mohammedans in Nepaul. There are generally three harvests or crops in the year; one of wheat, one of fine rice, and one of coarse rice, or pulse or vegetables. The capital, Catmandoo, is only remarkable for its great number of wooden pagodas; its streets are narrow, and the houses are built of bricks, which are uncommonly good, all over Nepaul, to the height of four stories, and covered with tiles. It extends along the river Bishenmutty about a mile, but it is no where more than half its length in depth. In cultivating this valley spade husbandry is preferred to the plough, and the women perform a great part of the labour. All the fruits and vegetables of India grow here, with many of those belonging to Europe. There is a great variety of game. They have very few manufacturers, although expert in working copper, brass, and wood. It is wonderful how they accomplish some of their undertakings with their tools, which are of the very worst description. It is said that the revenue does not amount to more than thirty lacks of rupees per annum, being only 375,000*l.*; but the government requires little for current expenditure, the civil and military establishments being provided for by assignments of land, and the whole territories let out in jaghires. All the coins current in Hindostan pass in Nepaul; but the currency of their own mint is a silver piece worth fourteen-pence, called a sicca, with several copper ones, the lowest of which is the 280th part of a sicca. The regular forces are clothed with English broad cloth, and armed with muskets and bayonets; but their irregulars have bows and arrows, matchlocks and hatchet swords. Their peace establishment may be about 10,000 men, but they can bring a very large army into the field on occasions of emergency; for when their war-standard, which is yellow, with the figure of Hanuman, the Munkey deity, on it, is unfurled, the chiefs flock to it with enthusiasm, war being their delight and vocation. The Nepaulese were never subdued by the Mohammedan invaders of India. This may account for their purity in many respects, and strict conformity to the Brahmanical institutions; yet it is extraordinary that buffaloes are here offered as sacrifices to Bhavani, and the Newars feed on the flesh. Bravery is the distinguishing trait in the high castes of Nepaul. The men are therefore open and candid, with a military simplicity of character. The Newars, or peasantry of the country, are of the middle size, well built, with strong limbs and broad shoulders, round faces, and small eyes. Their countenances are cheerful, and many of the women sprightly and pretty; all fond of ornaments; and, like the Nair fair ones of Malabar, they may have several husbands, it being lawful for them to divorce at pleasure. Their complexion is between a sallow and a copper colour. The vernacular languages are Parbutti, Newar, Dhenwar, Muggur, Kyraut, Hoovoo, Limboa, and Bhootea; but the Brahmans study Sanscrit and several of its ramifications.

The restrictions and monopolies under which commerce labours, have never enabled the merchants of Nepaul to compete with the neighbouring states. Their trade is confined generally to an annual intercourse with Tibet and Bootan. Caravans start, when the summer begins to melt the snow in the passes through the mountains, with grain, treacle, oil, sugar, cotton, chintz, iron, brass, lead, woollens, pearls, corals, cowries, or small shells that pass for money, dates and almonds, and return with salt, saffron, borax, dried grapes, gold-dust, cow-tails, musk, blankets, bezoar, porcelain, hill poneys, sheep with six horns, the cow of Tartary, called yak, dogs, shawl wool, and tea. No other animal can be used in passing these mountains for carriage but goats and sheep. These are not of the species with large tails, so common to the westward, but a small breed, possessed of great strength and activity. Small bags are tied on their backs, and a ram with a bell leads the flock, which generally consists of from 50 to about 200, followed by a couple of shepherds and their dogs. These sure-footed creatures pass over precipices with their small burdens which no human foot could traverse, and find vegetation among the crags sufficient for their wants.

Like all other countries, the history of the valley of Nepaul is involved in obscurity. The Brahmans of Bhatgong have lists of princes that reigned over it from times antecedent to our creation of the world; but nothing authentic is known till A. D. 1323, when Hur Sing Deo, rajah of Semrounghur, a descendant of the Surya Vansa, princes of Oude, conquered it. Under his posterity, Nepaul Proper continued till 1768, when it was entered by the victorious Parthi Narrain, rajah of Goorca. Runjeet Mull, of Bhatgong, the reigning prince, was beaten in a pitched battle, and he died some time after at Benares. The Goorcas then established their power at Catmandoo, and successively overcame all the neighbouring states, having now above forty-six petty princes tributary to them. In 1769 their aggressions were such on the Company's territories, that a force under Major Kinlock was sent against them, which penetrated as far as Sedowly, at the foot of the hills of Nepaul; and, although it was found impracticable to proceed further, yet such an impression was made on the government of Catmandoo, by the valour and conduct of our troops, that a friendly treaty was arranged between the two states, and part of Mocwanpore ceded to us. In 1790, the Nepaulese invaded Tibet with 18,000 men, and plundered the treasures of the Lama a second time, which, rousing the indignation of the emperor of China, he sent an army of 70,000 men against Catmandoo. The flower of the Nepaul infantry had been frozen to death in the gulfs of the Himalaya on their return, and the Chinese army beat the Goorcas in several battles, forced them to regorge the whole of the plunder to the Lama, and to become tributary to the emperor. For a considerable time after this, a great jealousy was shown to the Company's interest. Lord Cornwallis failed in his endeavours to establish a political treaty with the Nepaulese; but when the Chinese army had entirely evacuated the country, that object was effected. A friendly intercourse thence subsisted till 1808, when the government was usurped by Bheem Sing Tapah, during the minority of rajah Bicrama Say, who about that time succeeded to the throne, at the age of eight years. From this period, a system was pursued so hostile to British interest, and the safety of the frontier provinces, that in 1814 a most respectable force was formed from the Bengal army, and invaded it with success, but great loss, as shall be detailed in its appropriate place. *

* Vide Addenda, IV.

Bootan lies eastward of Nepaul, and extends to the wilds bordering on China. The inhabitants of its mountains are a small race of men, and subject to the extremes of heat and cold; for at Punakha, in one of the valleys, the vertical sun burns, while at Ghassa the people are chilled by eternal snow; yet these places are within sight of each other, and the difference is produced by altitude alone; so true it is, that climate depends as much upon locality as latitude. The Booteas are of Tartar origin, and their complexion is fair: they are an active, hardy, and warlike people; expert in the use of the bow and short sword. Many of those who inhabit the mild parts of the country, possess great personal advantages, being stout and broad-chested, of Herculean strength and undaunted courage. Nearly all the offices of husbandry are performed by the women. The government is monarchical, and the worship of Budha prevails.

Bengal is bounded on nearly its whole eastern line by the wild and extensive district of Tiperah, the mountains of which are inhabited by savages, who have now scarcely any knowledge of the Brahmanical code, nor indeed of any other, although, in ancient times, this was the seat of an empire which brought armies into the field of 200,000 infantry. From this region and Chittagong the government of India recruit their establishment of elephants, purchasing none under nine feet high. The inhabitants of Rajemal, a northern district of Bengal contiguous to this tract, are mostly of low stature, but stout and well proportioned. Many of them are not taller than four feet ten inches, with small eyes, flat noses, and thick lips. These savage men were reclaimed and civilised by the noble exertions of Mr. Cleveland, their judge and magistrate, who has a monument in the form of a pagoda, erected to his memory near Boglipore: he died at the early age of 29. An idea of his worth may be entertained from the tribute paid to his memory by the governor-general and council of Bengal, and which remains for a testimony to future times, engraved over his mortal remains. There he lies — "Who, without bloodshed, or the terror of authority, employing only the means of conciliation, confidence, and benevolence, attempted and accomplished the entire subjection of the lawless and savage inhabitants of the Jungleterry of Rajemal, who had long infested the neighbouring lands by their predatory incursions, inspired them with a taste for the arts of civilised life, and attached them to the British government by a conquest over their minds." To my understanding, this is one of the most honourable monuments that ever was erected, and worthy of being perpetuated till time shall be no more.

The eastern parts of Silhet, over which the Bengal government exercises authority, are within 350 miles of Yunan in China; but the intervening space is so wild, and the jealousy of the Chinese so strong, that no intercourse subsists between them. From the hills of Silhet, fine lime is sent to Calcutta, which is found in inexhaustible quantities there, although no where else in Bengal. Orange plantations are cultivated to such an extent in Silhet, that a thousand of that fine fruit are sold for half-a-crown.

To mention all the savage tribes along the frontier of Bengal, in the Tiperah mountains, would be tedious: a brief notice of one or two may be interesting. The Garrows are a very lively people, who live chiefly on raw animal food, and build their houses or villages on piles in a very curious manner: they are exceedingly fond of dancing. This amusement is thus conducted: Twenty or thirty men stand behind one another, each holding his hands round the waist of him, in his immediate front, thus forming circles, and hopping first to the right, and then to the left, on one foot, they keep time to a sort of drum, and a wild instrument like a clarionet. The women dance in rows in like manner, but do not mix with the men. Marriage is settled here by a regular courtship, and all the violence of love is felt. If the parents should refuse their consent after the young people have agreed, they are well beaten by their friends, and forced to submit to the wishes of their children on this point. The youngest daughter is always the heiress: if her husband die, she marries one of his brothers; which custom, noticed in our Holy Scriptures, is to be found in other parts of India; but here, if all the brothers die, she marries their father. They worship the sun and moon, also Mahadeva; drink to excess, and when their chief men die, the heads of several slaves are struck off, and burned with their bodies. Among the Kayns, the women have their faces tattooed all over in lines of a circular form, which gives them a hideous appearance. The Kookies live on the steepest and most inaccessible hills; they are engaged in constant warfare, and perhaps the most vindictive race in the world, being of opinion that nothing is so pleasing to God as to kill a great number of their enemies.

On the east of India, even to Canton, there are numerous Hindoos, and some of their temples: but the general worship, in all the civilised parts, beyond Tiperah, is that of Budha. There are thirteen Indo-Chinese dialects derived from the Chinese language, all written in a character so nearly alike, that in every part, the symbols convey the same meaning, though the words, used to express them orally, are so different as not to be understood perhaps at a few miles' distance from the town where custom has rendered them intelligible. Therefore fellow countrymen when they fail to comprehend one another have recourse to writing. In the Cochin-China common language, there are 3000 characters; the Chinese written tongue is understood by twenty different nations: it indicates real objects, not sounds.

Our numeral, algebraical, astronomical, and chemical signs, are like its wonderful alphabet*, which is, in fact, its dictionary.†

The foregoing remarks respecting the Indo-Chinese languages, apply generally to all the countries east of the Tiperah wilds, and Chittagong, but particularly to the kingdoms of Cambodia, Laos, Cochin-China, and Tunquin. These regions lie to the eastward of the Birman empire; and no further notice may be taken of them in this work. There is no native government, subject to one sovereign authority, at present existing in India, so extensive as the Birman empire; therefore, a brief account of it should be interesting.

It includes the space between the 9th and 26th degrees of north latitude, and the 92d and 104th of east longitude; about 1050 geographical miles in length, and 600 in breadth. To the north it has Tibet and Assam‡; to the south the Indian Ocean and the Siamese territories; to the north-east the empire of China; to the east Cambodia, &c.; and to the west the Tiperah mountains and the river Nauf. This extensive empire contains 194,000 square miles; comprising Ava, Arracan, Pegu, Martaban, Tenasserim, Junkseylon, Mergni, Tavay, Yunshan, Lowashan, and Cassay. It is

* Vide Addenda, V.

† Vide Dr. Leyden's account of the Indo-Chinese, Asiatic Researches, vol. ix.

‡ Vide Addenda, VI.

said to contain 8000 cities, towns, and villages, without including Arracan. Colonel Symes estimates the whole population at 17,000,000; but Captain Cox, who succeeded him as ambassador, does not go beyond 8,000,000, which is probably much nearer the truth. The principal rivers are the Irawaddy, the Keenduem, the Lokiang, and the Pegu. Its chief towns are Ummerapoor, the capital; Ava, the ancient capital; Monchaboo, the birth-place of Alompra; Pegu, Rangoon, Syriam, Prome, Negrais, Persaim, and Chagaing. The climate is very healthy. Its seasons are regular, and the extremes of heat and cold seldom experienced; the duration of the intense heat, which precedes the commencement of the rains, being so short, that it incommodes but very little.

No soil can be more fertile than many parts of the Birman empire. The south yields abundant crops of rice, and the north produces wheat, and the various kinds of small grain and legumes which grow in Hindostan. Sugar canes, tobacco, indigo, cotton, and the different tropical fruits, are indigenous. The tea plant grows very well near Ummerapoor, but it has scarcely any flavour. Besides the teak tree, which is superabundant in many parts, there is almost every description of timber that is known in India. There are mines of gold and silver, rubies and sapphires, iron, tin, lead, antimony, arsenic, sulphur, &c. It has amethysts, garnets, beautiful chrysolites, jasper, amber, and marble. The wells are found here which produce petroleum oil.

The Birmans carry on an extensive trade with China. Cotton, amber, ivory, precious stones, betel nut, and edible nests, are transported up the river Irawaddy, in large boats, as far as Bamoo; where they are bartered at the jee or mart, with the Chinese merchants, for raw and wrought silks, velvets, gold leaf, preserves, paper, and some utensils of hardware.—The British in India import to Madras and Calcutta, from the Birman dominions, about 200,000*l.* worth of teak timber, annually, which is paid for in English broad cloth, hardware, coarse Bengal muslins, glass, Cossimbazar silks, cocoa nuts, &c.

Like the Chinese, the Birmans have no coin, silver in bullion and lead being the current monies of the country. The value of these are estimated and approximated by artificial standards, so fluctuating that every foreigner finds it necessary to have a native banker to manage his money transactions. Rice is sold at the capital generally at the rate of eighty-four pounds for 2*s.* 8*d.*, but at Rangoon 250 pounds may be had for that sum.

The courts of Ava and Pekin resemble each other in many respects, particularly in excessive vanity and pride. Like the sovereign of China, the Birman emperor acknowledges no equal. Amongst his titles are, the sovereign of the earth

— the emperor of emperors — the sovereign esteemed for riches and happiness — the monarch of elephants and horses, and all good things — the lord of high-built palaces, of gold, &c. &c. There are no hereditary dignities. Gold chains are the badges of the order of nobility. The king wears twenty-four chains, his prime minister twelve, and the other nobles created for life or during office different numbers down to three, which is the lowest rank of nobility. One-tenth of all produce is exacted as the revenue of the crown, but the amount fluctuates so much that no average can be given. All we know accurately on the subject is, that the riches of the Birman emperor are immense. Every man in the kingdom is liable to be called upon to serve as a soldier. Their standing army is very small; but 60,000 men can be raised in a short time, when wanted, the great men of the state holding their lands by military tenure. The establishment of war-boats is very respectable; at a very short notice the emperor can collect 500, carrying from forty to fifty rowers, thirty soldiers armed with muskets, and with a piece of ordnance on the prow.

There is a striking contrast between the Birmans and the natives of India. The Birmans are lively, inquisitive, active, irascible, and impatient; their Bengal neighbours are exactly the reverse. In Ava the females are not concealed from the sight of men, though they are treated in a manner destitute both of delicacy and humanity. Their women are sold to strangers; but this purchase does not authorise a foreigner to carry a Birman female out of the country. As in China, women are not permitted to emigrate. In their features, the Birmans resemble the Chinese. The men pluck out their beards by the roots; and both sexes colour their teeth, their eyelashes, and the edges of their eyelids, with black. Marriages are not contracted until the parties reach the age of puberty. Polygamy is prohibited by law, but concubinage is admitted to an unlimited extent. They burn their dead. In their food the Birmans are gross and uncleanly. Even reptiles are eaten by the lower classes. The sitting posture is here the most respectful. Their houses are raised on wooden posts or bamboos, generally composed of bamboos and mats, and but indifferently thatched; but their temples are splendid fabrics, glittering with gold.*

This precious metal is the type of excellence among the Birmans. Every thing belonging to the king has the word *shoe*, or gold, prefixed to it. When a subject means to affirm that the king has heard any thing, he says, "It has reached the golden ears:" he who has obtained admittance to the royal presence, has been at "the golden feet." In short, what pleases the sight is delightful to "the golden eye;" and what gratifies the sense of

* Vide Addenda, VII.

smelling is pleasing to "the golden nose."* His majesty is sole proprietor of all the elephants in his dominions. It is a high honour to be permitted to ride on one. Male elephants are prized beyond females in Ava, though in Hindostan the females are in more estimation, on account of their superior docility. The henza, a wild fowl, called in India, the Brahmany goose, is the symbol of the Birman nation, as the eagle was of the Roman empire.

In Ava, Pegu, and Siam, the Pali language, which is derived from Sanscrit, constitutes the sacred text. The character in common use is a round nagari, formed from the square pali. It runs in circles and segments of circles, variously disposed, and is written from left to right. Their common books are composed of the palmyra leaf, on which the letters are engraven with styles.—The laws of the Birmans are of Hindoo origin. Their code is founded on the Dharma Sastra, which is a commentary on Menu. It prescribes, like Chinese jurisprudence, specific punishments for almost every species of crime that can be committed. Their laws are described as being wise, and pregnant with sound morality; and their police as better regulated than in most European countries. There are no distinctions of caste among them; nor are they restricted to hereditary occupations,

* Vide Addenda, VIII.

nor forbidden from participating with strangers in every social bond. It is said that every peasant can read and write the vulgar tongue; for all their monasteries are seminaries, where youths of all descriptions are educated gratis, by the rhaans or monks, who never buy, sell, or accept money. They are fond of poetry and music. Colonel Symes was shown the king's library; the books were innumerable, kept in boxes, ranged with great regularity, the contents of each chest being written in gold letters on the lid.

The Birmans are sectaries of Budha, who, according to Sir William Jones, reformed the doctrines contained in the Vedas, 1014 years before the birth of our Saviour. He is admitted by Hindoos of all descriptions to be the ninth Avater, or incarnation of the Deity, in the character of preserver.—The Birmans acknowledge to have received their religion from Ceylon. Their priests wear yellow clothing; they have a long loose cloak of that colour which they wrap round them, so as to cover most part of their bodies. Their kioums, or convents, resemble the architecture of the Chinese; are entirely made of wood, and consist of one large hall, open at all sides. There are no apartments for the private recreations of the monks or priests; publicity is the prevailing system of Birman conduct. They admit of no secrets either in church or state. These priests profess celibacy, and abstain from every sensual pleasure.

They have no salaries; never dress their own victuals, but receive the contributions of the laity ready dressed, and prefer cold food to hot. At the dawn of day they perambulate the different towns and villages of the empire, to collect supplies of boiled rice, oil, dried and pickled fish, sweetmeats, fruits, &c. During their quick walk they never lift their eyes from the ground, nor stop to solicit any thing. The provisions are thrown into a lackered box, which is carried on the right arm. They eat but once a day, at noon. Any surplus of provisions is always disposed of as charitably as it was given, to the needy stranger, or the poor scholars, who daily attend for instruction. Nunneries were abolished by law as injurious to population.

The early history of this country is involved in obscurity. During the successes of the Portuguese in India, they interfered in the wars between the Birmans and Peguers, but little was known of the interior. In 1752 the sovereign of Pegu conquered the king of Ava, which is the country of the ancient Birmans. But soon after Alompra, a man of low origin, rescued his country from that state of degradation, drove out the Peguers, and founded the present dynasty. In these wars the French favoured the Peguers, and the English assisted the Birmans. Alompra died in 1760, after most extensive conquests and the display of profound wisdom, leaving the empire to his eldest son,

Namdogee Praw.—In 1767, or 1131, of the Birman era, the Chinese sent an army of 50,000 men against the Birmans. But the whole were destroyed, except about 2500, who were sent in fetters to the capital, where they were forced to marry Birman wives, and encouraged afterwards to consider themselves as Birmans.—It appears that all strangers are invited to marry Birman women. This custom, in the East, is singular; for women are, nearly every where else in that quarter, degraded by intercourse with strangers.—Minderagee Praw, the fourth son of the great Alompra, ascended the throne in 1782. He founded the new metropolis of Ummerapoor, to which the seat of government was removed from Ava. Since which period the Birman power has been gradually increasing to its present height.*

No notice was taken of Persia in our western outline beyond its mere nomination. The same would be the case, with respect to China, were that country not more closely connected with the British empire in the East, by trade and locality. Persia, at this day, is sunk into a state of vice and moral degradation, which places it very low in the scale of national estimation; but China, in many respects, is one of the most curious empires that ever existed, even in the regions of imagination. Doubtless, fanciful writers have described it with

* Vide Symes, Cox, Leyden, F. Buchanan, Dalrymple, and Hamilton.

a tincture of utopian colouring; but its unquestionable antiquity, its amazing population, though certainly this has been much overrated by those who fixed the inhabitants of the fifteen provinces at 335,000,000; its civilisation in the lower branches of political economy, and the wisdom which directs the experience of the past to meet the exigencies of the present;—conspire to render the following brief notice of it perfectly apposite in an outline of India.

The jealousy of the Chinese government, or rather their experience of the encroaching dispositions of Europeans, has never permitted our curiosity to be gratified with a full view of the interior of that wonderful country. Lord Macartney, in modern times, had the widest field for observation. He arrived in Jangangfoe Bay, in the Yellow Sea, about the latter end of September, 1792, and travelled from the north-eastern coast through the great cities of Tyensing and Tong-tchew to Pekin, and thence to the emperor's summer residence at Jehol, in Tartary, beyond the great wall.* But in all this course the embassy was so strictly watched, and closely guarded, that except what occurred in their immediate neighbourhood, no opportunity was afforded of seeing the Chinese in their real character; and it may be presumed that the mandarins took care to exhibit their country

* Vide Addenda, IX.

in the most favourable and imposing light. Thus having passed from the northern to the southern extremity of China, and back again, Lord Macartney reached Canton in December, 1793; and we may therefore safely rely upon those remarks which Sir George Staunton has published as the basis of our best information.

In this most ancient empire, where upwards of two hundred millions of men have for ages been kept together under one government, knowledge and virtue alone qualify for public employments, and every person is eligible to rise to the highest honours; for although there are nine orders of mandarins, there is no such thing as hereditary rank: there is no state religion, and no man is questioned on account of mere matter of opinion. The laws are, like the civil code of Rome, founded on the principle of universal justice, which the Creator has stamped on human understanding.—There is every reason to believe that this empire has endured full four thousand years. It consists of fifteen provinces, exclusive of territories in Tartary and Tibet, spread over an area of about 3,350,000 square miles; the whole of which is in a state of cultivation far beyond what is seen in the most civilized parts of Europe. The very mountains are in some places tilled to their summits, and irrigated by artificial means; the rivers are conducted in all directions across the country, forming fine canals, upon which thousands of families live in boats. There are many fine roads, and curious bridges; but nearly all the magnificent edifices are for the public offices of the state, or for the honour of God, who is worshipped under various forms. Husbandmen are held in the highest estimation, and some of the Chinese emperors have risen from holding the plough. The fine arts have never advanced much in China. Their language is so difficult that few of them ever attain perfection in it: education is solely directed to wisdom, self-knowledge, and the science of life. There are regular posts or modes of quick communication with all parts of the empire. Justice is administered in every town, and criminals are punished with great severity: the form of oath is very solemn; and it is rendered striking by a piece of china ware being smashed with force on the ground, and similar destruction invoked on the soul and body for hesitation, evasion, or reservation in speaking the truth. War is not cultivated as an art. About one hundred and eighty years ago the Tartars conquered the Chinese, and they have given four dynasties of emperors, without changing manners, customs, and forms. Yet it must be acknowledged that the Chinese are far behind the Christian world in the conception of pure morality. Their notions respecting liberty are all slavish. Fathers have despotic authority over their children. Various kinds of slavery are permitted by law. Women are not permitted to quit the empire, that emigration may be discountenanced, and their condition is little better than bondage; for although the men be restricted to one wife, yet they may bring as many concubines into the house as they please, and divorces are allowed upon very frivolous pretexts.—The Chinese are, generally speaking, a dirty, cunning, deceitful people; with many of the lower virtues, but scarcely one that would exalt man to eminence in England. It must be allowed that Europeans have, by their own selfish conduct, drawn forth this dark side of the Chinese character. In our early intercourse with this extraordinary empire, its government did not evince that jealousy which is now extreme. Russia was permitted to establish a college and church at Pekin *; and the Portuguese were most hospitably received on the shores, as well as the Dutch, till time proved the danger of their encroachments.

Canton, situated in lat. 23° 7′ N. lat. 113° 14′ E., is now, however, the only place on the continent of China where Europeans are allowed a temporary residence for commercial purposes. It is seated on the eastern bank of the Pekiang river, eighty miles from its entrance into the Southern Sea; and near the city it is as broad as the Thames at London Bridge. The climate here is cool, and fires are necessary during the winter. Europeans may enter the suburbs, and one street is entirely

* Vide Addenda, X.

appropriated to their use; but they are not permitted in the body of the city, which is surrounded by high walls about five miles in circumference. The front of every house is a shop; and many of them have signs, such as we have in our towns, for attraction. Here the Chinese displays his wonderful equality of temper, in humouring our capricious tars, and his ingenuity in fleecing them of their cash.

All the river, for many miles, is covered with junks and boats. Some of the former carry one thousand tons, and are curiously divided into compartments belonging to the owners, one sometimes having an hundred proprietors. Their ships are so constructed, that they may strike on a rock without sustaining any serious injury; and if a leak springs in one part, the cargo in another will not be damaged. These junks trade to all parts of the eastern seas, and the same compass is used as in Europe; but with a needle pointing to the south, which is here considered as the attracting point. The foreign factories extend along the banks of the river: they are called hongs; and each resembles a long court, with four or five separate houses, built on a fine quay, with a parade in front, called the Respondentia Walk. In the neighbourhood are large warehouses. Below these are the chop, or custom-houses, under a tontiff, called by our mariners *John Tuck*. All transactions are conducted by foreigners with the hong merchants, who are a company in whom the monopoly of all the outward trade is vested by the government, under a charter of regulations. These hong merchants have sometimes property in their hands, belonging to our East India Company, to the amount of two millions sterling.

The English establishment at Canton consists of twelve supercargoes, and eight writers, whose allowances graduate from nearly 9000*l.* a year to 1500*l.* There are also a few medical, religious, and military posts, remarkably well paid. All vacancies among the supercargoes are filled up from the writers, who have a free table, and about 400*l.* per annum. They all reside three months at Canton during the commercial season, and then remove to Macao, where they have permanent houses.

Our exports to China are, woollens, camlets, lead, tin, &c.; and the average value is about 1,200,000*l.* But the Company's trade from India to China is more miscellaneous, and consists of cotton, pepper, sandal wood, putchick, sharks' fins, olibanum, elephants' teeth, rhinoceros' horns, pearls, cornelians, beads, betel nut, rattans, sea swallo, birds' nests, &c. Though opium is prohibited, a great deal of that valuable commodity is smuggled by the hong merchants; the average of which is 2000 chests, at 1200 dollars per chest. All this trade averages about 2,000,000*l.* per annum; but the returns, comprising piece goods, sugar candy, tutenague, camphor, tea, raw silk, nankeens, and china ware, &c. nearly equal the imports.—The private trade to China, carried on by individuals from Britain, authorised by the Company, does not exceed 300,000*l.* on an average. The exports from China are, tea, china ware, gold in bars, sugar, sugar candy, rhubarb, china root, snake root, sarsaparilla, leather, tutenague, Japan copper, varnished and lackered ware, drugs, leaf gold, utensils, cast iron, silk, raw and wrought, thread, nankeens, mother-of-pearl, gamboge, quicksilver, alum, dammer, red lead, vermilion, furniture, toys, and drugs. Of these exports the Company take annually to the amount of about 3,000,000*l.*, upon which they gain 35 per cent. The average in tea alone is about 30,000,000 of pounds weight annually, which yields a revenue to England of about 4,000,000*l.*; and the China trade produces a circulation in London of perhaps 20,000,000*l.* sterling every year. America takes away great quantities of tea, so does Russia from the Siberian frontier; so that it is easily conceived how China must be enriched. In 1678 only 4713 pounds of tea were imported annually by the Company; such has been the rapid increase in tea drinking.

The Chinese eat horse flesh, dogs, cats, hawks, and owls; yet milk is not used by them in any form: such is the strange capriciousness of taste, and the amazing diversity of customs.*

* Vide Staunton, Barrow, Milburn, Elmore, Johnson, Ellis, &c.

We are obliged to trade with China through the Portuguese settlement of Macao, which is an island situated at the mouth of the Canton river. This place was granted to that nation in gratitude for a signal service performed, which shall be noticed hereafter in the history of the Portuguese. Even at Macao the Europeans are enclosed by a great wall of oyster shells, which are found here of an enormous size, within very narrow limits. The Portuguese extent of territory on the island is not more than eight miles in circumference. They are therefore completely in the power of the Chinese government for their supplies of provisions, but the market is abundantly furnished from the continent. There are about 4000 Portuguese inhabitants, many of them half-castes, in the town of Macao, and upwards of 8000 Chinese, &c.; who have two large temples, while the former have thirteen churches. A mandarin is the real governor of the town; but the Portuguese are allowed to amuse themselves with the forms of government in a grand senate-house. Perfect submission is, however, the lease by which they hold possession; and they are obliged to submit calmly to all the encroachments of the Chinese. In 1806, when we attempted to garrison Macao from Bengal, the trade was stopped, and provisions withheld till the troops were withdrawn. In 1700 we were permitted to trade with Limpo and Amoy, as well as Canton, which circumstance speaks volumes. The present emperor is the fifteenth son of Tchien-lung, who died in 1799, at the age of 89 years, three years before which he resigned his throne, after a reign of sixty years. A Chinese salutes with a sort of salam, and the words "hou, poo hou," which signify, "are you well or not?" literally they are, "well, not well." All business with the Chinese is transacted in a jargon of English, of most laughable sound. A Chinese calls rice, *lice*, not being able to pronounce the letter *r*, but they are very ready at picking up what answers their purpose.

The town of Macao and the gardens around it occupy the whole of the little peninsula which belongs to the Portuguese. A long neck of land joins it to the remainder of the island, and across this the wall of oyster shells, before alluded to, is built. Beneath a lofty eminence in the town, Camoens' Cave is situated, in which, it is said, this celebrated poet wrote a great part of the Lusiad. The large oyster shells here are divided into thin laminæ, and being finely polished, serve for window lights. No foreign women are allowed to go up to Canton. The low Chinese, in their manners and habits, are brutal, and their immorality is so gross, that delicacy must leave to imagination what it would degrade human nature to describe. Many of their pictures are abominable; but no true criterion of national character can be deduced from the perversion of one passion. It excites our wonder in this country to behold some men, who are truly honourable, polished in manners, refined by the advantages of education, and delicate in many respects, yet gross to bestiality in one; and it certainly should not be urged against the Chinese, as a general charge, that many of them have been found so depraved, as to leave other nations as far behind in invention, as they go before in industry and perseverance. Their women scarcely ever appear in public, but the lower orders have been observed to be employed in household affairs, much like other oriental females. The small feet, so much talked of, are, like the artificial size of the mandarin, confined entirely to the higher classes, or men of large property, who can afford ideal refinements in substitution for bodily activity. Their peasantry, like our own, are too poor, and too busy, to think of much but their belly, their back, and the gross passions and appetites common to all humanity.

Thus we have travelled from the mouths of the Indus along three sides of Hindostan. It remains for us, in finishing our outline, to notice briefly the principal islands which are comprized under the general name of East Indies.

CHAPTER II.

THE ISLANDS OF INDIA.

We shall endeavour briefly to describe the southern outline of India under the heads Ceylon, Sumatra, Java, Borneo, Celebes, the Moluccas, and the Philippines.

CEYLON.

The southern triangular projection of Africa, and the western coast of New Holland, form between them a magnificent gap of about ninety longitudinal degrees, in the latitude of 32°. It is probable that at some remote period the great body of Asia extended, like Africa, in an unbroken state into the ocean; and that, in some of those wonderful changes of position which the sea is known to take, the waters rushed with irresistible impetuosity round the huge bulwark of the Cape of Good Hope, from the great Atlantic, through the defenceless flats of the East Indies, into the Pacific, leaving the highlands and mountains dry. This supposition is supported by tradition.

In the voyage to India round the Cape of Good Hope, after passing the great island of Madagascar, and the Mauritius, which lie eastward of it, no land is seen till the Maldives and Ceylon are approached. The Maldives project into the Indian Ocean to the equator, being the extreme point of a fine triangle, formed by the Arabian Sea on one side, and the Bay of Bengal on the other. This triangle is the Peninsula of Hindostan.

Ceylon, the Maldives, and Laccadives are traditionally reported as once forming part of the main land, though now separated by the sea. Ceylon lies at the western entrance into the Bay of Bengal, its shape being that of a large ham; while the Maldives and Laccadives run in a chain to the south and west off the Malabar coast. We shall briefly notice the latter two chains before Ceylon.

The Laccadives derive their name from *Laksha dwipa* (a lack or 100,000 islets); they belong to the bibby, or princess of Cananore, and are situated about 75 miles from the coast of Malabar, extending from the 10th to the 12th degree of north latitude. These islands were visited by Vasco de Gama in 1499. Though very numerous they are of small value, being of a barren and unproductive nature, except for cocoa-nut trees. The largest does not contain an area greater than six square miles. All the inhabitants are Moplas, Mohammedans, the descendants of Arabian settlers on the coast. They barter cocoa-nuts, jagory, or coarse sugar, made from the juice of that useful tree, oil made from the nut, ropes made from the husk of the same, boats manufactured from the trunk, and coral found upon the banks, with cochin, anjango, &c., for provisions and other necessaries of life. Their houses are entirely built with the stems of cocoa-nut trees, and covered with the leaves of that useful palm. Their beds and utensils are nearly all composed of the same material, with parts of which they make fishing-nets, sails for their boats, and cups for drinking.*

Malaya Dwipa, or the Isles of Maldive, run from the eighth degree of north latitude to the line. They are very numerous; separated from each other by narrow dangerous channels; and many of them are mere barren rocks. There are seventeen clusters of these islands inhabited by Mohammedans; but they still adhere to Indian customs, and are divided into a sort of castes; for one island is occupied by weavers, another by mat-makers, a third by potters, and so on, through all the trades and professions of the East. Their boats are made of the trunk of the cocoa palm. They carry on a brisk trade with the neighbouring coasts in manufactures of gold, silver, iron, and turtle-shell; all the produce of the cocoa-nut tree, and couries and salt-fish. They are most adventurous seamen, and during the N. E. monsoon, when the

* Vide Addenda, II.

steady weather prevails, they launch their frail barks into the great ocean, sail into the eastern seas with cargoes of shark fins, which the Chinese esteem as an ingredient for their delicious soups; carry dried bonetto to Acheen, and trade with Calcutta, bringing, on an average, merchandize to the amount of 30,000*l*., and taking away cotton, sugar, broad cloth, cutlery, silk stuffs, &c. to a great extent. Each island is under a separate government of a mild patriarchal form. No wars have occurred among them for ages, and all the inhabitants are described as a most inoffensive and hospitable race. They have several times behaved with the greatest tenderness to shipwrecked Europeans; and the French had formerly a small settlement among them. In their manners and customs they resemble the great continent; and they are equally credulous and superstitious. Their greatest ceremonies are at the annual launches of small vessels loaded with odours and flowers, which are sent adrift for the use of the king of the sea and the emperor of the winds.*

The island of Ceylon is known by several names. It is called by the aborigines, Singhala; by the ancient Europeans, Taprobane; by the neighbouring continent, Lanca; and by the Mohammedans, Serendib. It lies between 5° 40′ and 10° 30′ N.

* Vide Buchanan, Sonnerat, Elmore, Forrest, Leyden, and Hamilton.

and 79° and 82° E. The Gulf of Manar separates it from the Coromandel coast, which is 160 miles distant, at Cape Comorin, but the northern point of the island approaches Tangore. In extreme length, this fine island is about 300 miles, and in breadth it varies from 100 to 40. It is crossed by a lofty chain of mountains, which seem to be a continuation of the Ghauts of Malabar; for the monsoons are the same here as on the continent, and while it is raining for three months on one side, the sun is shining in unclouded splendour on the other. Hammalleel, or Adam's Peak, which name it received from the converts of St. Thomas, is the highest part of Ceylon. It lies about 60 miles to the north-east of Columbo.

We are informed by the Indians, that Ceylon and the Maldives once formed a great island, and that the whole was torn from the continent at a still more remote period. The astronomical calculations, in the ancient Brahmanical books, confirm this tradition, if their first meridian, which passed through Oojain, be correct; for the equinoctial point was Lanca, which does not now occupy that position, whereas the Maldives exactly agree, and the appearances between the two warrant the belief that they were once the same.

Agriculture on this island is in a very rude state. The soil is in general sandy *, and requires con-

* Vide Addenda, XII.

stant irrigation; when it is laid properly under water, it yields a good crop of rice, which is the chief sustenance of the natives; but a sufficiency is not raised for home consumption, and vast quantities are annually imported from Bengal. The peasantry, or husbandmen, live in straggling villages, composed of the most simple materials, which the forests furnish in abundance. They go nearly naked, and each village forms a sort of society, who have a joint property in the surrounding lands. All their labour is performed by regular contribution. They go out with their ploughs, which are nothing but crooked pieces of wood shod with iron, and drawn by a pair of miserably yoked oxen, and score the ground by going repeatedly over the same furrow, to a proper depth. The crops are divided according to immemorial custom, which awards a certain portion to the government, another to the clergy, a third to the village officers and necessary tradesmen, and the remainder to the cultivators. A very respectable old man is in general the magistrate, and organ of the society; who, assisted by a few others, compose a court that settles all litigated subjects at one hearing. Over these villages, the government has officers called moodaliers, who inspect their proceedings, and report to the highest authority. This is the remnant of ancient Hindoo civilization, which was overthrown by an invasion of Rama, the great rajah of Oude; who is mentioned in a poem called the Ramayuna, as having entered it over a bridge, which his army of monkeys constructed across the gulf of Manar, the remains of which, but whether natural or artificial, it is hard to say, still are visible.

The principal harbours are Trincomalee and Point de Galle; but ships can anchor very well off Columbo, Batacolo, Barbareen, Matura, Caltura, Negombo, Chilon, Calpenteen, Manar, and Point Pedro, during the fine seasons on each coast. There is very little inland navigation. The two chief rivers are called Malivagunga, and Mulivaddy, the former of which falls into the sea near Trincomalee, and the latter not far from Columbo. The Dutch left marks of their fondness for canals, and lakes at the latter place, some of which have been filled up by the British, for the promotion of health.

Ceylon produces fine elephants*, though not of the largest kind, wild horses and buffaloes, deer, elk, gazelles, hares, wild hogs, and small tigers, tiger cats, leopards, jackalls, hyænas, bears, and a variety of monkeys, but the fox has not been seen. All our poultry are domesticated here. Pheasants, parrots, and parroquets are numerous. Nearly all the species of game abound. The honey bird rifles the bee; and there are tailor birds, fly catchers, peacocks, and crows of the most impu-

* Vide Addenda, XIII.

dent description. Reptiles are innumerable, The covra capellas, covra manillas, and whip snakes are poisonous. There are rock snakes thirty feet in length, but they are only dangerous from their vast size. Some of the alligators are twenty feet long, and as thick as an ox. Guanas, toads, lizards, blood suckers, chameleons, leeches, flying lizards, and large bats abound. The rivers are well supplied with fish, and the gardens with fruit. There are apples, oranges, pomegranates, citrons, lemons, melons, pumpkins, squashes, figs, almonds, mulberries, bilberries, mangoes, shaddocks, mangusteens, rose apples, cushoo apples, and nuts, custard apples, plantains, jack fruit, and cocoa nuts. The plantations abound with pepper, cardamoms, coffee, the sugar tree, the betel palm, and four species of the laurus cinnamomum. In the woods are found the banyan, the cotton tree, mando wood, satin wood, calamander wood, and ebony. But what is still more curious, the tea plant has been found in the forests of Ceylon, in a wild state, though its properties are not the same as in China, and it is extraordinary, that the repeated trials to transplant its virtues have failed.*

Valuable minerals are found in various parts of this rich island. The ruby, topaz, diamond, amethyst, tourmalin, sapphire, crystal, cats' eye, opal, and cornelian are concealed beneath the sur-

* Vide Addenda, XIV.

face; while lead, tin, iron, and quicksilver lie deeper in the bowels of the hills. Fine pearls enrich the coast.

The inhabitants of Ceylon are of various nations. Its aborigines are the Cingalese; but the Portuguese, Dutch, Malays, and Mohammedans have left their posterity round the coasts in great numbers. The ceremonies, manners, and customs, resemble those of the continent. The Tamul and Portuguese languages are spoken generally over the island. Many of the Cingalese are ingenious artificers; others called Bedahs are wild men who live in the woods, and have their habitations on trees like monkeys. Some of them are as timid as antelopes. The apostacy of Budha, at an early period, made a great progress on the island of Ceylon, and the laxity it permitted in the Brahmanical tenets prepared the natives for easy conversion to Christianity. More than half a million of the Cingalese are now professors of our faith; and it is probable that the whole island will be converted in a short time, since no native government now counteracts the spread of our opinion and example.

From the arrival of the Portuguese on this island, in 1505, to the final conquest of it, by the British in 1814, it was always a scene of bloodshed, cruelty, and death. Both the Portuguese and Dutch were involved in constant warfare, not only with the Candians, but with the deadly marsh miasma of forests and mountains. At length the insupportable tyranny of the king of Candy roused the united resistance of his nobles, who, calling in the assistance of the British government, deposed their sovereign, and placed themselves at the disposal of the king of England, as shall be related hereafter.*

In 1802, Ceylon was constituted a royal government. It is placed under a council, consisting of the governor, chief justice, commander in chief of the forces, and the secretary. The revenues now amount to above 400,000*l.*, of which the East India Company pay 60,000*l.* per annum for cinnamon; and the pearl fishery yields about 40,000*l.* more. An European regiment and six native corps were usually kept on the island, but of course the military and civil establishment will now be considerably enlarged. Columbo is the capital, and seat of government; it is a strongly fortified Dutch town, with a population of about 50,000 or 60,000 souls.

Ceylon is a beautiful island, and a most valuable acquisition to the crown of England. Its appearance from the sea is a lovely diversity of green shade in the foreground, while the distant purple of the high mountains exercises the exquisite deceptions of hope.†

* Vide Addenda, XV.

† Vide Percival, Knox, Symes, Jones, and Hamilton.

SUMATRA.

Pulo Purichu, Indalas, Sumatra, also called Java Minor, by Marco Polo, and supposed by some to be the Ophir of Holy Writ, is about 1050 miles in length from Acheen to the straits of Sunda, and about 165 in its average breadth, through the extent of which there runs a high chain of mountains, some peaks of which are 13,842 feet above the level of the sea. A chain of small islands skirts its western coast, which appear to have once belonged to it; and on its eastern side is situated the island of Banca, whose tin mines are exceedingly valuable. It is separated by the straits of Malacca, from the long peninsula of that name, which extends 775 miles by 125, its average breadth, to the isthmus of Kraw, which joins it to India, beyond the Ganges. The western coast of Malacca is also studded with islands, which seem all to have once been a continuation of the continent. Pulo Penang, or Prince of Wales's Island, is one of great consequence; and the Nicobars and Andamans, which form a chain almost from Acheen to the head of the Bay of Bengal are curiosities, on account of the savages by whom they are inhabited. We shall therefore briefly notice this outline, before we retouch our principal figure.

The great Andaman, or the principal island of the cluster, or chain so named, is about 140 miles in length by twenty broad; and near the centre of it, mountains rise to the height of 2400 feet above the sea. Its inhabitants are supposed to be oriental negroes, of the same origin as those inhabiting the interior of Malacca. In the Andamans, their number does not exceed 2500, and they are perfect savages, living on fish and reptiles of all descriptions. Their hair is short and woolly, their noses flat, their lips thick, their eyes small and red, their skin a deep dirty black, and their appearance horribly frightful; for their limbs are very slender, their bellies protuberant, they go quite naked, smear their bodies over with mud as a preservative from the bites of insects, paint their hair with red ocre, and their countenance is a most disgusting picture of misery and ferocity. Their chief occupation is fishing, hunting, and searching for birds' nests among the rocks; for they know nothing of husbandry, at least they will not practise it. In stature they seldom exceed five feet.

Providence has furnished them with a superabundance of fish at one season of the year, which they dry in the sun, and lay up in their wretched huts for a time of necessity; but their stupidity and want of foresight is such, that they are often obliged to eat the most obscene reptiles; and it has been asserted that they are anthropophagi. They have among their numerous fish, mullet, soles, pomfret, rock fish, skate, gurnas, sardinas, roeballs, sable, shad, aloose, cockup, grobers, seerfish, prawns, shrimps, cray fish, small whales, and enormous sharks. Their chief vegetable is the fruit of the mangrove; and their animal food consists of lizards, guanas, rats, snakes, and the edible birds' nests, which are so much esteemed for soups by the Chinese. On the shores are found beautiful shells, gorgonias, madrepores, murex, and cowries.*

Our government in Bengal established a settlement here, about 1791. The beautifully picturesque spot called Port Cornwallis was chosen, in a short time after, for improvement and colonization with convicts from the British settlements in India; but it was found so unhealthy, that it was at length abandoned, and Pulo Penang fixed upon for that purpose.

The weapons of the Andamans are bows made of bamboo, arrows headed with fish-bone, spears made of heavy wood well pointed, and shields composed of hard bark. They salute each other by lifting one leg, and striking their thigh smartly with one hand. Their canoes are made out of the trunk of trees; and often merely by the help of sharp flint and fire. In language they are distinct from all the Indians. They worship the sun and moon, and chaunt wild chorusses to appease the spirits of the winds and waves. The Danish missionaries of Nicobar, though long near neighbours,

* Vide Addenda, XVI.

were never able to make any impression on these savages, who threaten to destroy all strangers, and who, beyond all doubt, have been in the habit of eating their enemies. Though the cocoa nut tree abounds in the Nicobars, it is not found in the Andamans.*

In the Nicobars, which islands are also numerous and some of them considerable as to size, the natives are a different race of oriental negroes, whose colour is of a copper hue; their eyes are small, their noses are flat, their lips thick, but their hair is long and black. They shave their eyebrows, blacken their teeth, and flatten the backs of their heads by compression of the occiput when infants. In civilization they have made considerable progress; carry on cultivation to some extent; and export cocoa nuts, areca nuts, fowls, hogs, birds' nests, ambergris, and tortoise shell; importing in return, cloth, silver, iron, and tobacco. They live in villages, composed of from ten to twenty huts, under a sort of patriarchal government so simple, that it resembles a family compact. Their food is chiefly the mellori bread, cocoa nuts, and yams. A narrow piece of cloth is wound round the waist, and passed between the legs, as in India; but here the end of it hangs down behind like a tail; and it gave rise to the opinion that there were men with tails, which Lord Monboddo

* Vide Symes, Col. Colebrooke, and Hamilton.

believed, and the Swedish navigator Kioping reported. Their notions of religion are confused, and their priests are sorcerers who make hideous grimaces, while they exorcise evil spirits and diseases. Their language is an almost unintelligible jargon.

The Danes established themselves here in 1756; and missionaries of that nation continued their unsuccessful exertions till 1787, when the settlement was abandoned, after having proved the grave of nearly all the Europeans that ever resided on Nancowry.*

Prince of Wales's Island, the N. E. point of which is in lat. 5° 25′ N., and long. 100° 19′ E. is computed to contain 160 square miles. It was received in 1785 by Captain Francis Light, of a country ship, as a marriage portion with the king of Queda's daughter. He transferred it to the East India Company, and being appointed governor of the infant settlement remained there till 1794, when he died. Its name was changed from Pulo Penang, in compliment to his present majesty, then Prince of Wales, and the new settlement was called George Town. Here is a fine harbour that affords perfect security to ships at all seasons of the year. The island is diversified with hill and dale; some of the former rise 2500 feet above the sea; and showers are so frequent, that, with the excep-

* Vide Haensel, Fontana, and Hamilton.

tion of January and February, rain may be expected every day in the year. Cooled by a fine sea breeze, the thermometer seldom ranges above 90°, and it is sometimes as low as 66°.

When the island fell into our hands it was covered with an immense forest, the trees of which were large enough for the lower mast of a seventy-four gun ship. Only a few fishermen occupied a small part of the coast; but at present there is a population of more than 50,000 souls, among which are British, Dutch, Portuguese, Americans, Arabs, Parsees, Chinese, Chulias, Malays, Buggesses, Birmans, Siamese, Javanese, Bengalese, and all descriptions of Indians. There is a large fort well furnished with cannon. Fine roads have been made for several miles round the town, and many bridges constructed by the convicts and company's artificers. Some of the forests have been cleared away, and the markets are well supplied with all the necessaries and luxuries of life; the various fruits and vegetables of Asia and Europe having been introduced with success, as well as many curious productions which enrich the colonists. For the soil is a fine rich black mould, produced from the vegetable putrefaction for ages.

Here are cultivated, pepper, betel nut, cocoa nuts, coffee, sugar, paddy, ginger, yams, sweet potatoes, mangusteens, rambosteens, pine apples, geravas, oranges, citrons, pomegranates, leechees; and cloves, nutmegs, cinnamon, pimento, kiapootee, colalava, and some other exotics have been transplanted successfully from the Moluccas, &c. The American gum-vine, called caoutchouc, or urceola elastica, is found here in great plenty. It creeps along the ground to a great length, and sends out roots from its various joints, the trunk being about the thickness of a man's arm; after which it mounts a high tree, and expands in branches, clinging to every support. A vast quantity of milky juice is procured by wounding the bark or cutting the vine in pieces; and this fluid, in its chemical properties, nearly resembles animal milk.

Prince of Wales's Island promises to be a settlement of mighty consequence, and the seat of universal commerce. From China are received tea, sugar, lustrings, velvet, paper, umbrellas, china ware, quicksilver, nankeens, tutenague, sweetmeats, pickles, &c.; in exchange for opium, cotton, rattans, betel nut, pepper, bird's nests, sandal wood, shark-fins, camphor, and tin, biche de mar. All the staples of Europe and India find a market here. It is, in fact, now what Ormus was in former times, a great universal bazaar resorted to by all nations. A governor and council subordinate, as Bombay and Madras are, to the presidency of Bengal, conduct the affairs of the company, who have expended a vast sum on this fine settlement.*

* Vide Leith, Elmore, Howison, Marsden, Johnson, and Hamilton.

Malacca Peninsula is inhabited by a variety of distinct races, the principal of whom are the Malays and Samangs. The Samangs are the oriental negroes before noticed, and supposed to be the aborigines. These live in a savage state in the wild mountains of the interior; but the Malays occupy the sea coasts, are an enterprising and commercial people, live under a feudal government, and have made some progress in arts and civilization. Their original country is said to have been the kingdom of Palembang, in the island of Sumatra, from which they spread by colonization and conquest over many of the coasts. The Malay language is represented as an elegant compound of Sanscrit, Arabic, and all the eastern tongues; even Portuguese words are found in it. In Malay literature are found translations of nearly all the popular productions in India, Arabia, and Persia. They have many original works of an historical and biographical description, with commentaries on the Koran; and amongst their poetical production is an epic poem, entitled "Hikarat Malacca," which recounts the founding of that city, and the wars between the Malays and Portuguese under Albuquerque. Previous to conversion by the Arabians to Sooni Mohammedanism the Malays belonged to the Brahmanical Institution.

At that period, they were governed by a rajah, who is now styled sultan; and under him are the dattoos or nobles, who exercise feudal rights over their vassals.

The city of Malacca was founded in 1252, and about forty years after, during the reign of its first sultan, Mahommed Shah, the Malayan empire extended over all the Peninsula, and the islands of Lingen, Bintang, Junkseylon, and part of Sumatra; but in 1511, Alphonso D'Albuquerque conquered the coast of Malacca, took the city, and forced the government to fly to Iohore, on the extremity of the Peninsula, where it still exists.

Gaming and cockfighting are the favourite amusements of the Malays. To these unconquerable propensities they sacrifice fortune, life, and character. Their last morsel, the covering of their bodies, their wives and children, are frequently staked on the issue of a pair of dice, or the life of a cock. If lost, the desperate wretch sometimes intoxicates himself with bang, or hemp leaf, unties his long black hair, draws his deadly creese, and runs the muck. This is so named, from his calling *amok*, or *kill me*, which he repeats, aiming destruction at all he meets, till he is cut down in self-defence, or seized alive. But this he prevents, by all possible means, and generally dies inflicting wounds till the last gasp. The Malays are active, restless, and courageous. But they are treacherous, ferocious, and vindictive. If you offend a Malay he stabs you privately; if you punish him, his impetuous temper knows no bounds, and he sacrifices his own life in immediate retaliation, by committing open murder. *

It would be uninteresting to describe all the small islands, that seem to have once been a continuation of Malacca, to Sumatra and Java. Equally unprofitable would be the tedious enumeration of those which stud the western side of our subject. Many of these are produced, along the coast of Sumatra, by the growth of coral banks.

Sumatra is cooled by fine land and sea breezes. The S. E. monsoon, or dry season, continues from May till September, when it slackens, and changes in November to the N. W. when the rainy months set in, and cease in March gradually, without those tempests common elsewhere.

The natural productions of this island are very numerous. Gold is found, in great abundance, in its rivers. Copper, iron, tin, and sulphur are also in plenty. The earth is, in many places, impregnated with saltpetre and oil, which latter article is a preservative of wood, &c. from white ants. † They have also plenty of coal; and several mineral and hot springs, resembling those of Harrowgate. Rice is the great article of general cultivation, and, in some places, husbandry is managed so well, that the earth yields 140 fold, but the common return is thirty for one. The cocoa nut tree, sago tree, and all the species of palms are

* Vide Marsden, Leyden, Elmore, Hamilton.

† Vide Addenda, XVII.

here, with the sugar cane, and plantations of maize; chilly pepper, turmeric, ginger, coriander, cumin seed, and hemp, are numerous. All the plants and shrubs of the East are found here. Silk worms are fed on the dwarf mulberry. The broad green castor oil plant gives its rich hue to the scene, and the indigo plant rewards the peasant with its purple dye. There are innumerable fruits, and the grape flourishes here, but the vine is only cultivated by Europeans. The poisonous upas of Java is also a native of this island; but the accounts of its pestilential atmosphere are fabulous. It is, however, a deadly poison. The camphor of Sumatra is not now plentiful; sometimes 300 trees are cut down in a forest, before one is found containing this valuable drug. In the deserts are elephants, tigers, bears, and all the varieties of oriental wild animals, and reptiles. Alligators are also natives of this island. Among their fish, they have the dugong, a large one, of the order mammalia, with two large pectoral fins, that answer the purpose of feet. They have all the birds and insects of the East, except the bird of Paradise *, and a few other peculiar ones, such as the cassowary and loory. Nothing can convey an idea of the brilliant illuminations which are sometimes occasioned by the fire fly; and at the commencement of the monsoon, the exultations of the frog species keep

* Vide Addenda, XVIII.

night awake. From the rocks are collected the Chinese dainties, called biche de mar, swalo, tripan or sea slug (*holothurion*). Pepper is not now grown to any great extent. The nutmeg and clove were transplanted hither from the Moluccas, and large plantations of these valuable spices are now cultivated. Benzoin, which is a highly valued incense and styptic, being the basis of Turlington's drops, is indigenous here, as well as cassia, the shrub cotton, the coffee tree, and lignum aloes, which is a wood that yields a fragrant scent while burning. Among their trees are the poon, the camphor, the marbau, the pinaga, the ebony, the kayu gadis, the wood of which is like sassafras, and the rangi, like manchineel or mahogany. They have also the large banyan of India, but not the teak.

All the various forms of government in Sumatra are feudal and patriarchal mixtures. Their laws are long established customs. A whole family is held responsible for the debt of any of its members. The father's property is divided equally amongst his children. All crimes, murder not excepted, may be expiated by pecuniary compensation to the parties seeking redress. Oaths are administered among the graves of their ancestors; and they swear, like the followers of Odin, over instruments of destruction, such as creeses and gun-barrels. Slavery and polygamy are allowed.

The natives are of a yellow complexion, with

flat noses and ears, standing at right angles with the head, both which deformities are effected by artificial means when infants. These are of course considered with them great beauties, as well as enormously long nails. They pluck out their beard, and file down their teeth even with their gums; sometimes leaving them in points like a saw, which they blacken with empyreumatic oil. Among the higher ranks of both sexes, the teeth are cased with gold, which by candle light, set off by the deep black tint given by the oil, has a splendid appearance. Their dress is very simple, and does not differ materially from the general Indian costume. They live in small villages, built on piles, and mount to their airy habitations by a sort of stair or ladder, which they draw up after them, as a security. Their chief luxury is smoking opium, which is imported from Bengal. They emit the smoke by the nostrils, and through the passages of the eyes and ears, keeping the mouth closely shut after taking a whiff. They live generally on vegetable food of the most simple form; and their rice is boiled in a green bamboo, which has so much sap, that it resists the fire during the operation. But every meal requires a new pot, which nature supplies in exhaustless plenty. Their wives are all purchased, and the chief wealth of a father consists in debts due to him on account of his daughters. The women are, therefore, slaves, and may be sold again by their husbands.

Along the coasts the natives are generally Mohammedans, and many of them are of Malay origin; but the real Sumatrans of the interior are in some cases savages, without any forms of worship, and in others wild idolaters. Mr. Marsden does not corroborate what Dr. Leyden has said respecting the cannibalism of the Batta tribe, who are rather a civilized people than otherwise. If they eat their criminals, therefore, it is out of detestation of their crime; and if they devour their old parents, it is from a custom founded on affection.

In the southern part of the island, the mangrove * nearly covers the whole marshy extent of the eastern quarter; and the branches form curious arches, curving from the trunk to the ground, so that near the sea, oysters and shell fish stick to them, and appear like fruit, which once gave rise to a belief in natural history, that there were oyster trees. Thus, we perceive how easily credulity may be imposed upon; and really it is no wonder, for man seeing both within himself and without, so many things that he cannot comprehend, is prepared to see, feel, hear, taste, and understand with the senses of others.

Bencoolen is our chief settlement on Sumatra. It is situated on the S. W. side of the island, in lat. 3° 50′ S. and long. 102° 3′ E. Near it there is a strong fort called Marlborough, which was founded

* Vide Addenda, XIX.

in 1714. It is subordinate to the Presidency of Bengal. The property of the East India Company at this place is estimated at 400,000*l*.

The Sumatrans in the vicinity of this settlement are polite and humane. Their principal punctilio consists in never pronouncing their own names, and a great embarrassment occurs when a stranger makes such an enquiry. Some of the women are very pretty, and have the same fondness for ornaments that females every where evince. Their hands are constantly cold. They are marriageable between ten and eleven years, but soon grow old, and even the men are short lived; sixty years being thought a great age. The Mohammedan boys are circumcised generally in their sixth year. All the diseases of India are known here. Burning fever is cured by pouring cold water over the patient, which brings on copious perspiration. There is a great difference between the Malay and Sumatran. The Sumatran is of the middle size, a yellow colour, and slender conformation; the Malay is sometimes tall, generally robust, of a dark complexion, inclining to a copper tinge, with broad features, and ferocious expression. There are not in the world more desperate pirates than the Malays. Their prows have attempted to board our ships of war. The excellence of the Sumatrans lies in the execution of most beautiful filagree works of silver and gold, which they perform like other Indians with extremely coarse tools, by unconquerable patience and industry. Silver is not a native of Sumatra; but gold is found, united with copper, in the mines, and in veins near Padang, where the Dutch founded a settlement subordinate to Batavia. It is said that about 20,000 ounces of gold are annually exported from Sumatra, with some large cargoes of pepper, in return for opium, English cloth, salt, &c.*

JAVA.

This island derives its present name from a misnomer of Ptolemy; for Yava signifies barley, which is not an indigenous grain, though now cultivated in the mountainous parts by Europeans. Java is separated from Sumatra by the Straits of Sunda; a channel of only twenty miles. The length of Java is six hundred miles, by an average breadth of ninety-five. It has a volcanic chain of mountains, which occasionally explodes. The soil is in general far richer than the neighbouring islands. In point of climate it differs but little. It is cooled by land and sea breezes, and the extreme heat of the marshes may be exchanged by a short journey for the bracing atmosphere of the mountains, where nearly all the grains, fruits, and vegetables of Europe flourish.

* Vide Marsden, Macpherson, Bruce, Elmore, &c.

The Javanese proclaim their honourable descent from the Wow Wow, which remarkable species of ape inhabits their forests, and he is held in great reverence. They are divided into five principal governments, Bantam, Jacatra, Cheribon, the empire of Soesoehoenan, and that of the Sultan. All these are subjected to the Dutch East India Company's government of Batavia, which I have described in the historical account of the trade of Holland with India. It is estimated on good authority that Java contains 3,000,000 of inhabitants, a considerable number of whom are Malays and Chinese; but the mass of the people are a distinct race, that formerly professed the doctrines of Brahma and Budha. They were converted to Mohammedanism in 1406, by Sheik Ben Israel, an Arabian, who became a powerful sovereign. The kings of Bantam and Cheribon are descended from him; and his mausoleum, situated near Cheribon, is one of the most curious and magnificent antiquities of the east. There are splendid remains of Hindooism at Borong Budor and Brambanan; and also in the districts of Mataram and Ballanbouang.

Java swarms with life; and its inhabitants may be said to eat and drink animalculæ, for every thing exhibits innumerable forms of living matter. The forests are impenetrable from thick underwood, creeping plants, spiders' webs of great strength, and every description of snake and venomous reptile. In the waters are prodigious numbers of all the eastern monsters and fishes, while the air teems with insects, and night blazes with phosphorescent flights of the fire-fly tribe. From the great cassowary to the little humming bird, the mountains and woods abound in the feathered race, and the boa constrictor is found here thirty feet long, and as thick as a buffalo, of which he makes but one meal.

But man* should be the great object with man; and if curiosity respecting our fellow creatures be a general inclination of our nature, the Javanese character furnishes a melancholy subject for contemplation. Here the government has been for ages one of the most terrible forms of complete despotism that ever disgraced the records of mankind, which has sunk human nature below the most sordid description of animal meanness with which we are acquainted. The will of the prince is law. He is restrained by no institutions, either civil or religious. Surrounded by a set of men whom he raises to honour or depresses to nothing by a breath of his mouth, the people are abject slaves, and these temporary nobles, sycophants who fawn and grovel in the filth of capriciousness, for the privilege of inflicting misery on their inferiors. A Javanese approaches his prince in a crawling manner, and

* For an account of the Dutch on the island of Java, vide the history of the East India Company of Holland, in another part of this work.

endeavours to appear in his presence an idiot and a pauper, to express emphatically the immeasurable inequality of his condition, compared to that of his sovereign. An inferior never presumes to stand in the presence of superior rank; he approaches and withdraws like a beast, and sits like a monkey covered with rags; for his best apparel is never exhibited in the presence of his king, as it would shew something like an equality of enjoyment. The Javanese are in body as in mind filthy, fond to excess of intoxicating liquors, notwithstanding the prohibitions of the Koran; careless about the chastity of their women; depraved in their morals, and addicted, like the Malays, to a passion for gaming and cock-fighting, in which they are imitated to a wonderful degree by the Chinese settlers. Their principal weapon is the creese or serpentine dagger of the Malays, which is made of Japan steel, and inflicts a ghastly wound. In clothing, household furniture, accommodation, ceremonies of marriage, &c. they do not differ materially from the natives of India on the continent. The young bride* is paraded about with similar noise and ostentation, after which she becomes the slave of her husband to all intents and purposes, and he may purchase as many wives as he pleases. Their colour is a deep brown, their eyes and hair jet black, their nose broad and flattened, and their teeth ebonied and

* Appendix, note 3.

decorated with gold. The women wear their hair in a knot on the top of their head, ornamented with jewels and flowers.

Java produces exceedingly fine rice, good pepper, valuable sugar, excellent coffee, and coarse cotton, with tobacco, which, added to bang, betel, and opium, charms away the cares of the natives. The fruits here are of the finest flavour; and the mangusteen of this island is delicious and beautiful beyond conception. It grows on a tree bearing at the same time, like the orange, both fruit and flowers. As it ripens, the fruit changes from a bright to a dark purple, and in shape it resembles a perfect sphere, resting on a green calyx, surmounted by a corona, divided charmingly into as many rays as the fruit consists of lobes. The upas, or anchar tree, is here without the deadly poisonous atmosphere attributed to it by Foersch, and believed to be fact by Dr. Darwin, with nearly all the forest trees of the eastern islands.*

This island was taken from the Dutch and French by Sir Samuel Achmuty, in 1811, under the auspices of Lord Minto, but restored by the peace of Paris. While it remained in our hands, very considerable improvements were introduced, and a mildness given by equity to the native character which may be the foundation of political happiness at a future period.†

* Vide Addenda, XX.

† Vide Stavorinus, Marsden, Barrow, Leyden, Hamilton, and Raffles.

BORNEO, CELEBES, AND THE MOLUCCAS.

Several small islands lie to the south-east of Java, but I think it would be uninteresting to notice them.

Between Sumatra, Java, New Guinea, the Philippines, and Cochin-China, are situated the two large islands of Borneo and Celebes, separated from each other by the straits of Macassar; and immediately to the eastward lie the cluster called the Moluccas. All these islands are inhabited by races of men like those already described. The Malays and Chinese are settled round the coasts; but in the interior the natives are savages, and some of the tribes anthropophagi, who drink out of the skulls of their enemies, and, at least once in their lives, must embrue their hands in human blood. They are known by the general name of Horaforas, and, being found not only in these islands, but in many other parts of India, there is strong reason to suppose that they are aborigines. These natives are divided into tribes, and some of them are advancing towards civilisation under rude governments. They cultivate the land, raise various crops, and carry on commerce with the coasts; exchanging gold, diamonds, spices, gums, &c. for opium, and different manufactures. One tribe of these singular people are called Biajoos, and live constantly in boats, on the sea, wandering about like gipsies, or itinerant fishermen, from isle to isle. They delight in the ceremony practised by the Maldivians, of launching little vessels loaded with their sins and misfortunes, which, they believe, will fall upon those mariners who may chance to meet their unlucky barks. Another tribe of them are called Tiroons, whose desperate acts as pirates are famous in the eastern seas. The Macassars and Buggesses of Celebes are expert workmen in iron, copper, and gold.

Borneo is 750 miles long, by 350 in average breadth. It is therefore by far the largest of the Asiatic isles; but the interior is little known. Some of its rivers, such as Banjarmassin and Passir, are large and navigable. There are fine elephants on this island, and its forests are inhabited by a large specimen of the ourang outang. The Dutch, French, and English have had settlements on Borneo, but none of them succeeded well. In 1774, the English East India Company established a factory at Passir; but the climate was so unfriendly, and the natives so treacherous, that it was abandoned. The French ship L'Epreuve was cut off here in 1774, and the whole crew assassinated, in the most horrible manner, by the attendants of a Malay chief, who was dining with the captain. An expedition was soon after sent from Chandernagor, to revenge the murderous act, and three hundred, perhaps innocent people, were butchered in the attack on the town. The French council's instruction to the captain was, "To seize a number of prisoners on the coast, and to put them on shore again, after having cut off their noses, ears, and hands."* Perhaps the barbarity of the former act could only be equalled by the latter; so true it is, that civilised nations become savages, when they give way to passion and vindictive ferocity. In 1700, the New English Company established a factory at Banjarmassin, where the Dutch had long been settled, but in 1707, they were nearly all massacred by the natives.

Celebes is 500 miles in length, and 150 in average breadth. It is deeply indented by two gulfs. The southern one is called Buggess Bay, while that to the north-east is named Tominee; near which, on the peninsula formed by it, is Fort Amsterdam, a Dutch settlement, whence much gold is received in exchange for opium, &c. In 1512, the Dutch got a footing in Macassar, on the south-west coast, and in time subverted the empire of that name, which was the principal one of the Buggess tribes, and perhaps the original seat of their language, laws, and government. The Dutch settlements were taken possession of by the English, in 1812, but restored at the pacification of Paris.

The Molucca islands comprise all those clusters,

* I give this on the authority of Hamilton's Gazetteer, p. 651.

which lie between Celebes and New Guinea; but the name is generally restricted to the Dutch spice isles of Amboyna, Banda, Ceram, Ternate, Tidore, and Batchian. Here the natives are the same as in Borneo and Celebes, with a mixture of Papuas, or Oriental negroes, who are supposed to be the aborigines of New Guinea, as they are found there in great plenty. These have been noticed before in our account of the Andamans and Malacca, and mention being made, in the history of the Dutch East India Company, of these spice islands, it would not be profitable to dwell on the subject here.*

THE PHILIPPINE ISLES.

Magellan, when he discovered these islands, called them the Archipelago of St. Lazarus; but Ruy Lopes de Villabolos named them the Philippines, in compliment to Philip II., of Spain, then prince of the Asturias. They are very numerous, lie between the 5th and 20th degrees of north latitude; and the principal ones are called Luzon, Mindoro, Panay, Marandique, Negros, Masbate, Zebu, Bohol, Leyte, Samar, and Magindanao. They were anciently called Bisayas, or Painted Islands, because the natives painted their bodies like Indians of old. Over all these, the Spaniards

* Vide Hamilton, &c. &c.

assume sovereignty, but they are in constant warfare with the pirates, who are a most unconquerable race, and start up in new places, when expelled from their old haunts and strong-holds.

Cheered with constant showers for a great part of the year, the soil of the Philippines is very fertile : but terrible hurricanes sometimes occur, that entirely destroy whole cultivated districts. The intolerance of the Spanish government has been such, with respect to religion and improvement, that these fine islands have remained under Europeans, in a languishing state, though rich in gold, and nearly all the productions of the eastern seas. The natives live on rice, sago, plantains, bread fruit, yams, and fish, and are so extremely indolent in the interior of the large islands, that they are only induced by necessity to move. Even the gold mines are worked so feebly, as scarcely to defray the expences. Here the Bisayans go nearly naked; their houses are huts of palm leaves; and they require no doors to secure their property, for a green bamboo serves them for a pot, a plantain leaf for a plate, their fingers and thumb are their forks, and a palm mat their cool bed. Many of the Papuan negroes, whom the Spaniards found here, were so wild and unapproachable, that they were thought to be satyrs, and men with tails, some of them are still found in the eastern isles, scarcely a degree above the beast in intellect; and their likeness to the ourang outang, has given rise to the belief, that he knew the use of fire, and dressed his own victuals. It is said, that the Bisayans are foreign intruders, and have nearly extirpated the Papuas, who were the original possessors of the Philippines. But there are many different tribes in this island, all agreeing, however, with the general characteristics already described in the other islanders. These people are governed by petty chiefs, and their laws are long established customs. They purchase their wives, are allowed only one by law, but as many concubines as they please; and the bridegroom often serves a number of years for his partner, as Jacob did heretofore, for his two helpmates. Many obscenities take place at a marriage ceremony, which is performed by sacrificing a hog.

Tagala is the general language, which is highly esteemed for its melody; and the literary natives had historical poems, and songs innumerable, till the Spanish missionaries took such pains to destroy these idolatrous records. Their religious ceremonies are performed in woods and arbours, like the Druids, at which a priestess presides, who, with a lance, pierces a hog, and works herself up to phrenzy, while the blood is flowing. The carcase is then divided and eaten, and the whole ends with dancing. They bury their dead, and place clothes, arms, and food on their tomb, believing that they still enjoy the things of this world, but their notions of a future state are exceedingly complex and confused.*

On the day of St. Lazarus, 1521, Magellan discovered these islands. In 1571, Legaspi conquered Luzon, or Luconia, and established Manilla as the capital of the Spanish possessions. Had the government countenanced industrious Chinese settlers, the Philippines would be, at this day, the garden of the East; but it was contrary to their policy. In 1574, their infant settlement was attacked by a Chinese pirate, with an army; but he was repulsed.

In 1590, the Spaniards successfully attacked the pirates of Sooloo. After the Dutch settled at Batavia, several wars ensued between them and the Spaniards. In 1762, Manilla was taken by the British force, under General Draper, but it was restored in 1764. The Spanish trade is now a mere trifle, and the colonies, neglected by the mother country and unsupported by Mexico, are sinking beneath the savage encroachments of numerous enemies.†

* Vide Addenda, XXI.

† Vide Zuniga, Sonnerat, Leyden, &c.

CHAPTER III.

GEOGRAPHICAL DESCRIPTION OF INDIA.

INDIA, or Hindostan, the country of the Hindoos, lies between the 8th and 35th degrees of north latitude, and the 72d and 92d of east longitude. Hindoo, in the Persian language, signifies black, and *sthan*, country. From the most early times this region was inhabited by the Indians, or black men. It comprehends an area of 1,020,000 geographical square miles.

As Cashmere, Nepaul, &c. have been already noticed, we have only briefly to describe the remainder of Hindostan Proper, the Deccan, and the Peninsula.

Hindostan Proper is generally subdivided into Lahore, Mooltan, Guzerat, Ajmeer, Delhi, Agra, Malwa, Allahabad, Oude, Bahar, and Bengal.*

The Deccan contains Aurungabad, Khandeish, Beder, Hyderabad, Nandere, the northern Sircars, Berar, Gundwana, Orissa, and Bejapoor.

* Vide Arrowsmith's Map of India.

It ought to be observed, that the British possessions in India are subdivided by the local authorities into civil and military districts. These, being often changed, need not be mentioned. In the Peninsula there are several tracts of country which received new names when they were ceded to the Company, or conquered by our arms. As nearly the whole now belongs to us, I shall not mention those partial designations, but confine myself to a natural subdivision of it.

The Peninsula comprehends the Carnatic, or all that region below the ghauts on the Coromandel coast; the Mysore, or all the countries above the ghauts to the river Krishna; and the Malabar coast, which is the usual name of that region westward of the Malabar ghauts, from Cape Comorin to Bombay, although it contains Canara, Cochin, Travancore, &c.

So extremely curious are the climate and natural history of India, that philosophers of all ages have been surprised, and their wondering speculations awakened by these subjects. It is never so hot in Canton as in Calcutta, nor so cold in Calcutta as in Canton; yet these places lie nearly in the same parallel of latitude, and at about equal distance from the sea. The seasons in India are called the two monsoons*; one from the south and another from the north, which extend from Africa

* Vide Addenda, XXIII.

to the longitude of New Holland and the east coast of China, and from the Himalaya mountains to the latitude of the trade winds in the Indian Ocean. But from the direction of the coasts, the intervention of mountains, the variation of the compass, &c., the monsoons visit India from the S.W. and N.E., and are thus denominated. The south-west monsoon brings with it black clouds and storms from the Indian seas. These clouds, filled with rain, and urged forward by the winds, open their flood-gates on the Malabar coast, in May, with frightful storms, and astounding thunder explosions. The monsoon would thence spread, in a regular sheet, over the Peninsula of India, were it not stopped by the ghauts on the coast of Malabar. Being turned northward by these lofty mountains so as to expand over the table-lands of Mysore, the Deccan, and Hindostan Proper, it visits these regions in regular succession, but in a much milder form than it bursts forth on the Malabar coast; for it makes astonishing struggles to conquer the lofty ghauts, and seems to exhaust itself in the loudest peals of thunder I ever heard against their huge heads. The rain falls here for several days together, literally in torrents. When the clouds reach the Himalaya range, the strength of the monsoon seems to revive from the opposition it meets with there. Being again turned from its natural course, it seems to visit Bengal from the north-west. The clouds are impeded in their progress so as not to reach the Coromandel coast till October, when the stormy season commences there. All ships belonging to Madras are then forced to fly for safety to the western coast of Ceylon, or round to Malabar. The rains having spent their fury on the Malabar coast in three months, and gone off with the storm called elephanta, such fine and lovely weather prevails there in October, that zephyr scarcely ruffles the ocean, while all the fury of the elements is felt on the other side of the ghauts. When the south-west monsoon, which commences in May and ends in October, prevails on the western coast of India, the north-east monsoon holds steadily on the eastern side of the Peninsula. In short, the winds and seasons on the two coasts are continually opposite.

Thus, although the operations of nature are regular throughout the whole of India, yet the interposition of localities has produced great variety, diametrical opposition, and wild eccentricity, at which the finite wisdom of man must pause in wonder, without being able to explain the causes to the satisfaction of his understanding. But whilst he is lost in incomprehensibility, he is filled with admiration at the infinite ways of the Almighty. Man seems to be every where like the atmosphere he breathes. On the mountain he is hardy, in the plain he is soft; in all situations he is liable to alternations of calm, gloom, agitation, and storm; but in India, where the law of local peculiarity governs nature, the people are also under the same influence, and still, like their atmosphere, they are endless in variety, diametrical in opposition, and wild in eccentricity; which character is exemplified both in national and particular individuality.

The inhabitants of India may be thus enumerated:—1st. Hindoos, who are said to be ten distinct nations *, but who come under the denominations of Brahmans, Jains, Budhists, Seiks, and Pariahs. 2d. Mohammedans, who are chiefly of the sect called Soonis. 3d. Parsees, who are followers of Zoroaster, and worship fire. 4th. Armenians. 5th. Jews. 6th. Nestorian Christians; and 7th. Europeans, who are Portuguese, Dutch, English, French, Danish, Spanish, and Swedish, with their spurious offspring by intercourse with the Indian females, now forming a very numerous race. The followers of Mohammed are to those of Brahma in the proportion of one to ten; but the other classes are not near so numerous. It is on the western coast only that the Parsees are settled. The Armenians are in all the great towns as merchants; the Jews and Nestorians are chiefly in Malabar; the Europeans all round the coast, which is now occupied by their descendants, in the proportion of one to ten of the natives; but although an exact census be very desirous, none has yet been taken, and the following is the nearest approxim-

* On the authority of Colebrooke in the Asiatic Researches.

ation to the whole population of India and the islands.

Under the direct government of Britain	60,000,000
Under our influence indirectly	40,000,000
Under independent chiefs beyond our control	20,000,000
In the islands of the Indian seas	20,000,000
Total population of the East Indies	140,000,000

The chief rivers of India are, the Brahmapootra, the Ganges, the Indus, the Sutleje, the Krishna, the Godavery, Jumna, Nerbudda, Cavery, Goggrah, Tuptee, Mahanuddy, Megna, Soane, Chumbul, Beyah, Gunduck, and Ravey. Its mountains are, the Himalaya ridges, which cross the country from the Brahmapootra river to Persia, rising one above the other, and producing the three great rivers, Indus, Ganges, and Brahmapootra; the mountains of Kemaoon and Sewalic; the eastern and western ghauts; and the Vinchyan chain, which crosses India parallel to the Nerbudda. The great cities are, Surat, Benares, Calcutta, Delhi, Madras, Bombay, Agra, Lucknow, Patna, Moorshedabad, Dacca, Poonah, Hyderabad, Nagpoor, Catmandoo, Oojain, Jyenagur, Amritsar, Lahore, and Seringapatam.

There are, generally speaking, two harvests,

called Khereef and Rubbee; the first in September and October, the latter in March and April. The general food is rice, and the implements of husbandry are simply awkward. It requires three or four strokes of their ill-formed plough to produce a furrow. This instrument is often only a piece of crooked wood, shod with iron, and drawn by a pair of ill-yoked oxen. Their harrow is like a short ladder, upon which a man stands, whilst he drives the bullocks that draw it to break the clods with his weight. The cart, or car, called hackery, generally used throughout India, is a bamboo frame, supported by two wheels, the shape of which frame is that of an acute triangle, and the point of it passes up between two oxen, and rests on a sort of ladder, in which their necks are placed. What we perform with a spade and shovel, the Hindoos do with a sort of hoe in a sitting posture. Their reaping-hook is a short crooked knife; and they tread out the grain in the fields by means of oxen that are driven round a threshing floor of baked clay; after which it is secured in earthen bee-hive-shaped granaries, about the size of barrels, smeared over with cow dung to guard it from white ants. In the vicinity of large towns the implements of husbandry are better: but I am speaking generally of the country. The inhabitants of small villages or towns have, in some places, a joint interest in the crop, the labour being performed by contribution, and the cattle grazed together; but in numerous cases, the fields for tillage are private property, while those for pasture are common to all. A fixed rent, which is estimated according to the value of the crop, is paid for the land to the zemindar, or person who holds it from government, and the cultivator has, for his share, barely what keeps him from absolute want. There is in every considerable village and town a dhuramsallah, or inn, for strangers, with a person to attend and furnish what may be required. Each village has a magistrate, and many of them a court called pancheat, or five old men, who decide upon all matters of minor import at one hearing. Superior courts are held at fixed places, both civil and criminal, where the laws are administered according to the Hindoo and Mohammedan written codes and customs. The Hindoos have an admirable collection, said by them to have been composed by Menu, many millions of years ago, with commentaries by learned pundits, a considerable part of which has been translated by Sir William Jones, and some of their laws carefully digested by Sir H. T. Colebrooke. They form a magnificent testimony in favour of the great antiquity and civilisation of the Hindoos.

These laws establish some curious points. They must have been compiled at a time when civilisation had attained a place which it never surpassed in India. At that period the Brahmanical authority must have been in full force, for the laws are all in favour of priestcraft; where that is not concerned, they are often framed on the broad and universal basis of natural equity. These laws display a wonderful degree of refinement and barbarism: on commercial points, on the duties of kings and magistrates, and on the various modes of lending money and securing property, the most acute wisdom and knowledge of human nature are indicated; but in the various regulations for preserving power and producing implicit obedience, inhumanity, perjury, and slavery are resorted to: children and wives being made slaves to their parents and husbands, the people were subjected to the despotism of kings, and kings to the tyranny of priests. The great difference then, between the eastern world and the western in civilisation is this, that whereas religion was formed in the latter for a support to government, in the former government was produced to support religion. The treatment of women too forms another grand difference between Europe and India. These particulars certainly divide the whole world into east and west, giving a peculiar character to the institutions of each.

What distinguish the Hindoos, in general, are the delicate and slender form of their bodies, their equality of mind, their living on vegetable food, their distribution into castes, their early marriages, and their painted faces, which have continued the same since the time of Alexander the Great. But in travelling from Madras to Cashmere, up the centre of India, the greatest variety is obvious to superficial observation. There are not greater differences between the French, Italians, English, Swedes, and Russians, than between the different nations of India, who speak distinct languages, and inhabit the several parts of Hindostan, which are together nearly as large as all Europe.

The Vedas, or sacred books, of the Hindoos, are written in Sanscrit, which is now a dead language, as well as the Purannas, which are commentaries on them. There are also the Prakrit, the learned language of the Jains; the Bali, the sacred tongue of the Budhists; and the Zend, in which the books of Zoroaster are written, all derivations from Sanscrit, now unknown as living tongues. But besides these very ancient languages, there are ten distinct tongues, supposed to have been spoken by ten different nations, which form the groundwork of all the dialects of India. These are the Saraswata, the Kanoge, the Gour, the Tirhoot, Orissa, Tamul, Mahratta, Carnata, Telinga, and Gurjara.

Among the Hindoos, there are no titles of nobility in the gift of their rajahs, or kings, as in Europe, but they can reward by bestowing a jaghire, or gift of land, with an honorary appellation, which is not hereditary. The Hindoos are divided into many religious sects. Five worship a single deity; one adores the five great divinities; several worship Chrishna under different forms, others Vishnu, some Mahadeva, and several Bhavani. Great alterations have taken place in the Brahmanical institution: and rituals founded on the Purannas and Tantras, have obsoleted the Vedas. Besides these are several philosophical sects, whose refinements equal those of Greece, Rome, &c. Vishnu is worshipped under ten avaters, or incarnations, and he is expected shortly in the form of a horse. But it is not by prayers to their gods, that the Hindoos expect to work out their perfection, but by such mortifications as Tarika performed, who is reported to have nearly dethroned the king of heaven by their powerful efficacy. These consisted in standing for a length of time in positions that produced excruciating pain. Various modes of suicide are believed to secure future happiness. A woman is promised paradise, who burns herself with her husband's dead body. Men are promised the same, for starving themselves, burning their bodies in dry cow dung, burying themselves in snow, at the source of the Ganges, giving themselves to sharks and alligators at Saugur Island *, cutting their own throats at Allahabad, burying themselves alive, and throwing themselves from precipices. Long and expensive pilgrimages are also made to ensure salvation, or happy transmigration; and a journey of 1000 miles is sometimes

* Vide Appendix, note 4.

performed, by tumbling all the way. To cut and mangle the body, to be crushed under Juggernaut's car, to renounce the world, and to live in deserts, are other modes; but it may be generally observed, that the Brahmans seem to have invented these various torments, pilgrimages and sanctifications for purposes of deep policy; for when they elevated the man to fame who sacrificed himself, they opened a road to ambition, and either sent troublesome spirits out of the world, or gratified them with the praises of men while in it. Peter on his pillar was as vainglorious as Alexander at Babylon.

The Brahman religion has no visible head of the church, each great pagoda being dependent on its own fame and sanctity. Some Hindoo sects shave the whole head, except a tuft of hair on the crown, unless when undergoing mortifications, when it is allowed to grow wild, and to mat with oil and ashes, so as to appear frightful. Some of the Brahmans take a vow of celibacy, others marry. All Brahmans are not priests, but they are nevertheless held sacred, and placed above the law as to life; for it is the greatest of all crimes to kill one of them, under any circumstances. The four great castes of Hindoos never intermarry, nor eat together, except at some great sacrifice that levels all distinction for a moment. This happens in the presence of Juggernaut. The same caste is not an introduction to society in different parts of India, where a man is a stranger. A freemason will be admitted into a lodge in a strange country, by a sign and word, but a Hindoo remains an outcast, when at a distance from his own little circle. But he must scrupulously observe the rules of his own society, or he would be expelled, and never again be admitted to any other sect; for the Hindoo religion, so far from aiming, like the Mohammedan at conversion, will not receive a proselyte; yet it looks with perfect charity on all worshippers, as pleasing to God, and objects of his care. The Mohammedans and Hindoos now live together in perfect harmony, though at first some persecuted Hindoos were circumcised by force. It is supposed that the Brahmans were philosophers, who came into India, while it was in a barbarous state, and subverted the horrid practices which still prevail in the Eastern isles.

In Hindostan they reckon that four ages, consisting of many millions of years, have elapsed since the creation, but the Chinese and Hindoos are surpassed by the Jains, who believe that they never had a beginning, and that the world was never formed.

Polygamy and slavery are permitted by law, but the customs and privileges of women are very different in the various tribes of Hindostan, as well as their ceremonies, both civil and religious. The Hindoo character is in general parsimonious, except on occasion of marriage, and in the celebration of annual sacred feasts, at which vast sums are expended in ostentatious display. In the marriage ceremony, the young bride and bridegroom are paraded about with all the magnificence of wealth which the parties can command; and at festivals, the idols are drawn through the public streets, on gorgeous carriages, with amazing pomp and noise. The lower orders have seldom more than one wife, who is as little secluded from society as a peasant's wife in Europe. Nearly all the children go perfectly naked for two or three years, but many of them have a silver plate, in the form of a heart, suspended from a string tied round their loins, to hide the sight of what modesty prompts all nations to conceal. The females are immoderately fond of ornaments, and their noses, ears, wrists, fingers, ancles, and toes are loaded with rings and jewels, in proportion to their circumstances. Every where companies of dancing girls will be found, who are devoted to pleasure. They take great care of their beauty, preserve their breasts from injury by keeping them in artificial forms, or moulds, which fasten behind, while their beautiful and delicate bodies are rendered soft and glossy by constant ablutions, champoing with the fingers, which opens the pores, and anointing with perfumed oils. Their jet black hair is tied up in a knot, decorated with white flowers and gold, their eye-lashes are painted black, and their teeth often stained with the same colour; but sometimes of an ivory whiteness, from their simple vegetable food. Their small delicate feet and legs are bare, as also their arms, and part of their bodies; for the Hindoo female dress is in general one long piece of white, coloured, or embroidered muslin, or cotton, wound round the loins, so as to form a petticoat, while the end of it is drawn gracefully round the breast, and serves for a veil to cover the head occasionally, or to hang on the smooth playful arm. The Hindoo male dress, of the lower orders, is nothing but a langutty, or loin cloth, but the higher ranks wear rich turbans, trowsers, and gowns, with party coloured sandals or slippers, and gorgeous shawls, sparkling in gold and silver.

The whole of the Mogul empire may now be considered as transferred to Great Britain. In the reign of Acber, it yielded a revenue of 36,000,000*l.* per annum, and was governed by an unwieldy army of plundering irregulars. In 1812, the East India Company's total revenue was 17,000,000*l.*, but it has since greatly increased by conquests in the Deccan. It now exceeds 22,000,000*l.*, which will under proper management gradually improve, as population advances and security is felt. The combined debts of the three presidencies amounted, in 1812, to near 30,000,000*l.*, which, owing to wars and increased expenses, is not yet much reduced. However, the assets of the Company are immense, and their affairs must be considered very prosperous; for although the free trade has slightly injured their commercial profits, yet they have still the monopoly of all that is truly valuable. Supported by an army of 30,000 Europeans, and 150,000 natives, well organised, commanded by British officers, and kept in constant activity, the stability of our empire rests at present upon a firm basis. But the fabric of human wishes is always in a tottering state; and vain are the prognostications of short-sighted mortals! There are in India about 40,000 British born subjects, in the Company's service, as civilians, military officers and soldiers, free merchants, and mariners, lawyers, shopkeepers, and settlers. The civil servants are about 2000 in number, and the establishment of the three courts of judicature above 300.

Females appear to be more numerous in Hindostan than males. Perhaps I may be wrong in this surmise; for in some tribes several men have but one wife; yet in others, for centuries past, the female children were destroyed. The following are facts in support of my assumption. Scarcely a Hindoo ever remains unmarried till twenty-five; indeed they are all fettered with wedlock when children; many of them have ten or twelve wives in the course of their lives; young widows never marry again; the companies of dancing girls are prodigiously numerous; and the number of Hindoo females that attach themselves to Europeans is very great. Women in India ripen soon, and wither fast; they are mothers in their eleventh year, and decrepid with age at thirty; but among men the wear and tear of life are not so, for many of them enjoy health of body and mind till ninety years old, and some reach a period considerably beyond 100.

Rice is their general food, with much spice, and but little animal addition. To its use may be attributed the slender form of their bodies, and the even texture of their minds, free from many of our perturbations, and calmly patient under sufferings, which in Europe would rouse most dangerous passions into immediate action.

The varieties of men have perhaps been thus formed imperceptibly, by accidental causes, influenced by peculiarity of climate. A Hindoo lives on rice, he is soft and watery; a Chinese may derive some of his qualities from tea; as an Arabian does from coffee, a Laplander from fish, and an Englishman from beef and ale. Men are every where radically the same in disposition and propensity. Colour, in such instances as have come under my observation, makes no difference in the texture of the mind. Genius has been found in slavery, and talent in chains. National physical superiority is flattering to pride; but in reality civilised man is the creature of institutions; he is, generally speaking, elevated or depressed in the scale of human estimation, just in proportion as the community to which he belongs is wise or foolish. *

* Vide Addenda, XXII.

Having made these introductory remarks, which are supported as well by personal observation as by numerous high authorities, we shall proceed rapidly to describe the divisions of India.

THE PENINSULA OF INDIA.

That part of the southern triangle of India, which extends from the river Krishna to Cape Comorin, called the Peninsula, is divided into three parts by the hand of nature: these are the Carnatic, Mysore, and Malabar. Malabar is, in its extended sense, all that country lying along the western ghauts, next the sea, from Cape Comorin, where they rise, to the river Tuptee, where they change their direction eastward, and run off till lost in the neighbourhood of Boorhanpore. This region is in breadth from forty to seventy miles, which is the general distance of the ghauts from the sea shore. From the western ghauts, in the latitude of about 15° N. a chain of mountains runs off eastward, and winds round northerly till it reaches the Krishna river, on the Coromandel coast. These ghauts rise to unequal heights, many of them towering far above the clouds, but generally supporting a magnificent terrace of 3000 feet above the level of the sea, called the Mysore. Many of the mountains rise above that country from three to four thousand feet. All the low country is called the Carnatic, on the eastern side of the western ghauts, and the one coast is denominated Coromandel, while the other is styled Malabar. The whole country, therefore, below the ghauts, we describe by the names of Carnatic and Malabar; and all above these mountains, to the river Krishna, by the appellation of Mysore.* From the source of the Krishna, which is in the western ghauts near Sattara, only about fifty miles from the sea coast of Malabar, this fine river courses about 650 miles, in many beautiful meanders, and falls into the Bay of Bengal, near Masulipatam, where a considerable portion of the Carnatic, along the eastern ghauts, is called the Northern Sircars. The Krishna in its course is joined by five other considerable rivers, called the Warnah, Malproba, Gutpurba, Beemah, and Toombuddra, besides a multitude of other smaller ones, and at its junction with the sea, it forms a magnificent body, though it is not navigable far inland.

There are four principal rivers in the Carnatic, which have their source in the western ghauts of the table-land. These are the Palar, the Cavery, the Pennar, and the Vaggaroo; but the country is nevertheless in many parts ill supplied with water; to remedy which deep wells are dug, and large tanks constructed, that yield a supply for indispensable irrigation, thrown up by very simple machinery.

* Vide Hamilton's East India Gazetteer.

The soil is in general sandy, the climate the hottest in India, from local position, but not subject to hot winds, on account of the sea and land breezes, which blow in daily alternation. Vegetation is parched during the dry season, and few trees grow without much care and labour; the melia azadarichta and the robinia mitis being, I have been informed, the only ones which flourish spontaneously in some parts of the interior. But the coasts are beautified with palms, and many parts inland luxuriantly green from the effects of patient industry; yet the Carnatic requires annual supplies of rice from Bengal, &c., which are paid for by an extensive exportation of piece goods, in the manufacture of which the people have been long celebrated.

The Nabob of the Carnatic, and the various chiefs and Polygars who composed the government of the country, before our influence in it, have now no political power; they live on pensions or jaghires of land, and may be considered in the light of independent gentlemen, or petty nobles. Their power in the administration of justice has been transferred to the Company's civil servants, who as judges, magistrates, and collectors, have the whole country divided into districts, and hold native courts according to ancient custom.

In no part of India are there so many great pagodas as in the Carnatic. The Hindoo idols are worshipped in these magnificent fabrics with gross enthusiasm. The bull is a general object of adoration, and in some villages, one is kept as a living idol, and when he dies his body is buried with great pomp. There are not many Mohammedans in the Carnatic, but Christian converts are numerous in the vicinity of Tranquebar *, and some other places. It is computed that there are 50,000 Christians. The Brahmans have nearly the monopoly of all the different offices in the revenue and judicial departments. Many of them, being of the secular order, hold large tracts of land, which are cultivated by their slaves. Nearly all the peasantry are of the Sooder, or fourth caste. There is a wandering tribe, called Chensu Carir, who have no fixed habitations, and whose wealth lies in droves of small asses, which convey them with their children and mat houses, round the country, like gipsies.

Malabar also belongs entirely to Great Britain, in a political point of view, though a small part of it be in the possession of the rajah of Travancore, who exercises over it the rights of an independent sovereign; but he is restricted in all external power. The revenue he pays the Company is considerable. There are in Travancore † about 90,000 Christians, and 30,000 Jews, and in the whole of Malabar full 300,000 Christians of all descriptions; but the mass of the inhabitants are pure Hindoos with peculiar customs and manners, though Moham-

* Vide Appendix, note 5. † Ibid. note 6.

medans and Parsees are also very numerous along the sea coast. In no part of India is the pride of caste more upheld than here. Some time ago, it was common for a Brahman, or a Nair, to cut a low caste man, or a Pariar down, like a noxious reptile that presumed to approach so as to come in contact. There are castes here held so infamous as not to be allowed to approach the habitations of others, and these miserable outcasts live in the woods, like wild men. In some tribes on this coast, the husband never cohabits with his own wife; she remains in the house of her brothers, and bestows her favours on whom she pleases; generally on the Namboory Brahmans, who are thought to be the most honourable fathers for offspring. Thus no Niar is said to know his father. Inheritance therefore runs in the female line, the sister's children being equal heirs to all property left by the head of the house. There are about thirty different sects of Nairs; many of them eat animal food *, and in general they are fond of intoxicating liquors. They are of the royal race of Malabar, second in rank to the Brahmans, and under them there are several other tribes of freemen and slaves. The astrologers of Malabar are still held in high estimation. Infanticide, from their predictions, was arrested by the Portuguese, and it is now unknown. Formerly, thousands of

* Vide Addenda, XXIV.

infants, it is said *, lost their lives in Malabar, whose stars were ascertained to predict misfortune ; as if it were in the power of man to rob destiny by committing murder.

The exports of Malabar consist chiefly of coir, cocoa nuts, fine timber for ship building, which grows in the ghauts, and is a species of oak called teak, rice, ghee or clarified butter, dry ginger, piece goods, cardamoms, pepper, sandal wood, sapan wood, turmeric, arrow root, betel nut, and iron.

Malabar is a lovely country of hill, dale, and valley, with a magnificent horizon on one side, rising to the sky, and on the other a blue cheerful sea. The rivers are very numerous, but having a course only from the ghauts, they are of little consequence as navigable streams. There is an interesting diversity in this province, not to be found in other parts of India, for the inhabitants live in single houses scattered all over it, peeping beautifully from amidst plantations of cocoa nuts, pepper vines, and plantain groves.

Many of the villages are romantically situated, and embellished with great taste. The Brahman and Teerettee girls of Malabar are very beautiful, and their dress is simple and becoming. An European may here purchase a blooming young female, for a few pounds sterling. It is not lawful for a proprietor of slaves to sell man and wife in separate

* By the Abbe Raynal.

lots, but children may be separated from their parents. Men are sold for about 7*l.*, and children for 2*l.*; and parents who are freemen have power to sell their own children. But it is to be hoped that Great Britain will establish universal freedom in India, and rescue human nature in the East, as well as in the West, from degradation and bondage.

The whole of Mysore, with the exception of a small part, nominally under the rajah, elevated from obscurity upon our conquest of the country, in 1799, belongs to the East India Company. It it watered by several fine rivers which flow into the Krishna, or towards the eastern ocean through the Carnatic. It is generally a fine fertile country, yielding rich crops of rice, several kinds of pulses, (among which is the cynosurus coraeanus, called raggy,) ricinus palma Christi, poppy, tobacco, cocoa nuts, and betel. The cattle are cows, buffaloes, small horses, sheep, and goats, with nearly all our varieties of poultry, a fine display of fruits, and excellent vegetables. No climate in India is finer than that of Mysore; the air being refreshed by showers during the breaking of the two monsoons, and cooled by elevation, without being subject to the rarefaction of the more northern parts. Mysore yields a considerable quantity of iron ore; and nearly all the butter used in the Carnatic is exported from it in a preserved state without salt; which is effected by keeping the butter till rancid, and then boiling it till every watery particle evaporates, after which it is called ghee, and put up in large flasks made of leather.

Although Mysore was for a long time subject to the Mohammedan sway, yet there are not many moslems in it; the mass of the people being rigid Hindoos, It is, on the whole, in a flourishing state; and certainly a far finer country than the Carnatic. The people live in villages and towns, and their houses are generally built with stone or mud, and covered with tiles, whereas in the Carnatic, and in many parts of Malabar, the dwellings are composed of wood or mud, and thatched with palm leaves.

The star pagoda, value about eight shillings, is a current gold coin, in the Carnatic, Mysore, and in Malabar; and rupees, of different denominations, in value, averaging two shillings the silver ones, with a copper piece of different small standards, like our pence and half-pence. In most other parts of India, the gold coin is a mohur, worth about thirty shillings, with silver and copper mediums, similar to those just mentioned. The day is generally throughout Hindostan divided into sixty parts, and an hour, or one portion, into twenty-four minutes. Distances are computed by miles of an hour each, that is the length commonly travelled over in twenty-four minutes, or about two and a half English miles.*

* Vide Addenda, XXV.

Both in Mysore and in part of Malabar, the Jains are numerous, and there are some interesting remains of their skill in sculpture to be seen. The palaces of Seringapatam are now, like many things that have been, of little interest, and a heap of ruins will soon mark the spots where they once proudly stood claiming immortality. Such is the fleeting nature of human grandeur.

THE DECCAN.

Deccan means the south, and formerly signified all the countries of India southward of Hindostan Proper. It is so understood by the author of the circumnavigation of the Erythrean sea; but the word is now restricted to the high country between the rivers Nerbudda and Krishna, while the region below the ghauts, or northern part of Malabar, is called the Concan.

The Nerbudda has its source in lat. 22° 54′ N. and long. 82° 15′ E. at a sacred well called Omercuntuc, and flowing westerly in almost a straight line, falls into the sea, after a course of 750 miles in the gulf of Cambay, after watering the fine province of Guzerat for a considerable way. This quarter of India is also fertilised by the Tuptee river, which rises in the Ingardy hills, and falls into the sea at Surat, after a course westerly of about 500 miles, part of which is through the strong province of Kandeish; and also the Godavery, which has its source in the western ghauts, about seventy miles north of Bombay, and flows easterly to the Bay of Bengal, after a winding course of about 850 miles, where its mouths form several navigable harbours.

From this river to the south-western archipelago of Bengal, the country is called Orissa. It is about 530 miles in length by ninety in average breadth, and in general character it is a mountainous region, inhabited by the Ooreas, who are a wild and uncivilised race of aboriginal Indians, driven to the most barren parts by the Mohammedan and Mahratta conquerors. The sea coast, in many parts, is however an exception; and the great temple of Juggernaut has for ages attracted such prodigious numbers of pilgrims, that for many miles around there is a polish of manners not surpassed in any part of India. Orissa is watered by the Mahanuddy, by the Byturnee, and Subunreeka rivers, which flow, like the Godavery, into the Bay of Bengal, after courses of considerable length. A rugged chain of mountains extends from the Godavey to the Mahanuddy, and forms a strong barrier inland along this coast. The whole of Orissa may now be said to be under the direct influence of the company; for much of the political power of the rajah of Berar is at an end.

To the westward of Orissa, lies the province of Gundwana, a great part of which is also wild and barren. The best parts are inhabited by the Mahrattas, and the worst by the Gounds, who continue almost in a state of nature. In the centre of the Deccan, are situated the territories of the Nizam, where a considerable portion of the population are Mohammedans, and southward to the Krishna lie the territories lately belonging to the Peishwa, which are now part of the British empire, for very little has been restored to the Sattara rajah, and he is entirely without external political influence. To this great acquisition has also been added the province of Kandeish, ceded by Holkar at the termination of the late Mahratta war, at least all his share of it; so that the whole Deccan, and Concan virtually belong to the Company, for both the Nizam and rajah of Berar have received subsidiary British forces, which entirely places their political influence at the disposal of Great Britain.

The whole of the Deccan, with that part of Guzerat south of the Nerbudda, is a remarkably fine country. In point of climate and natural advantage, it ranks with any part of India, but long distracted with war, famine, and plunder, it is in many places very thinly inhabited. The people live in walled towns, and every where the ruins of former grandeur present a melancholy picture to observation. The mountainous parts are inhabited by wild tribes of various denominations, almost in a state of nature; but the Mahrattas occupy the best districts, and conform to the principles, manners, and customs of the Hindoos; though it is said they were originally Persian emigrants*; but this is involved in great obscurity, and a difference of opinion prevails respecting the origin of this martial and restless race.

Every thing in the Mahratta states wears a warlike appearance. The summits of hills and mountains are strongly fortified, the towns are fortresses, and nearly all the inhabitants go armed. While these ambitious people had political independence, civilisation and peace could never exist very long in India. Their plundering excursions destroyed civilisation, and never permitted peace to afford security, which is the great object of all social aims.

Near the ancient city of Dowlutabad, are the famous caves of Elora, which are certainly most magnificent monuments of the Hindoo religion. Here the whole side of a mountain has been excavated, and the living rock formed into such endless variety, as would baffle the most laborious description.

The finest diamonds in the world are found in the Deccan, for which the mines of Golconda have been ever celebrated, and the whole region is teeming with natural and artificial curiosities.

* On the authority of Major Wilford, in the Asiatic Researches.

HINDOSTAN PROPER.

It has been remarked, that from the river Nerbudda southward, India forms a fine triangle. Another triangle may be said to be formed by the countries northward of the Nerbudda; for the great rivers, Indus and Ganges, which are the western and eastern boundaries of Hindostan Proper, have their sources, at no great distance from each other, in the Himalaya mountains.

Of all the great rivers in India, the Ganges is the most useful to man. It performs a winding journey of full 1500 miles, from its source to the Bay of Bengal, receives a great number of fine navigable rivers in its course, and fertilises the richest provinces of Hindostan, bearing commerce on its bosom, and affording employment to 300,000 of the natives. During the monsoon, the Ganges rises thirty-two feet above its lowest level, and overflows its banks, in some places being then 100 miles in breadth, with the inhabited parts like islands scattered over its glass-like surface. When at its lowest the principal channel varies from 400 yards to one and a quarter mile wide, but is commonly about three-fourths of a mile in breadth. At 500 miles from the sea, the channel is thirty feet deep, when the river is at the lowest. Taking the medium of the whole year, the quantity of water discharged by the Ganges is about 180,000 cubic feet, per second of time.

We shall now proceed to notice the principal provinces that compose Hindostan Proper. But as the three seats of British government, Calcutta, Madras, and Bombay, are described in another part of this work, no particular mention is made of them here.

Bengal is about 350 miles in length by 300 in average breadth, and its richness of soil is amazingly great. Its general character is that of a flat campaign country, yielding prodigious crops of rice, wheat, and barley. The Delta of the Ganges is annually enriched by the mud of the river, and there is not a stone to be found in it. The important productions of Bengal are tobacco, sugar, indigo, cotton, silk, and opium *; and to all the Indian fruits, are now added some from China and Europe. Vegetables are in great plenty. The potatoe flourishes here and in most parts of India; and the rivers yield a great variety of fish, among which is that called the mangoe fish, from its supposed resemblance in taste and flavour to the delicate fruit so named. I say, supposed taste and flavour, because, though I often eat the mangoe fish in Calcutta, I never could discover these qualities. All nature teems with life, from

* Vide Addenda, XXVI.

the elephant and royal tiger *, to the fire-fly and musquito.

The inhabitants of Bengal are very numerous, and generally average 200 to a square mile. In the eastern districts, the Mohammedans are almost as numerous as the Hindoos, but elsewhere they do not constitute a fifteenth of the inhabitants, who are rigid followers of Brahma. The Bengalese are a quiet, soft race of men, who have generally submitted to foreign dominion, without any efforts for freedom.

Bahar, which is an equally fine province, lies westward of Bengal, and contains about 26,000 square miles. It is more subject to the hot winds than Bengal, and yields a vast quantity of saltpetre, which is largely produced during their continuance. It has, therefore, been supposed that these winds are essential to the formation of nitre in this quarter. Cultivation is here carried on with such care, that in the vicinity of Patna, the fields look like fine English gardens.

Westward of Bahar, lies the province of Allahabad, which is 270 miles in length by 120 in average breadth. It is watered by the Ganges, Jumna, Goomty, and Caramnassa, and it contains the famous cities of Benares and Allahabad, two of the most sacred places of Hindoo pilgrimage. Its exports are diamonds, saltpetre, opium, sugar, indigo, cotton, manufactures of cotton and silk, &c.

* Vide Addenda, XXVII.

The kingdom of Oude lies to the north of Allahabad. It is in length about 250 miles by 100 in breadth, and produces, with all the varieties before mentioned, a considerable quantity of lapis lazuli, which is very valuable. This province is intersected by the Goggrah river, and bounded on the west by the Ganges, while to the north and east lie the territories of Nepaul. The Hindoo race in Oude is much superior, both in mental and bodily qualities, to the natives of Bengal. They retain the warlike characteristics of their ancestors, the conquerors of Ceylon. In this province Mohammedans are very numerous. The king of Oude holds his court at Lucknow; but his political power rests entirely with the Company, who defend his kingdom from foreign aggression.

North of Oude, is the province of Delhi, in which the Mogul emperors long exercised despotic dominion over the East. It is about 240 miles long by 180 broad; but having been long the scene of plunder and desolation, it is thinly inhabited, and in Delhi, heaps of ruin every where meet the eye. The best parts of it are in our possession, and the worst are occupied by petty chiefs, belonging to the Seik confederacy, who, instead of supporting the national rank which their founders gained, now weaken each other by constant civil war.

All these provinces may be ranked as directly under the control of the East India Company, together with the greatest part of Agra, which is about 250 miles long and 180 broad; and they constitute the British possessions in the eastern and northern quarters of Hindostan Proper, along with the districts of Kemaoon, &c. lately ceded by the Goorca government of Nepaul.

The territories of Dowlut Row Scindea, who is now the most powerful of the Mahratta chiefs, are situated principally in Malwah. He retains a considerable share of independence, which he secured by judiciously bending to necessity, at the commencement of the last Mahratta war; while Holkar, and the rajah of Berar, by trying the fortune of battle, placed their political consequence in the hands of Great Britain. The Rajpoot states lie in the province of Ajmeer, almost in the centre of Hindostan Proper; and the inhabitants are among the bravest and noblest races of the Hindoos; considering themselves descended directly from the ancient royal race, they are actuated by very high principles of patriotism and honor *; but being divided by the feudal system of government, which prevails among them, they never pursue a combined effort for empire. Mooltan and Lahore, which lie northward of Ajmeer, are possessed by a few petty chiefs, who by their continual feuds retard the progress of improvement, and barbarise their subjects. The province of Lahore, which

* Vide Addenda, XXVIII.

extends to the northern mountains, 320 miles in length and 220 in average breadth, is one of the finest in India, as to natural advantages, being watered by five fine rivers, which form what is called the Punjab; but, for the reasons before mentioned, it is now but thinly inhabited, and under a most disorganised government, amounting nearly to complete anarchy. In this province the Seik government, which is a theocracy and republicanism, was established by a philosopher, named Nanac, who apostatised from the creed of Brahma to pure Deism, and received converts from all religions, permitting them to retain their original manners and customs. But as some account of this curious nation is given hereafter, we shall merely say in this place, that the Seiks are the only state in India, which ever seems to have imbibed republican principles, and in the confusion which followed the death of Aurengzebe in 1707, those principles, and the ambitious views which then expanded, raised the Seiks to a formidable and dangerous height of power; but they have since sunk into political insignificance, and are now divided into separate interests and irreconcilable feuds.

By late conquests in Cutch, and the state of our connection with the government of Baroda, the whole sea coast, from the mouths of the Indus, round to Bombay, is subservient to the East India Company, who may be said to command all the resources of Guzerat and Kattywar.

The large and fine province of Guzerat occupies nearly the same place on the west of India, as Bengal does on the east, and yields, generally speaking, similar crops; but cotton is the great article of export. In length, this province is about 320 miles, including that part of it which lies south of the river Nerbudda, and 180 in average breadth. It is rich in precious stones, such as cornelians and agates, and at this day, as in 1582, when Abul Fazel compiled the institutes of Acber, it is famous for painters, carvers, and handicraftmen.

This province is inhabited by various classes of Hindoos, some of whom, in the mountainous and barren parts, are professed thieves, and the most expert pilferers in the world; others are receivers of stolen goods, by public occupation; and these tribes have given rise to a set of men, who stake their lives as security for the safety of persons and property. These are the Charons and Bhauts, who are of Brahman origin, and are held sacred by the Bheels, or thieves, who account it the most horrible crime to shed their blood; upon this prejudice the securities act, and when they fail in protection, mutilate themselves in a most dreadful manner. The tribe called Banyans are also very numerous in Guzerat. They have a great respect for animal life, and establish hospitals for the old and sickly of the brute creation. Here also are numerous establishments of Jains, of whom an account is given hereafter, who carry fans made of feathers to frighten away insects, lest they should inadvertently deprive any thing that exists of life.

Besides the Hindoos, Guzerat contains a great many Mohammedans and Parsees. These fire worshippers came to India during the Mohammedan persecutions, and being encouraged by the native princes, on account of their great industry and inoffensive dispositions, they have greatly increased, and acquired much property along the coast, even to the extremity of Malabar. Their women are placed on a complete equality with the men, and their morality is so pure, that a single breach of the marriage vow has not occurred for many years, nor is there an instance of female depravity permitted among these very curious people, who are in fact the Quakers of India. Like the Hindoos, the Parsees contract their children in marriage, when infants, but their widows, instead of burning, or remaining single, marry widowers; for the relations of the deceased are bound to find the survivor a partner, of the description mentioned. They do not bury their dead, but leave the bodies in open sepultures, to be devoured by birds; which is one of their most extraordinary customs. The Parsees support each other like the Quakers. When embarrassments occur, an enquiry takes place, and assistance is given, if the person's conduct be correct; that is, if misfortune have caused his losses, instead of neglect or extravagance. All their pursuits are of a commercial nature; and they are by far the best ship-builders in India.

In this province also are numerous Boras, who are the Jews, or hawkers of the east. They profess the Mohammedan religion, but in every other respect have the appearance of sons of Abraham; and they form every where a separate community, having their head quarters, or high priest, at Boorhanpoor, in Kandeish.

The principal towns are Surat, Baroda, Ahmedabad, Broach, and Cambay; and the chief rivers, besides the Nerbudda, are the Myhe and Sabramutty.

Throughout the whole of Hindostan Proper, the inhabitants generally live in walled towns and go armed, having been long accustomed to irruptions of plunderers. These towns have a gloomy hostile appearance that banishes the idea of security and happiness, notwithstanding their high walls and proud towers. Vast tracts of fine country have been converted into jungles by famine and war; and ruined towns and villages every where proclaim the frightful effects of depopulation.*

The author is aware how very defective these geographical recollections are; and that a full detail would have led him into volumes when he pro-

* Vide Addenda, XXIX.

posed to confine himself to the third of an octavo; but he trusts that, in the succeeding pages, and in the miscellaneous remarks of his third book, the enquiry of the reader will be awakened, to pursue the subject into its proper depth.

MEMOIRS OF INDIA.

BOOK II.

The history of India suggests two natural divisions: one from the most early ages till the discovery of a passage from Europe round the Cape of Good Hope, and the other from that important period down to the days in which we live. Yet much difficulty would arise in writing on India according to this suggestion; for the Mogul empire having continued to influence the whole system in Hindostan till very lately, it would be necessary to make repeated breaks, in the narration of European transactions, which are to us the most interesting. Indeed, it has been justly observed by Goldsmith, that all history increases in value the nearer it is to our own time. It is proposed, therefore, in the first place, to travel briefly over the ancient and modern history of India down to the present period; then take a view of the rise and progress of European affairs in the east, and rest in a more particular manner upon the public occurrences since the administration of the noble Marquis Wellesley. In the ancient part we shall take Dr. Robertson and other authorities for our guides; and in the modern, or European history of India, we shall follow the plan of Abbé Raynal; not, however, taking him for the best authority, but invoking the spirit of truth to enable our judgment to collect a fair statement from the various authors* who preceded him, and others who have carried the subject forward till the period when we became, as it were, identified with recorded facts.

CHAPTER I.

HISTORY OF INDIA FROM THE MOST EARLY AGES, UNTIL THE PRESENT TIME.

Those countries which make a jest of the age given to the world by the Holy Bible, have been always found the most deficient in historical materials.—One of these is Hindostan. But the fairest examination of the documents, alleged to have been in the possession of the learned Brahmans, has only tended to confirm scriptural record. The greatest oriental scholars have added their weight to the internal evidence which that sacred volume car-

* Vide Addenda, XXX.

ries along with it. Sir William Jones wrote in the last page of his own Bible:—"I have regularly and attentively read these Holy Scriptures, and am of opinion, that this volume, independently of its Divine origin, contains more sublimity and beauty, more pure morality, more important history, and finer strains of poetry and eloquence than can be collected from all other books, in whatever age or language they may have been composed."

It is, therefore, from this unerring source that we learn many things concerning the early history of India, which are to be found no where else. It was the spices of the east that the Ishmaelites were carrying down to Egypt, to whom Joseph was sold by his brethren; and even at this early period, upwards of three thousand years ago, the camel was used for the same purpose as it is at present to cross the deserts of Arabia, and to carry the productions of Hindostan to the west. The science of this country was also at a very remote time in the highest repute, for the wisdom of Solomon is compared to it; and he is said to have excelled all the children of the east and of Egypt in understanding.

There is reason to believe that this communication between the east and the west was long carried on by land before it was attempted by water; but at length great rivers and arms of the ocean were made subservient to purposes of commerce.* The Persian Gulf and the Red Sea soon became mediums through which the merchandise of India was transported; and the gulf still bears its ancient name, but the Erythrean sea has received the appellation of *red*, not from any disposition in the water or shore to that colour, but from an Arabian king named Erythras, or the red. Down this sea the Egyptians and Phœnicians soon began to carry on trade with Hindostan; and from the aversion of the Egyptians, as well as the Persians, to a sea-faring life, the enriching commerce of the east at length centred in Tyre and Sidon, admirably situated on the shores of the Mediterranean for communication with all parts of the then civilised world.

In the early history of all nations, there are few materials for authentic records. Men, in the first formation of societies, are too busily employed about the present to think much of the future; and it is not until the days of Herodotus, who flourished about one thousand years later than Moses, that we have annals of time upon which we may depend.

According to this most ancient heathen author, we find that the Persians, under Darius Hystaspes, established themselves in India; and that Scylax, a Greek in command of a squadron fitted out for the purpose, sailed down the Indus from its navig-

* Vide Dr. Robertson's India.

able source, and completed a voyage of discovery thence to the Arabian Gulf in two years and six months.

It is very probable that some of the Persians settled on the coast about Surat at this time; for there is a tradition to that effect, which would induce us to believe that these settlers became Hindoos.* According to the best information † we possess, there are ten nations of Hindoos now inhabiting India; and the ancient opinion that the Brahmans never received proselytes seems to be erroneous, on the authorities I have quoted. It is true, that an individual would not be received into any of the four castes, but the Hindoo religion being considered by the Brahmans as the only true one, all men are allowed to belong to the fifth class, and in transmigration may be born into any of the superior orders. The Brahmans never hesitate, upon being paid, to make offerings to idols for Europeans, or any other class of men. They will offer up prayers and invocations, and perform certain ceremonies for us as well as for Hindoos; and Major Wilford says, if any body of men, rich enough to endow pagodas, and pay Brahmans, were willing to embrace Hindooism, there is no doubt but they would find priests, and be in time considered orthodox followers of Brahma. Thus

* Vide Major Wilford's Essay, Asiatic Researches, vol. xi.

† Vide Sir H. Colebrooke's Essays in the Asiatic Researches.

it is said the colony of Persians, before mentioned, embraced the tenets of the Rajpoots whom they found about Surat, and assumed the privileges of one of the highest sectaral divisions of that warlike race, adding the title Maha, or royal, and so forming the word Maha-rajpoots, or Mahrattas.*

Although Greece looked upon all the rest of mankind as barbarians, it is evident that the commerce of India engaged the attention of some of her greatest men, whose aims were bent on turning that grand source of wealth to her advantage; and about one hundred and sixty years after the death of Darius Hystaspes, Alexander the Great invaded Hindostan. There is both external and internal evidence sufficient to show, that amidst all the excesses and inconsistencies of this wonderful man, he kept his eye fixed on the grandest objects, and meditated not only universal empire by land, but also over the ocean. The glory and strength of Tyre had roused in his breast the ambition of appropriating the trade of the east to himself, and in founding the city of Alexandria at the mouth of the Nile, after his conquest of Egypt, he contemplated no less than making his namesake the emporium of the rich commerce, which he clearly foresaw would flow through it. Accordingly we find that Alexandria continued the seat of the Indian trade for a long time after, notwithstanding

* Vide Major Wilford's Essay, Asiatic Researches, vol. xi.

many revolutions, which clearly shows how admirably well the site of it was chosen.

At the time that this young hero crossed the Indus, the limits of India were the same as at present. It was divided into two parts, India on this side and India on the other side of the Ganges. But Quintus Curtius supposed, what is now admitted by most geographers, that those countries, lying between Persia and the river Indus, partly belonged to Hindostan. Ptolemy describes it as having Paropamisus, Arachosia, and Gedrosia bordering on Persia, upon the west; mount Imaus, the same as the Himalaya mountains, on the north; the Ganges, and those countries in the vicinity of that river, to the east; and the Indian ocean to the south. We are informed by Arrian, that at this period the Hindoos had no slaves among them, which, if true, shows that their notions of liberty have undergone a material change; for in our days there are slaves in several parts of the country recognised by their code of laws. They erected no monuments in honour of the dead; which is generally the case still, with some exceptions. All the historians of Alexander's campaign in India divide the Hindoos into seven classes or castes; but it appears that either the Brahmanical institution was afterwards revised, or that these accurate writers mixed up some of the civil departments of government with the general division; for the arrangement does not correspond with the modern institution according as we find it established over the whole country.

It was very easy for authors, in other respects entitled to perfect credit, to fall into error on this intricate subject; for they were but a short time in the country, and received their information through interpreters, who were perhaps not well acquainted with the language of India. It is supposed that the classification was described rather from observation, than from accurate inquiry into the Brahmanical institution; for, under the name *overseers*, a distinct caste is mentioned as one of the seven. These officers were appointed by the Maha Rajah, or emperor, as private inquisitors into the conduct of magistrates, and all men invested with power. Their duty was daily to send a written report to court of what they saw and heard. The reputation of these overseers was so high for sincerity, probity, and patriotism, that we are told not one of them was ever accused of telling an untruth. Perhaps these disinterested officers were of the Brahman caste, which was then, as it is still, divided into the sacerdotal, ascetic, and lay orders. If these three orders were classed separately as castes with Khetris, Vyasees, Sooders, and Pariars, the seven classes of the antients would agree with the present distribution. Nothing gives us a more advantageous opinion of the government and civil policy in India at that period, than the establishment of such officers. Indeed the Mogul emperors were so well convinced of the superior civilisation of the Hindoos, that they gradually fell into their system of government; and we find, in modern times, that overseers and public news-writers were stationed in every soubahship and province, in order to communicate daily to court the result of their observations.

The interesting particulars recorded respecting the Brahmans, and the costume of the Hindoos, at that early period show, that although there is still a strong general resemblance, yet that material changes have been introduced. Many of the Brahmans may yet be seen, in India, quite abstracted from the things of this world; but the present dress of the Hindoos conforms a good deal to that mixed costume introduced by the Mohammedans.

Some of the Brahmans with whom Alexander conversed, by means of an interpreter, boldly answered his Majesty, that the only difference between him and them was, in restlessness and ambition. "You," said they, "like us, will die at last, and possess no more space than any other mortal!" * They were held in great veneration by the people, and as at present were the depositories of science, devoting their time to the study of astronomy, and pretended divination. Their sentiments respecting the creation, the majesty of

* Vide Rollin's Ancient History — India.

God, and the elements or principles of all things, did not much surprise the Greeks; and, according to Strabo, were not very different from their own; but the austerities of the naked Gymnosophists, and their wonderful patience, are recorded with all that exaggeration which surprise occasions. Some of them continued whole days standing in the same position, with their faces exposed to the rays of the sun, and held it glorious to burn themselves alive on the approach of old age, or sickness; deeming it beneath the dignity of a man to permit death to surprise him. But others looked upon suicide as an act of cowardice, and considered it honourable to bear all things, and run the course assigned by God. Thus, even at that early period, we perceive conflicting opinions among these sages. But in many respects their resemblance to the Brahmans of modern time is strong. Their food was roots and water: — they held the doctrine of transmigration, as at present. However, it is a singular circumstance, that no mention is made of any monstrous images in their temples, or of any thing very repugnant to the Grecian idolatry, which is a strong proof that the Brahmanical fabric was essentially similar to the general worship of the western world.

Nearly all the authentic information which the ancients possessed respecting India, was received from the historians of Alexander, and from the memoirs of Megasthenes, who was for several years ambassador at Palibothra, in the court of Sandracottas, maha rajah of Hindostan. But a stronger proof of the undefined notion which the Greeks had of the east, and also of the inaccuracy and paucity of Hindoo records, is, that the most learned moderns cannot agree as to the situation of that ancient capital; although there is nothing more certain than the high civilisation of the country at that time; fine roads, with shady trees planted on each side, being numerous, and the most regular system of police established throughout the empire.

When the Romans became possessed of Egypt, the pearls, diamonds, and silks of the east, flowed to them almost exclusively. It is probable that the trade of India was the great attraction which drew their arms thither; for such was the rage for silk in Rome, that it sold for its weight in gold. The avidity of the ladies for ornaments was so great, that a pearl from Ceylon, given by Julius Cæsar to Servilia, was worth 48,457*l.*, and Cleopatra's ear-rings were valued at 161,458*l.* Upon the decline of the Romans, the trade of India was divided between the Greek emperors of Constantinople, and the Persians. The eggs of the silkworm were brought from China by two Persian monks, and the mode of procuring that valuable commodity, by rearing these insects, became known to Europe. But when the doctrines of Mohammed began to be propagated by the sword of conquest, all communication from Christian countries was interrupted, and trade passed only through the Arabians, from the sixth to the thirteenth century. This enriching commerce excited the utmost rivalship among the commercial states of Europe. It at length became centred in Venice; but an account which the adventurous Marco Polo published of China, through which he had travelled, exciting the speculation of Columbus respecting a western passage to the East Indies, led to the discovery of America, and also to the voyage round the Cape of Good Hope by Vasco de Gama. This transferred the commerce of Hindostan to the Portuguese, and laid the foundation of their future power.

About the year of our Lord one thousand, the Mohammedans commenced their destructive irruptions into the provinces of Hindostan. A.D. 1011, Mahmood of Ghizni penetrated so far as Indraput, now Delhi, and conquered the rajah of that place. He was at that time only made tributary to the Afghan sovereigns; but in 1193, Cuttub ud Deen, the slave of Mahomed Ghori, dethroned the Hindoo prince of that place, and commenced the dynasty which reigned till subverted by Gengis Khan. Tamerlane took and pillaged Delhi in 1398, and partially subdued various parts of India; but it was not till 1525 that Sultan Baber firmly established the Mogul empire, which was consolidated by his son Acber, who died at Agra in 1605, leaving a great name behind. He is esteemed as a most magnificent prince. His vizier, Abul Fazel, author of the Ayeen Acbery, was murdered by banditti in the 47th year of his age. In the reign of Acber's successor, Jehangeer, Sir Thomas Roe was sent to India, as the first English ambassador, and resided some time at his court in 1615. From 1678 to 1707, the famous Aurengzebe had been absent from Delhi, effecting the conquest of the Deccan, which had never been completely subdued; and this long absence from his capital, laid the foundation for the decline of the Mogul empire. Major Rennel says it attained its full measure of extent in his reign. From this time forward, the court became a prey to faction, and several of Aurengzebe's successors were murdered. In this confusion the Mahrattas, who had been driven to the mountains of the Deccan, became powerful, and in 1735 they burned the suburbs of Delhi. The viceroys of provinces also, taking advantage of the weakness which they perceived in the government, established separate kingdoms for themselves. In 1738 the Nizam of the Deccan called in the Persians under Nadir Shah, who entered Delhi, and demanded thirty millions sterling for its ransom. The emperor, Mahomed Shah, being unable to pay this vast sum, the city was given up to plunder. It is said 100,000 of its inhabitants were massacred, and sixty-two millions sterling of booty collected. During this horrible scene, which happened in March, 1739, Nadir Shah sat at the Roshun ud Dowlah mosque, to behold the butchery. In 1747 the Carnatic and Bengal had been formed into independencies as well as the Deccan. The Rohillas, a mountainous race of native warriors, had re-established themselves within eighty miles of Delhi, and soon after the whole empire was split into as many petty states as could assert their rights by the sword. Anarchy now reigned in Delhi; one emperor was deposed, or murdered, after another, till the accession of Shah Allum in 1761, who at length fled to the British for protection at Allahabad, which was taken by the army under Sir Robert Fletcher in 1765. Shah Allum returned to Delhi in 1771, where he was blinded with a dagger by Gholaum Kaudir. This cruel and blood-thirsty Rohilla chief, after inflicting the most heart-rending tortures on many of the royal family, was himself put to death by Scindea, the Mahratta chief, in whose hands Delhi continued till 1803, when Dowlut Row Scindea was defeated near it by Lord Lake, since which time the whole power of the Mogul has merged in the East India Company.

We have not ventured to hint at the way in which Hindostan may have been originally colonised.—The subject is of course involved in great obscurity, and it is easy for a sceptic to raise arguments against received opinions, grounded upon scriptural authority. From the Bible we learn, that the children of Noah aspired to build a tower whose top might reach to heaven. It may not be inconsistent with the metaphorical style of the Scriptures to suppose, that this is a representation of the divisions and feuds which separated the posterity of Noah. Some of them, no doubt, penetrated through the natural openings, into the fertile plains of Hindostan, where population, left to its own prodigious increase, would soon replenish the east. Indeed, the researches of orientalists into the depths of Sanscrit lore, lead to the belief, that it was the antediluvian language of Noah's ancestors; for its ramifications have been found to pervade every tongue spoken on the globe, from the regions of China to the wilds of America.

It appears, from the experience of mankind, that civilisation advances much more rapidly in an island of small extent, than on a continent, where men are at liberty to choose that savage freedom, which is dear to uncultivated human nature. The early Hindoos, therefore, in all probability, extended themselves over the face of India, and in the course of a few generations lost all recollection of their origin and the institutions of their forefathers. Following the dictates of instinct and terrified imagination, they, like other barbarians, worshipped those objects which most readily presented themselves to their hopes and fears. We have testimony sufficient to assure us, that they fell into the most frightful forms of idolatry, shedding the blood of their children in profusion, to appease the supposed anger of revengeful and cruel deities. Their principal object of adoration was called Brahma; but whether this name indicated the sun, or the supposed first cause of all that meets the wondering eye of human intellect, is now unknown.

Tradition, and the concurring testimonies of philosophers, lead us to believe that the Hindoos were found in this state by some of the priests of the western world, who were tinctured with the laws of Moses and the learning of Egypt. Perceiving the ease with which credulity may be converted to self-interest, a plan was devised by them for framing a system of government, deriving its origin directly from the Almighty Father of Creation.

These priests, assuming the name of Brahmans, were received as messengers from heaven. They taught that Brahma had created all things, and divided men into four great classes, consisting of the natural components which constitute a congregation of people. viz. priests, warriors or nobles, the gentry or middle ranks, and the lower order. The first were represented as having sprung from Brahma's head, the second from his arms, the third from his body, and the fourth from his legs. During life, these classes were confined to their lots; but they were instructed, that by strict conformity to certain rules of sanctity, a transmigration would promote them through the higher ranks, till at length being born a Brahman, they would be absorbed in eternal felicity, The ambition of the nobles was gratified by the exercise of pompous duties of state. From them, the rajahs or kings were selected, who, deriving all power from the Brahmans, found that it was their interest to suppress the other orders. The roving appetite of the lower classes for change and preferment, was also provided for, by the fame conferred on religious knight errantry, and self devotion. Opinion was concentrated upon one point, which gives a peculiar feature to the Brahmanical institution in its original form. It was made the business of every man to keep him down, who was down. But, that it was at first extremely simple in its construction, cannot be doubted. All the seeming inconsistencies in the works of creation were accounted for by the operations of the preserving and destroying powers, which were figured as Brahmas, brothers under the names of Vishnu and Seeva, who became, in time, the great objects of adoration,

As civilisation advanced, the machine of government became more complicated. Revisions were found necessary, and these were effected by priests, who, under the title of incarnations of one of the great deities, held an all-powerful influence over opinion. The Vedas and Purannas were thus produced as the instructions of God, and ignorance was called in as an auxiliary to power. Death was the punishment inflicted upon the man of low caste, who presumed to read the scriptures; boiling lead was poured into his ears, if he opened them to the voice of his maker; and his eyes were sealed with burning wax, for directing them towards the records of his faith.

If, however, he was kept in darkness, he was well supplied with the means of subsistence*, for which implicit obedience and ready faith were required. Menu framed his code of laws, which are in some respects admirable, and various commentaries upon the Vedas in a great measure superseded their simple doctrines, substituting a most complicated and bewildering system of church government in their stead as ever proceeded from human ingenuity.

There is every reason to believe, that originally the worship of Brahma did not differ materially from that of Zoroaster's followers, or of the disciples of Budha; and that the disgusting images of beasts and monsters were then unknown, which at present shock the sight in every part of India. Surya, or the sun, was the great object of worship in Hindostan, in early times. I have seen his image, that of a well shaped man, in a most ancient temple in the fortress of Kantkote, in the province of Cutch. He holds a sun in each hand, and has behind him four diminutive attendants, with instruments something like tridents.

* Vide Addenda, XXXI.

Indeed the gross deviations from the simplicity of the Brahmanical institution occasioned several successful attempts at reformation. In an age so early as to baffle the research of antiquarians, Budha apostatised; and, denying the divine origin of the Vedas, began to worship God under the figure of a circle. It does not appear, however, that the followers of Budha ever became very numerous in Hindostan; but in all the neighbouring countries, that faith soon superseded ancient idolatry, and still holds its ground, having the great Lama of Tibet for its head. The Budhists are not divided into castes at present, except on the island of Ceylon, where it is said* they still adhere to the Brahmanical classification, with merely the difference of placing the warriors before the priests.

In the reformation of Budha, the discipline of Brahma was much relaxed, and a considerable latitude given in the use of food; but the founder of Jainism made the care of animal life one of his most particular injunctions; establishing it as the divine will, that nothing should be deprived by man of existence, and teaching that the world never was created. Their ideas of time are, therefore, the most complex that can be conceived.† They offer no kind of sacrifices in their religious rites, which are simple ceremonies conducted by their priests in two sorts of temples. One is covered, and much like

* Vide Lord Valentia's Travels in India.

† Vide Appendix, note 7.

the Hindoo pagoda ; the other is open above, having merely a high wall round colossean statues of much respected men; such as are to be seen at Kurcul, in the province of Canara, and at Baligole, in Mysore. The Jains believe nothing but what they can perceive; and the only objects they worship are the deified spirits of holy men, who are represented in a state of divine abstraction in their temples, on altars of white marble. I have seen several of these temples in Guzerat; and the following is a brief description of one.

The images were of white marble coarsely sculptured, but with tolerable proportion. There were ten of them seated on an altar; all exactly in the same posture. The centre one, on an upper pedestal, was larger than life, to which the others bore an exact resemblance, though different in size. These idols were situated in the temple, under a great pyramid, to which you enter by first going up a fine flight of steps, and passing through two circular, or rather octagon, apartments, over which there are large domes. The first impression is that you stand before representations of women with large ears; but on enquiry, it will be found, they are all intended for men, and that the form is merely feminine, to shew the superior beauty a spirit acquires by transformation from flesh.

It is impossible to describe the solemn grandeur of the sanctum sanctorum, in which the idols are placed, when lighted up with large brass chandeliers, with attendant priests, while the great hall in the centre, as well as the two wings and the vestibule, are crowded with worshippers, who go through a number of salutations, prostrations, and ceremonies. I was permitted to go close up to the images, upon leaving my boots under the great dome; and certainly, amidst all that surrounded me, I felt a considerable degree of awe and respect.

Indeed a man of sensibility, in the presence of even marble statues, that represent a state of mental abstraction, in which the Hindoos conceive there is real perfection, or the likeness of God, feels an elevation of sentiment towards the great Creator, who has so visibly revealed himself, in every atom, that meets human optics, and yet lies so completely veiled with his own magnificence, as to be seen by different imaginations in a vast variety of particular forms. Such a man, so situated, is apt to be impressed with the Brahmanical idea, that all forms of natural adoration must be pleasing to God; and, while he pities the delusion of mortal inconsistencies, he will enlarge the sphere of his charity, and believe that a pure heart, under any mode of faith, will meet with favour in the sight of the Almighty.

That Jain worship was a reformation in Brahmanism cannot be doubted. Any one will admit its pretensions to superior purity, who compares the simple forms of it to the complicated system of Hindooism, and the monstrous idols which the

Brahmanical pantheon displays, many of which are too shocking for delicacy to describe. It would be uninteresting to exhibit such monsters; and it seems only necessary to observe, that they are obviously creations of grossness and ignorance, which have crept into Brahmanism in its day of degeneracy; for originally there is nothing very repugnant to human reason in its construction. Even in some of its incarnations, particularly that of Chrishna, there is a remote resemblance to the history of our Saviour.

The last attempt, made by a native of India, to substitute a new form of worship in Hindostan in room of the Brahmanical institution, was made by Nanac, the founder of the Seiks, towards the middle of the fifteenth century. He was born at a village called Tulwandy, in the province of Lahore. His great success in converting the Hindoos to pure Deism, proves that they may be roused by persuasion alone to change their religion, and imbibe principles of enthusiastic republicanism, with more ease than is generally supposed. The Seiks, or disciples of Nanac, are now very numerous, and besides nearly the whole province of Lahore, they have the Punjab, part of Mooltan, and the greatest share of the country between the Jumna and the Sutleje. Their converts are permitted to retain the manners and customs of their castes, in a great measure. The cer mony of initiation is a solemn oath, to devote themselves to the use of the sword in defence of the state. Their priests are called Immortals, and preside at a great assembly, which meets, in prosperous times, at Amritsar, where the chiefs, having taken a sort of sacrament, by eating together of consecrated cake, transact the business of the government, which is a theocracy; but this invisibility has induced each chief to constitute himself the head of the state, and, therefore, the Seiks are weakened by internal divisions, and constant struggles for power.

In Hindostan it is believed that the world has existed for 7,205,000* years, which period is divided into four ages, that bear names conveying the same ideas as the golden, silver, brass, and iron times of classical notoriety. The present is called the black age, and about 395,000 years of it remain.

Having thus briefly run over the general history of India, we shall next proceed to describe the discoveries and conquests of the Portuguese, and other European states in the East, which portion of this work, we fondly hope, will be found pregnant with entertainment and utility.

* Vide Appendix, note 8.

CHAPTER II.

THE DISCOVERIES AND CONQUESTS OF THE PORTUGUESE IN INDIA.

AFTER the extinction of commerce and literature in Europe, it was long a prevailing opinion that the central regions of the torrid zone were uninhabitable, from the burning nature of the sun's rays. The intercourse of the Arabians with Spain and Portugal gradually removed this prejudice. Writings of antiquity, saved from the destructive devastations of ignorance, imparted new ideas respecting geography; mariners became bold, with the compass for their pilot; and Henry, son of John the First, king of Portugal, caused those seas to be explored in which Diodorus Siculus had placed the island of Atalantis: under his direction, in the year 1419, Madeira was discovered, which some learned men have considered as the remains of it; for Plato, in one of his dialogues, says that this once extensive region sunk into the sea, and disappeared in an instant. There are men every where, whose ardent spirits will always push forward if supported by hope. Under the terrible expectation of being perhaps burned to a cinder, the Portuguese navigators adventured;

and coasting along the western shores of Africa, at length doubled its southern extremity, which was then called the Cape of Storms; but John the Second, foreseeing vast consequences from this discovery, named it the Cape of Good Hope. Animated by the success of Columbus in 1492, and in pursuance of that grand object, by which a new world had been found, the discovery of a passage by sea to India, Vasco de Gama was furnished by King Emanuel with four ships, and doubling the Cape in 1497, reached the Malabar coast after a voyage of thirteen months.

In all successful undertakings there is a concurrence of favouring circumstances. At Melinda, situated on the eastern coast of Africa, which was then a place of considerable trade, Gama received most valuable information respecting the state of India. Among those who crowded to see the interesting strangers from Europe, he discovered a Moor of Tunis, who understood the Portuguese language. He was intimately acquainted with the affairs of India, and disposed to be a firm friend to the Portuguese. Under his guidance, Gama shaped his course for Calicut, the capital of the Zamorin, where he was received with all that fond hope which admiration excites. Through his intelligent interpreter the Moor, he was enabled to communicate with the natives, and being at length introduced to the emperor, who was here styled as before mentioned, he made a favourable impression on that sovereign, and obtained the promise of favours and privileges for his country.

Gama was conducted to the palace with great pomp and ceremony, through an extensive, rich, and populous city. Wonder was on tip-toe: and such multitudes pressed upon the numerous guards, palanquins, bands of music, and dancers around, that several persons were crushed to death. He was welcomed at the palace by the chief courtiers; and the high priest of the Brahmans, taking him by the hand, led the way through many spacious apartments guarded by centinels, into a magnificent hall of audience. The walls and floors were covered with rich tapestry, and silk carpets embroidered with gold. Here the Zamorin was seated on a low throne, surrounded by his nobles, who sat likewise on artificially decorated elevations, rising one above another. The Zamorin's dress was of fine cloth of gold, most curiously flowered, and adorned with diamonds of great value. He wore sparkling pendants of precious stones in his ears, and a sort of crown covered with pearls and rich gems on his head. His bare feet were decorated with costly rings, and his neck and fingers glittered with the wealth of Golconda. Gama presented the rich gifts which had been sent by King Emanuel, with a letter; and, in an appropriate speech, informed his majesty that his master, moved by the renown of his greatness, would have attended to offer his affectionate respects in person, had not the vast distance proved an invincible obstacle. The Zamorin replied—" I have no doubt of the friendly intentions of my brother Emanuel, king of Portugal, having convincing proofs before my eyes, in the honour of this splendid legation; and I am willing to enter into strict league and amity, with all the benefits of free commerce." Rich perfumes were then presented, with a preparation of betel and areca nut, in golden vessels, while a return of presents was introduced, borne by attendants on silver trays. *

The Arabian and Moorish merchants, dreading the consequences of this treaty, conspired to destroy it in the bud. Fortunately, at the critical moment, Gama received, through the instrumentality of his faithful Moor of Tunis, such information as enabled him to baffle the dark designs of his enemies; but such was his personal danger, that apprehensive of his detention on shore, and of the destruction of his companions by the Zamorin, whose jealousy and fear had been artfully roused, he directed his brother, who was on board, in the event of his imprisonment or death, to set sail immediately, and inform the king of the particulars of the voyage, instead of coming to his assistance, or seeking vengeance.

What a noble instance of the magnanimity of man! Regardless of himself, Gama thought only

* Vide Addenda, XXXII.

of forwarding the interests of others. Yet, in doing so, he secured, without aiming at it, fame with posterity, the second dearest object to every elevated mind. So true it is, that virtue rewards her followers with honour here and hereafter, while vice repays devotion with oblivion and torture, deceiving in agency, and giving the embrace of despair where hope was courted.

Gama, however, got privately on board; and, like a man of talent, zealous to serve his country, instead of openly charging the Zamorin with a conspiracy against his life, he, by a most insinuating letter, roused his majesty's jealousies and fears respecting the Moors and Arabians, and convinced him of the great advantages which would arise from cultivating the friendship of the king of Portugal. Stimulated by imaginary prospects of gain and power, the artful Asiatic prince sought to heal the breach, by promising to punish the Moors and Arabians, who had deceived him by false representations. In a letter to king Emanuel, he assured him, that the arrival of his admiral and fleet had afforded him high satisfaction. "The same sentiments I shall always cherish," said he, "provided your subjects regulate themselves so as not to give any occasion of disturbance here, and that the treaty I have entered into with your majesty may not prejudice my amicable correspondence with all other nations." Upon which Gama sailed for Europe, and lived to see the glorious result of his success, not having paid the debt of nature till 1524.

The Portuguese were at first surprised into a reverence for the Hindoo idols, seeing them only in the obscurity of the great temples at Calicut, and at the awful distance permitted by the Brahmans. Ferdinand Lopes de Castanheda in his history says, that they fell down and worshipped the images, from finding the ceremonies of idolatry so much like their own superstitions. But the priests and enthusiasts of the Catholic faith soon observed such horrible differences, that all the national energies of Portugal were roused, by not only the motives of gain and the extension of empire, but by the zeal of conversion.

Inspired by the Pope with all the folly of conquest, and put in possession of the coasts of India by the benediction of the church, thirteen vessels soon sailed from Lisbon, under the command of Alvares Cabral. Like the memory of Columbus, that of Gama is stained, by having carried away with him some of the natives of India. They were, of course, treated with all possible attention, and upon their return made most favourable reports to their countrymen on the power of the Portuguese nation. But this invasion of human right, and the impression made on the Zamorin by the private representations of the Moors and Arabians, caused Cabral to find a very cool reception, and fifty of his men were massacred. In return he sunk the vessels in the harbour which belonged to the instigators of this treachery, and cannonaded the town.

Hostilities having thus commenced, Cabral found many of the native princes along the coast ready to join him in despoiling the Zamorin of power and territory, anxious to free themselves from bondage and tribute, and too blind to perceive that they were only, like the fish in the fable, getting off the gridiron into the fire. In this way, from first establishing themselves at Cochin, and building forts in different places, they soon got possession of nearly all the trade of the whole eastern shores; for under the wise and gallant conduct of Alphonso Albuquerque, they were every where victorious.

The courage and conduct of the Portuguese on their arrival in India were admirable. It has occurred to my understanding that there is something in adventure to India peculiarly rousing. The energies of the various nations that have made conquests in the east have been most powerfully excited for some time, and then lulled into a calm which led to the grave; philosophically indicating that, like the tempest of Hindostan, the human mind there is roused by nature to expend itself at once, and then to retire into long repose; but unlike the unknown property, which gives to the monsoon, as well as the face of the globe, periodical undiminished force and resuscitated youth, it is unable to recover the spring of action. This curious phenomenon is exemplified in the history of the Hindoos, Mohammedans, Portuguese, Dutch, and French; it remains to be pointed out by the finger of time, whether or not the course will be progressive in application to the English settlements. The same law has operated invariably on individuals who settle or serve in India. For some years they are the most active men in the world; but a premature imbecility follows, which, if they remain too long in the country, they never recover.

Fertile in genius, resource, and ability, Albuquerque aimed at empire for his country over the east. His first object was to establish a capital, in a situation easily defended, and with the advantage of a good port for ships. After an attentive survey, therefore, of the coast of Malabar, he fixed upon the island of Goa, admirably and centrically placed. The approach to this harbour, one of the finest in the world, is defended by the two fortified peninsulas of Salsette and Barda. Rendered beautiful by the hand of nature, the island, which is about thirty miles in circumference, presents a most interesting variety of hill and dale, with the blue ghauts towering to the clouds on one side, and the cool ocean bathing the other; while a variety of natural canals, formed by a fine river, which flows from the mountains, gives cheerful diversity to the scene, also pleasingly varied by wild woods, green meadows, villas, pagodas, cottages, and churches. It belonged at that time to the extensive kingdom of Vijaya-nagar, but Adul Khan, the governor, was in rebellion against his sovereign, and during his absence on an ambitious project, Albuquerque sailed into the harbour, and took the fort by storm.

He was not at this time, however, able to retain it, for Adul Khan returned rapidly, with a vast army, and the Portuguese had to retreat to their ships, being sorely pressed by famine, and disappointed in receiving succour from Cochin.

Albuquerque had entered the city of Goa triumphantly on horseback, under the acclamations of the people, who were very willing to change masters; a Dominican carrying an ensign with the cross in it, and another the keys of the fort before him; but he had to quit it in the darkness of night, being attacked not only by Adul Khan's whole army, but the treacherous citizens. When on board his ships, his men were reduced to the greatest misery for want of water and provisions. In working down from the island along the windings of the river, he was attacked constantly by the enemy, who had possession of the two forts situated on the points which defend the harbour. Batteries blazed upon him during the day, while his men were dying of thirst and hunger, having had only dead horses and rats, with the fish of the river, for some days before their retreat. In this exigency Albuquerque determined upon a most desperate thing. The event proved, that in extremities the boldest undertakings are often the best. Landing about 300 men, in the dead of night, he suddenly scaled the two forts, where he found the garrisons entirely off their guard, as he expected, put them to death, carried away their cannon, and made himself master of their ammunition and provisions.

A short time after, being reinforced by the arrival of a fleet from Europe, he attacked Adul Khan, conquered his army under the walls of Goa, and took the city by storm, when a vast slaughter of the inhabitants ensued. This happened on the 25th November, 1510, since which time it has continued under the controul of the Portuguese. To repeople the city, Albuquerque ordered all his young officers and soldiers to take native wives, who were baptised, and forcibly converted to Christianity.

Like the rape of the Sabines, this violation of human rights increased the good fortune of the Portuguese. — The natives on the island and continent, particularly the women, observing the happy state of the Indo-Portuguese matrons, came in thousands to be baptised, and soon formed a vast Christian society. In 1548, the convent of Dominicans was erected; and in four years' time 17,290 Indians were baptised. The Jesuits and Franciscans converted, during the life of St. Francis Xaverius, in the east, upwards of five millions of souls, and erected so many churches, that there is now scarcely a pagoda to be seen in the vicinity of their stations, but the cross peeps from every shade in whose gloomy recesses the mysteries of idolatry once prevailed.

Most wonderful things are related by John de Lucena and Daniel Bartholi of this eminent saint, whose piety, zeal, and charity made an impression upon the natives so favourable to Christianity, that the horrors of the inquisition were scarcely sufficient to remove it. His death happened in 1552, in China, occasioned by fever, after having spent eleven years in various parts of the east. His body was placed in a coffin filled with quick-lime, that his bones might be transported to Goa, when the flesh was consumed. After some time it was still found fresh and sweet, unchanged in colour, and having the placid smile and lively appearance of life. The coffin, however, was deposited in the earth at Manilla, till an opportunity occurred of sending it round to Malabar; but five months afterwards a travelling Jesuit, being desirous of seeing its state, found the whole in perfect preservation. Didacus Pereria, therefore, pronouncing it miraculous, had a magnificent coffin, adorned with gold and silk, made for the body, and the saint arrived at Goa surrounded by the emblems of mortality, but with all the appearance of enjoying a tranquil sleep. The viceroy, accompanied by the whole city, and a great part of the continent, went out to meet the procession with incredible demonstrations of respect; joy, that his body had arrived amongst them, and sorrow, that they should be no more cheered by his heavenly exhortations. The coffin was deposited in the chapel of St. Paul, where thousands of the natives embraced the uncorrupted body, laying their beards upon it, bathing it with their tears, and champoing or rubbing it with their hands, in the hope of rousing the almost speaking clay to life. All tongues spoke loudly in praise of his uncommon zeal, piety, charity, mildness, dangers encountered, chastity, temperance, fasts, prayers, miracles, constancy, prudence; and the Jesuits were so apprehensive that his body would be rubbed away, or carried off piecemeal, that the coffin was surrounded by an iron palisade.

These particulars are given merely for entertainment, not on account of any veneration for superstition. It was easy for the Jesuits to embalm the body of Xaverius, and to impose on the credulity of fanaticism; but the whole relation, taken as biographical fact, establishes the high value set upon the character of this worthy man; and that his acts of benevolence in the service of his fellow-creatures, together with his fidelity to God, were no fictions. But to place him at the bar of judgment, it is only necessary to quote a few of his sentiments from an address he made to his friends, in reply to their affectionate remonstrances against his departure for Japan and China, on account of the dangers attending the voyage.

"I am surprised that ye who dedicate your lives to the praise of God's power and mercy should fear for my person. Have you forgotten that he is the supreme governor of the universe, and that every thing is ruled by his will? As we see ambassadors of temporal princes, relying upon their characters and the power of their masters, pass confidently through an enemy's camp; so it becomes us, the interpreters of the divine law, and teachers of the heathens, to rely upon heavenly assistance, which, without weapons, can carry us safely through earthly dangers by sea and land, by fire and sword, or by whatever may seem to oppose the accomplishment of Almighty will. It is true, the victory is not always ours; but all miseries are to be looked upon as trials of faith and constancy, and no disappointment ought to stop a zealous minister in attempting every thing that may conduce to God's honour and the salvation of souls. If a soldier, animated by perishable fame, adventures his life,—if a mariner for gain leaves the shore and exposes himself to the merciless waves, would it not be shameful for a minister of Christ to shrink from hazard in God's service?—Should he not look upon every thing as a trifle in comparison of the kingdom of heaven and its increase? Let no such thoughts enter your minds; for no consideration of personal safety should hinder us from promoting the interests of God."

Goa thus, in a short time, became the great centre of Indian commerce, and Calicut ceased to attract the ships of foreign nations.

The Venetians, soon after the arrival of the Portuguese in India, apprehensive that the rich commerce of the east, which they had long enjoyed, would be transferred from its channel through Egypt round the Cape of Good Hope, excited the Egyptians and Arabians to oppose the settlement of the Portuguese on the shores of Malabar. Albuquerque foresaw the aim of this confederacy; and before their projects were ripe he made himself master of Socotoro, an island situated so as to command the mouth of the Red Sea. It was taken possession of by Tristan D'Acunha, after the slaughter of all the Arabians, who defended their posts with undaunted courage, and refused quarter. Though this island did not answer the purpose of preventing the Egyptian fleets from passing into the Indian seas, yet it was found valuable on account of its fine aloes; and a Portuguese fleet stationed near it watched the proceedings of their enemies and destroyed their ships and forces in detail.

This was, however, so expensive to the viceroy of India, that he attempted to seize Suez, but the difficult navigation of the Red Sea baffled his abilities; and after wild speculations of his genius, respecting the practicability of turning the river

Nile, and conquering Arabia with four hundred horse, he turned his views to the possession of the Persian Gulf.

At the mouth of it stands the island of Ormus, which was, at the beginning of the fifteenth century, entirely a city, — for its site is a barren rock; but as it became the centre of trade between Persia and India, and had two good harbours, foreign merchants from all commercial countries crowded its streets at particular seasons, which were screened from the sun by awnings. In short, a combination of lucky circumstances made it at this time not only the seat of universal commerce, but of politeness, gallantry, and pleasure.

Albuquerque, in his first attempt to get possession of this important station, was foiled by the treachery of his own captains, after he had displayed consummate skill and unsinking fortitude. But, upon being reinforced from Europe, he resumed operations against the place, and at length firmly established the Portuguese flag in the Persian empire, the sovereign of which had the confidence to demand tribute from the conqueror; but he, producing some of the destructive implements of war, told the envoy that this was the kind of tribute paid by his master. The conduct of Albuquerque in attacking Ormus, with the chief of which he had no cause of quarrel, is another proof that ambition will not be stopped by the weak barriers of justice; and the dissensions which produced his failure, demonstrate the power which cunning and gold have often over genius.

The Portuguese being now firmly established in the western parts of India, by the valour and conduct of Albuquerque and his predecessors D'Almeyda and Ferdinand Cautinho, began to extend their settlements eastward; and Albuquerque effected the conquest of several parts of Ceylon. This fine island presented many inducements to the viceroy for his chief settlement, but he rejected them in favour of the Malabar coast.

He was, however, still debarred from full participation in the trade to China by not having a settlement to command Malacca, which was the centre of attraction for the merchants of all nations. Albuquerque longed for a pretext to attack it; and the jealousy evinced by the Malays to the growing power of Portugal soon afforded him a just one. Several of his men were massacred in a most inhuman manner, and their viceroy soon appeared before the place, and notwithstanding desperate opposition, succeeded in establishing a settlement there in 1511. Thence he sent a detachment to plant a colony in the Molucca islands, while he returned to Malabar to consolidate the extensive conquests he had made.

The temperate and contented inhabitants of the Moluccas had lived, undisturbed by foreign invasion, amidst their volcanic rocks on sago and cocoa-nuts, without suspecting that they possessed a treasure, which would raise them to general notice. But the clove and nutmeg, unknown as spices to the ancients, were here discovered accidentally by the Chinese, and soon became a productive article of commerce.

These valuable productions render the natives quite independent, and, satisfied with the plenty which nature has provided, they are averse to labour. The sago tree is a kind of curious palm. It is not, like the cocoa nut tree, common over India near the sea shore, nor is it found in the interior, as that useful production is in some places. It grows to the height of thirty feet by six in circumference; and beneath a thick bark the sap is found which falls into sago flour. Its maturity is known by the long leaves of the tree being covered with white powder, and by its trunk shedding great numbers of long thorns, which protect it while young. Being cut down it is sawed into pieces, the sap is diluted in water, and strained through a sieve for use, either baked, boiled, or formed into a delicious jelly.

The cocoa nut tree is, perhaps, the most useful production in nature. Of a beautiful form, it rises with stately grace, sometimes to the height of seventy feet. Its trunk is nearly straight and cylindrical, marked with circular rings. The wood is of a spongy nature, and not valuable for solid work; the leaves are used for covering houses, for umbrellas, sails, fishing nets, and for writing on with a brass style. These leaves grow on the top of the tree, and seldom exceed twelve, but they are very broad and long, and covered when young with a net work, of which sieves are made. The nuts grow from the centre of this tuft, and hang down in an interesting manner between the leaves. Each is of an oval form, and about six inches in diameter; there are about six in a cluster, and perhaps, the same number of clusters on the tree. This fruit is covered with a thick coat, of which excellent ropes are made. Underneath is a good sized nut, which the Indians form into cups, and a variety of useful things. The pulp is agreeable food, and it yields a great quantity of fine oil. In the centre of the nut there is a drink of clear sweetish liquor, which is both refreshing and wholesome. By cutting off the bud of one of the flowers, and placing a vessel under it, a considerable quantity of juice is procured every day, of a whitish colour, and an agreeable taste. When this sours, it is good vinegar; if distilled, it yields a strong spirit called arrack; and if boiled with quicklime, it gives tolerable sugar. This juice is called toddy, and in a plantation the native reserves a number of trees for fruit, and a proper proportion for juice, because the buds which are cut become for that season abortive. It is curious to see the Indians mount those trees to prune the buds, and replace the earthen jars, into which the liquid oozes. A string is tied to each ancle, to prevent the feet from separating more than the diameter of the tree. The man who mounts, first sharpens a pruning hook in the sand, by grinding it alternately with the heel of each foot. It is fixed in the girdle, which supports the only covering or clothing round the loins, and an earthen pot is slung on the other side. The trunk of the tree is then seized by a twisted cord round the wrists, and the foot cord is placed against one of the circular rings, by which the body is raised, the feet are then drawn up, and so on, till the top or tuft of leaves is gained, for there is no impediment on the long stem of the tree.

Albuquerque died at Goa in 1515. He was the greatest of all the Portuguese. It is impossible while we drop a tear over his faults, not to reverence his virtues. Long after his death the poor and oppressed Indians repaired to his tomb, as to the shrine of a god, to pray for his protection against the rapacity and injustice of his countrymen, and their own. He was too elevated and noble not to be envied; and his king began to suspect that ambition of a disloyal nature lurked in a heart, that only beat for his country's glory, and honest fame. Inspired by him and the great commanders, which the enterprises in India formed, the Portuguese feared no odds; they fought and conquered one against an hundred, from the Persian Gulf to the confines of China.

His successor Lopez Soarez, who was also a

humane and talented man, pushed the interests of his country to China, which had been contemplated by Albuquerque. At this period nothing was known in Europe of that vast and curious empire, except from the account published by the Venetian traveller, Marco Polo. Some of his apparently fabulous descriptions were confirmed by representations transmitted to Lisbon, from the viceroy of India; and in 1518 a squadron sailed for Canton, commanded by Ferdinand Andrada, having on board Thomas Perez, an ambassador from the king of Portugal to the emperor. He was politely received by the mandarins of Canton, and conducted with great ceremony to Pekin; and though he had but slight opportunities of seeing much of the interior, yet the observations made during his journey convinced our authorities of the antiquity, vast population, political economy, and civilisation, to a very curious extent of China. The towns were large; the villages numerous, and beautifully situated; the roads were in the most perfect order; the country was intersected by navigable canals; even the hills were cultivated to their summits, and irrigated by machinery or reservoirs; and the multitudinous inhabitants of both land and water were mild in manners, sagacious in aspect, and polite and attentive to each other.

The Chinese government did not then seem prejudiced against Europeans. Perez was favourably received at court; and the ports of the empire were upon the point of being opened, when Simon Andrada, the brother of Ferdinand, appeared on the coasts with another squadron, and disconcerted the good understanding. He treated the Chinese with haughty superiority; built a fort, by seizing forcibly part of the island of Taman, and pillaged the country; carrying off young girls; making slaves of the inhabitants, and exercising all manner of atrocities. Roused by indignation, the Chinese attacked him, drove his troops into the sea, made the ambassador Perez answerable for his invasion of right, by imprisoning him, where he died some time after, and banished the Portuguese from China.

Some years afterwards, however, permission was granted for their ships to trade with the port of Sancian, and a fortunate occurrence soon gave them an establishment of their own. The island of Macao, situated at the entrance of Canton bay, was seized by a formidable pirate, named Tchang-si-lao, who desolated the coasts of the empire, and destroyed all trade with Canton, by besieging that city. Alarmed by his conduct and the strength of his forts, the mandarins called upon the Portuguese ships of war, then at Sancian, for assistance. The siege was raised, the pirate destroyed, and the emperor in reward for such signal service, bestowed the island of Macao on the Portuguese, under certain conditions, where they built a town in 1540. This soon after led to their discovery of the rich trade to Japan, for a vessel being accidentally wrecked on that extraordinary coast, the sailors were hospitably treated, and upon their return to Goa inflamed the authorities and missionaries with further desires of conquest and conversion.

The Japanese opened their ports to the Portuguese with willingness, and a most extensive market was discovered for the productions of Europe and India. In return for which gold was paid, for Japan is a mountainous country, abounding in that metal, and other valuable minerals, but not so fertile as to supply its numerous inhabitants with the necessaries of life. But here we again see the bounty of Providence, and a manifestation of the wish that all parts of the earth should be covered with men; for places, which are apparently so barren as to resist the industry of husbandry, are generally found rich in hidden treasures, which may be bartered for the superfluities of other countries.

In this manner the Portuguese established their power round all the coasts of the East, from the Cape of Good Hope to Japan; giving laws to the natives, and setting what price they pleased upon the productions of Europe and India, having a complete monopoly of all the branches of trade. From Japan they drew annually about 600,000*l.* in gold, silver, and copper; from China, the teas and silks that were exchanged in Europe for the wealth of Mexico and Peru; from the Moluccas, cloves and nutmegs; from Bengal, the fine muslins of Dacca; from Coromandel, the various productions of the Peninsula; from Ceylon and Malabar, the pearls, precious stones, and spices of those regions, with the ivory produced by the elephants of the forests, and the sandal wood which perfumes the ghauts; from Guzerat, cotton, and the different rich manufactures of Hindostan; from the Persian Gulf, the wealth of that extensive kingdom; from the Red Sea, all the riches of its shores, and from the coast of Africa, the precious minerals of Zanguebar. Besides which they had some of the islands in the Indian Sea, and in the Atlantic Ocean, between Europe and the Cape of Good Hope. They had settlements thence along the coast of Tunis. In short, their power was wonderful, and the conduct and virtue by which it was acquired admirable.

But from this they degenerated and became such oppressors of the natives, that a general conspiracy was formed against them by nearly all the powers of India, in the reign of king Sebastian, who sent out Ataida, a man of consummate military knowledge, to reanimate expiring virtue. He and his lieutenants bravely repulsed the treacherous attacks of the Zamorin in Malabar, the king of Cambay in Guzerat, the king of Achem at Malacca, the king of Ternate in the Moluccas, the Great Mogul at Surat, and the queen of Onore. The noble soul of one man, however, could not retard the rapid course of his country's falling star, though he lived not to see it set in the eastern ocean. Luxury, profligacy, corruption, and oppression, reigned at all their settlements in India; while the mother, whose breast supplied them with strength, fell under the dominion of Philip, the second king of Spain. On the downfall of Portugal, the sun of Holland rose, equally bright in the morning, as glorious nearly at noon, but tinged with a dirty and bloody red in its short evening.

Goa and Macao belong still to the Portuguese; but those monuments which they fondly hoped would endure for ever, are now crumbling into dust. Such is the perishable nature of earthly hope! What sensitive heart has not to heave a sigh over the grave of its own wishes! So true is the reflection of the poet Southern, "All things pass away and are no more." But before this pass from under my pen, let the virtues and vices of the Portuguese in India be briefly portrayed.

During an overwhelming attack made by the Egyptian fleet that had passed down the Red Sea unexpectedly, on a small squadron under Laurence D'Almeyda, after a most determined resistance, his vessel struck on a flat. It was impossible for the other vessels to get near him, for Hocenus, the Egyptian admiral, with his native auxiliaries surrounded the wreck, assailing this unfortunate ship on all sides. The battle continued during a whole day, and at night a boat was sent to bring off the

Portuguese admiral, but he replied, " I shall never leave those who have been my companions in danger, nor desert this ship whilst hope or life remains to defend and save her for my country." Next morning the battle was revived, and one of Almeyda's thighs was shot away, but he ordered himself to be placed in a chair on the deck, and continued to give his orders with coolness till another ball carried away part of his breast and ribs, when he expired. The Egyptians then boarded the vessel, when Laurence Catus, a servant of the deceased admiral, who was wounded in the eye with an arrow, and who had thrown himself on the body of his master, started up, and with his sword killed several of the assailants, while another sailor, named Andrew Van Portua, who had lost his right hand, and received a musket-ball in his shoulder, fought to the last with his left, dealing destruction around. When Almeyda's father heard of his son's death, he said, " It is mine to sustain his place," and, brushing away the tear of mortal weakness, he proceeded with a fresh force to attack Hocenus, destroyed his whole fleet in the harbour of Diu, took that important little island, and amazed the continent by his valour and humanity.

In this engagement the brave Nonnius Vasques Pereria was killed; he passed through the enemy's batteries that lined the shore with his single ship, and boarded Hocenus amidst his own fleet.

Old Almeyda did not live to see the termination

of his commenced success, for having fallen into disgrace with king Emanuel by some misunderstanding, he was recalled, and killed at the Cape of Good Hope, by a pointed stick having been run through his body, in an affray between some of the natives and his sailors. But Nonnius Acunia took the fort of Diu, and the fortified island of Betel, where the desperate Turks, having burned their wives and children, being determined to receive no quarter, rushed upon the Portuguese like lions, maddened by revenge, and were not destroyed till they had slaughtered seventeen officers and one hundred and fifty men belonging to the force under Nonnius.

James Bottelho, a brave officer, having incurred his king's displeasure, determined to remove it by an uncommon instance of self-devotion. He set sail from Goa in a boat eighteen feet long and six broad, with hands sufficient to manage this frail skiff, and arrived safely at Lisbon, with advice of a glorious victory in India. He received Emanuel's pardon, and a look of approbation dearer to his heart than life.

Antonius Sylveria was left governor of Diu with a small garrison. He was soon after attacked by 3000 Turks, supported by 20,000 irregulars, belonging to the king of Cambay, while the Egyptian fleet, which had got into the Indian sea for this express purpose approached the walls. This great naval force was commanded by Solyman, basha of Egypt, and consisted of sixty-four stout galleys belonging to the Grand Signior, manned by experienced seamen, and having on board a large force of Janissaries, then considered the bravest troops in the world. Fire-ships were pushed up to the fort, to involve the place in smoke, while the general storm of it was attempted both by land and sea, but one of the most steady defences ever made repulsed the attacks. Mines were then carried under the walls, and the roar of battle, day after day, was heard not only under the burning sun, but in the cool dark bowels of the rocks. Maffæus, the historian, says that some of the Portuguese soldiers, when short of ammunition, charged their pieces with their own teeth. At length Diu was relieved; and this noble defence made such an impression on the king of France, that he sent for the picture of Sylveria, and had it set in gold.

When Albuquerque attacked Malacca, his friend Arañjo was a prisoner there, and the enemy threatened to put him to death, the moment the siege should begin. Anxious to save his life, operations were suspended; but he wrote to his general: "Think of nothing but the glory of Portugal, and let not a thought of me prevent you from pursuing victory."

At a time when Ataida was much in want of troops, and sorely pressed by enemies, he ordered the ships to sail which every year carried the tribute to Lisbon. His officers remonstrated, and insinuated that all assistance was required for the defence of India. "We shall be enough without them," said he; "the state is in distress, and its expectations must not be disappointed."

In the hottest part of a furious engagement the son of Lopez Carasco was told that his father had been slain. "We have one brave man the less," said he; "we must conquer, or deserve to die like him."

A beautiful young female was sold to the amorous Thomas de Souza, as a slave. She had been betrothed to a lover who almost adored her, and who rushed into his presence frantic with grief, offering to share her chains. Souza was deeply affected at the interesting sight: — "I give you liberty," said he, presenting the youth with a purse of gold; "go and live happy elsewhere." This high-minded officer knew how to imitate the Roman, and to captivate the human heart by conquering his own.

Some of the viceroys were also, from motives of humanity and benevolence, active in preventing the human sacrifices in India, occasioned by the horrid practices of idolatry and superstition. In some parts of Malabar a custom prevailed of always consulting magicians with respect to the destiny of children: if prognosticated to be happy, the infant became the object of parental affection; but if calamity was indicated, the innocent little stranger was deprived of life. To the honour of Lopez Soarez, he abolished this inhuman usage. *

But in reversing the picture, we are forced to acknowledge that vice sunk the Portuguese character lower than ever virtue raised it in India. In the hour of its profligacy, when only the courage of a robber remained to redeem it from contempt, an Indian said, "Providence has decreed that there should be but as few of them as there are of tigers and lions, lest they should exterminate the human species."

The sepulchres of the Chinese emperors were plundered by one, and the pagodas of Malabar destroyed by another, while all who came to weep were massacred. To impose upon man, oaths were taken on song books, that they might be broken by tarnishing honour with an insult on religion. Deceit and perfidy of every description became common. Kings and their children were carried off and murdered. The native peasantry were reduced to slavery. But providence has decreed that depravity should die by the injection of its own poison. When man is false to himself, he cannot be true to his friends. From robbing Indians, the Portuguese learned to rob each other. But all their atrocities were surpassed by the Inquisition which they established at Goa, where the

* On the authority of the Abbé Raynâl.

most monstrous cruelties were exercised under the sanction of religion.

Mar Joseph, the venerable bishop of the Syrian Christians of Travancore, was seized and sent to Lisbon. Their churches were pillaged; their books were burned; while archbishop Menezés from Goa, in 1599, marched, singing a hymn, round the flames. In short, this innocent race, like the contaminating Pariars of Malabar, had to take refuge in the forests, fearing less from the wild elephant and tiger, than from the ferocity of fellow-creatures, who worshipped the same God. So like is the resemblance between the fanatic and the heathen.

But certainly it is wrong to charge the misery inflicted by the Inquisition on the Portuguese government of India. In this instance the church of Rome was alone criminal. But punishment overtakes the servants of iniquity. Governments embraced the terrors of that tribunal as an engine of power, not from conscientious conviction of its being serviceable to God. Against the Portuguese in India it excited universal fear, with its companion hatred; and now two thousand priests have two hundred mouldering churches, some of them still magnificent structures, with scarcely a soul to attend the ringing of their bells. The processions of the *auto da fe* will long be remembered, with the shrieks of victims, so pathetically described by the

French physician Dellon *, who was immured in the dungeons of Goa for two years; the black dresses, the horrid executioners, the ghastly confessors, the *san-benitoes* painted with the holy cross, the grey *samarras*, the paintings representing human creatures placed upon burning torches, with demons seizing upon their fleeting souls, the *carrochas*, the ringing of great bells, the *parrains*, the military array, the viceroy in all his glory presiding as the slave of a Dominican, and at last the actual flames curling about dying wretches, whose groans and shrieks pierced the soul. The voluntary sacrifices of the Hindoos excite no such feelings of disgust: we pity but we admire. A smile plays round the beautiful lip, while kissing the husband's body on the funeral pile of the living and the dead. The devotee, placing his head under the wheel of Juggernaut's car, says, "This is my delight." A Christian may hate the one as well as the other, but a Hindoo makes a wide difference between giving what we must pay, and taking what we cannot bestow.

There is a description of the Portuguese in India by Baldæus, in 1670, which equally applies to their descendants: "They are," says he, "generally very idle, applying themselves seldom to any business, leaving the management of their concerns to slaves, and even the women committing the

* Vide Appendix, note 9.

care of their children to ignorant female servants, who also give them suck. Marriages are frequently formed with the natives by the men, but this is not such a general practice now as formerly. The children from this connection are called Mistices, and their offspring Castices. Fornication and adultery are considered as errors of little moment, and the men are so fond of variety that I have known three female slaves in *the straw* at one time to the same master. But they are averse to drunkenness, notwithstanding which, quarrels and murders are frequent among them. The men are excessively proud, and fond of snuff; as they walk along the streets, they are continually stroking and setting up their whiskers. So jealous are they of their wives and slaves, that the women seldom appear abroad unveiled, and the windows of their apartments are so contrived, that they can look upwards, but not down into the streets."

Goa is situated in the province of Bejapoor; lat. 15° 30′ N. long. 73° 42′ E.; distant from Poonah 245; from Bombay 292; from Delhi 1158; and from Calcutta 1300 miles.

The old city of Goa, which contains so many fine and magnificent specimens of Gothic architecture, is eight miles further up the river than the new town, in which the viceroy and chief Portuguese inhabitants reside. It is at the mouth of the river, within the forts of the harbour. In the old city, one of the cathedrals is in imitation of St.

Peter's in Rome, and its grandeur surpasses what has yet been attempted in any other part of India by Europeans. The statue of Vasco de Gama is placed over the palace gate of the city. There are in the Portuguese territories, which extend about forty miles in length and twenty in breadth along the coast, in the vicinity of Goa, 200 churches, and about 2000 priests, many of whom are exceedingly ignorant; and they have the old city nearly to themselves. The Inquisition is of course no more. It is the chapel of the palace, which is an accurate model of that paragon of architecture St. Peter's. The church of St. Dominic is beautified with paintings by Italian masters. In the Augustinian convent there is a very valuable library of theological works, mostly printed in the sixteenth century. The monument of St. Francis Xaverius is exquisite; and his coffin is enchased with silver and precious stones.

Although the Portuguese kept up a very considerable force, their conquests never extended far from the sea coast. But from the Cape of Good Hope to China, there are numerous descendants of those settlers who colonised the different places along the shore. Many of them are now blacker than the neighbouring Hindoos; which is a curious circumstance, that shews how soon a new race of men may spring up by crossing the breed; for those to whom I allude, are all castices, that is the offspring of an European Portuguese father and a native. Their language is a dialect composed of Portuguese, Hindostannee, and Malabar: and pronounced so in some places as to be nearly unintelligible to a native of Portugal. Even at Goa, the national language is now a corruption which, in time, will form another of those numerous dialects which are found in India. Such is the poverty of the inhabitants of this once famous city, that women descended from the best families, earn their subsistence by making lace or artificial flowers, and working muslin. Necessity obliges them now to be industrious, and the productions of their needle are sometimes very beautiful. Cochin lace is the most durable of any in India. The Portuguese have besides Goa, small establishments at Damaun, and on the islands of Timor and Macao, in China; but their trade is inconsiderable. In 1580, their power was at its summit, after which it came down by degrees, till almost totally destroyed by the Dutch.

CHAPTER III.

ON THE EAST INDIA COMPANIES OF HOLLAND, FRANCE, DENMARK, OSTEND, SWEDEN, PRUSSIA, AND RUSSIA.—ALSO ON THE TRADE OF SPAIN WITH INDIA.

THE Hollanders, like the other states of Europe, had received the fashionable productions of India through Portugal, till the conquest of that country by Philip of Spain, who prohibited his new subjects, in 1594, from corresponding with his enemies. But these brave republicans had now become soldiers and sailors, and they determined to seek at the fountain head, what monopoly refused to share down the stream. Cornelius Houtman was dispatched with four stout ships, by a society of merchants, called the Company of distant Countries, and succeeded in reconnoitring the coasts of India. He returned with a cargo of pepper and valuable spices; and reported that the Portuguese were every where hated.

A plan was immediately formed at Amsterdam, for establishing a settlement on the island of Java, and Van-Nec, in 1598, arrived there with eight ships. He was so fortunate in his negociations with the native princes, that he returned to Europe loaded with riches, and excited such emulation, as nearly ruined the first company; for different associations were formed, whose interests clashing with each other, threatened the destruction of the whole. At length, with the assistance of a wise government, these jarring elements were harmonised into a body of men styled, The East India Company, armed with absolute power to make peace or war in all parts beyond the Cape of Good Hope, to legislate for themselves, and to retain such territories as they might conquer.

This was quite an original idea. The Portuguese had traded to India for the purpose of enriching the king. Their viceroy had to act merely in agency for the government of his country, while in the case of Holland, one republic was formed within another, made mutually dependent by interest, yet both masters in their own concerns.

Success is the child of energy. Admiral Warwick, with a fleet of fourteen ships, soon laid the foundation of Batavia, formed a connection with Bengal, beat the Portuguese, and established a high character in the East for the courage of his country. In 1624, Fort Zealand was commenced on the western coast of Formosa, an island near China, which soon became the centre of trade with Java, Siam, the Philippine islands, Japan, and all the East. In 1621, the Portuguese were driven from the Moluccas, and the trade in cloves and nutmegs fell into the hands of the Dutch. These valuable fruits grow on bushes resembling our birch and pear trees. Cloves preserved in sugar are eaten as a dessert to promote digestion; nutmeg is said to be a poison, if used immoderately, but, as a spice or medicine, it strengthens the stomach and bowels, expels wind, and is serviceable in dysentery.

The Dutch soon formed settlements also in the fine islands of Timor, Celebes, and Borneo; the last of which is perhaps the largest in the world. It produces abundance of fine pepper, and some diamonds; but the inhabitants of all these are barbarous, treacherous, and cruel. Some of them are Christians; but in general they are converts to Arabian missionaries, whose tenets have only inflamed their natural ferocity.

In Sumatra, Banca, and Siam, the Hollanders also speedily formed settlements. From these rich and extraordinary regions they got tin, elephants' teeth, gum lac, sappan wood, gold, pepper, and camphor. The tree which produces the camphor, is one that grows as tall as our oak, with a leaf like the laurel, having numerous clusters of white flowers, which form into black berries as large as peas. Oil is procured by the application of fire from all parts of the tree, which is cut in pieces, soaked in water, and being heated, the camphor rises into an iron receiver. This is the case all over

Japan, where the coarse camphor is plentiful, but the Sumatra drug is the finest in the world, lodges in a smaller species of plant, and is yielded without distillation. But it is now very scarce, all the trees having been nearly cut down. It is deposited in the trunk of the tree in flakes. The Indians use it for removing obstructions. It also strengthens the stomach, and combined with other medicines, it increases their efficacy.

On the island of Ceylon, the Portuguese had made themselves detested by the foulest murder and perfidy; and when king Janiere was inhumanly sabred in their council chamber, the beautiful young princess to whom he had been betrothed, predicted their destruction, for said she " Of whatever crime he may have been guilty, you ought to have given him a legal trial. Rest assured this treacherous act will turn to your ruin. Who will not curse you that hears it? How can any one trust you again? Alas! You have involved me in misery. Be therefore upon your guard, for you will pay dearly for having rewarded a man thus, who had done you such signal service." And they were afterwards massacred and driven out of all their settlements by the combined forces of the Ceylonese and the Dutch; who then pushed up the Malabar coast, stormed Cochin, and seized upon all their forts and territories except Goa. Malacca even was at last taken, which for some time held out in the eastern parts: and in less than seventy years, the Dutch became in India what the Portuguese had been in the meridian of their glory. The Portuguese colonists embraced their yoke with the docility of Hindoos; and changed masters without a regret for their country. Their forefather's stern virtues were extinguished by the luxury, indolence, and effeminacy of Asia. Thus Holland became master of the areca, betel, cinnamon, and pepper of Ceylon; which are in themselves mines of gold, were there no other treasures in this paradise of the East.

The areca is a small solid nut, which grows on a most beautiful species of palm, neither so tall nor so thick as the cocoa; the betel is the leaf of a plant that climbs like ivy, and the areca nut, whose kernel is analogous to nutmeg, is wrapped in the betel, powdered with lime, made from shells, and chewed all over India by male and female, both by day and by night. Ladies of gallantry breathe it on their lovers. It is presented when friendly visits are paid, and offered as a pledge of regard when departure is intimated. They say it strengthens the stomach, and excites inclinations of love. The cinnamon tree is a species of laurel, the root of which when distilled, yields coarse camphor. Its fruit is a small berry, and from it is extracted, by boiling, a perfumed white gum, of which candles are made for very great men. There are three layers of bark, two of which are cut every eighteen months as cinnamon, till the tree dies, or falls into a decline, when, being removed, fresh shoots spring up from the odoriferous stem left in the ground, equally prolific.

When the Hollanders had conquered India, they were anxious to have a proper station for the refreshment of their ships on the passage, and under the guidance of Van Riebeck, the Cape of Good Hope was colonised in 1650, and in twenty years upwards of two millions sterling expended on Cape Town, its fine gardens, walks, and fortifications. It is certainly an uncommonly fine settlement, and at this day presents an interesting sight.

Under the mild government of England, the Dutch inhabitants, who are now so numerous as to form a populous city, which may be called the capital of Southern Africa, seem contented and cheerful. The climate is healthful; nearly all the fruits of Europe and Asia flourish here; and the people, instructed by beautiful forms of Lutheran and Calvinistic Christianity, are simple in manners and frank in their deportment. The females are very pretty; in some instances, that fell under the author's observation, he thought them possessed, in a high degree, of what the French term *naïveté* —a certain undescribable something, which we admire in children, and almost adore in a young mistress; but which, we would call credulity, if the innocence of the lip was not a redeemer of the prattle that falls from an unsophisticated tongue; and if an arch, sparkling, chaste eye did not speak wit to the imagination, which the words were not calculated to impress on the understanding. Indeed it is said that the young girls here reverse our mode of courtship. If so many happy marriages, as are reported, be the consequence, let utility plead a pardon for indelicacy. Perhaps Dr. Gregory may have been cold, when he told his daughters never to let their husbands know the extent of their love; for the sentiment has the freezing feel of cunning, instead of the honest glow of a candid heart. The Dutch farmers, however, in the country, are in some instances rude specimens of the effect of rural retirements when not influenced by contact with advancing civilisation; for the march of the human mind in solitude is that of a crab. Memory, intellect, every faculty of our nature, grow and gain strength by intercourse with the world.

Batavia, the capital of Holland in India, called after the ancient name of the Dutch, who are descended from the Battæ of Hesse, is situated in the island of Java, lat. 6° 10″ S. long. 106° 51″ E. It is a parallelogram of 4200 feet by 3000, ornamented with fine wide streets, canals, public edifices, churches, mosques, and Chinese temples. In 1811, it surrendered to Sir Samuel Achmuty, Lord Minto, our Governor General, being present, superintending the operations of the attack. General Jansens defended his fortified camp at Mester Cornelius, to which he retired, with skill and obstinacy; but on the 25th August, he was defeated, and Fort Cornelius taken by storm. At the peace of Paris it was restored; and the Dutch received it back much improved as to salubrity. Their establishment is now prosperous. There are about 5700 taxed houses, which, with the villages around, in a circle of ten miles, contain a population of about 120,000, and there are subordinate to it upwards of 200,000 souls. Fully 10,000 of these are Dutch, or free citizens, and their wives, descended from Hollanders; the rest are Javanese, Malays, Chinese, and 20,000 of them are slaves.

Acute inflammatory febrile diseases are very destructive to life. The unhealthiness of Batavia must certainly be occasioned by the miasma of its morasses, ditches, and canals; for all the inhabitants of this capital are sickly in appearance, but recover their colour and spirit by a short residence in the neighbouring mountains, which they soon lose upon their return. Death is so common and sudden, that it scarcely excites emotion in the survivors. At the Cape of Good Hope and Chinsurah, the Dutch are possessed of sensibility, and at Cochin, some of their descendants are far from phlegmatic; but at Batavia an apathy prevails, which deeply affects the heart that can behold it. In fifty years it has been ascertained that 47,000 soldiers and sailors died in the hospitals of Batavia, though the European military forces on the island were always but a handful of men. Beauty is here without motion, and lifeless. The sparkling eye of Cape Town is no where to be seen. It is true, the mode of living here is destructive of health and life. Luxury and debauchery are called in as auxiliarics to climate, and the poison of mud reeking constantly with putrefaction.

When the Dutch came to India, they were a sober, industrious, temperate, and simple people; their valour was admirable, their prudence was conspicuous, and their integrity such that they sometimes only punished native perfidy by withdrawing their factories; for it was their policy to impress on the Indians, that in settling upon their coasts, and guarding them from the rapacious Portuguese, they were doing them a signal favour. The cloven foot of self-interest, which was afterwards substituted for public principle, did not then appear. Hambroeck in magnanimity equalled Regulus; for being taken in a sally, he was sent to persuade the surrender of Fort Zealand, under penalty of death; instead of which, his object in going, was to inspire the garrison with fresh courage. Their tender solicitations, backed by the tears of his two daughters, that he might break his promise of returning, were unavailing. "I have pledged my honour," said he, "and my memory shall never be sullied with reproach." He then calmly returned to meet his fate in the Chinese camp.

At Malacca, the Dutch got possession of the fortress by bribery, after many fruitless attacks at different periods. When this golden key had opened the gate, the governor was massacred to save 30,000*l.*, which had been promised in reward for treachery. The Sabines were here imitated, but on a different principle. Tarpeia was crushed by their bucklers for her perfidy. Odious oppressions were at length every where practised; the spice trees were rooted up, that a complete monopoly might belong to the Dutch company; the poor natives were reduced to beggary, and butchered when they wept for the loss of their vegetable gold; kings were dethroned, and tyrants raised for purposes of subserviency; the will of man was substituted for the wish of God; and murder was called in to accomplish what open force could not so well achieve. In short, the noble Hollanders became Asiatic Portuguese; and the simple republicans ceremonious despots. Such is the inconsistency of man. We are creatures of imitation. Vanity may whisper a different tale; but let truth be told, and it will be found that man is every where the same creature. All nature aims at conquest. Animate and inanimate matter once in motion, go on till stopped by their own friction; and as in the ocean, what flows to it fresh becomes salt, so in nations, the small body mixes with the mass, and partakes of its qualities. The conquerors of England became Britons; those of India Hindoos, in all but name.

Alligators and noxious reptiles are very numerous near Batavia, and the river Caiman takes its name from the numbers of the former in it. There are no stones near the city; marble and granite are imported from China. The sun's heat is not excessive, for the thermometer ranges from 84° to 90° in the heat of the day, during the whole year. Several islands protect the mouth of the harbour from the swell of the ocean, and the anchorage is very safe. The campong of the Chinese, or town, is situated near the walls inland. It resembles a great bazar, of 1500 mean houses, huddled together, containing 20,000 inhabitants, and 40,000 swine. These industrious people cultivate the rice grounds, sugar plantations, and gardens around, carry on all kinds of manufactures and trades, and contract for the supply of all things required in the civil, military, and marine departments.

The trade of Batavia is considerable. Opium, camphor, benzoin, pewter, iron, saltpetre, gunpowder, and all warlike stores, spices, &c. are monopolised by the company. From Bengal come opium, drugs, and muslins; from Sumatra, camphor, benzoin, birds' nests, and ivory; from Cape Town, garden seeds, butter, and wine; from China, porcelain, teas, silks, nankeens, alum, borax, brimstone, cinnabar, mother-of-pearl, paper, sweetmeats, and tobacco; from Japan, copper, sabre blades, camphor, soy, and curious articles of furniture varnished, and flowered with mother-of-pearl. The exports are pepper, sugar, coffee, rice, and arrack, with other indigenous varieties. Batavia arrack is the best in the world. It is manufactured by the Chinese, who call it sanchoo, or burned wine, from various kinds of grain; but the produce of the sugar cane is, I understand, the principal of Batavia arrack. The composition is mixed in hot water, and the other ingredients are liquorice root, aniseed, garlic, and the juice of the cocoa tree. Exportation of specie is prohibited; the duties are heavy, and a free trade is prevented by restrictions.

Accounts are kept in rix dollars, an imaginary coin of forty-eight stivers; but the currency is doits, stivers, dubeltjees, schillings, and rupees; the ducat, Japan copang, English guineas; mohurs from India; doubloons, florins, and guilders, with all money in gold and silver, at a value proportioned to its purity.

Affairs are administered by a governor general, who is president, a director general, entitled governor of Java, nine counsellors, and two secretaries. The authority of this body is absolute; and the governor general can exercise all their functions on his own responsibility. A fiscal is at the head of the police and criminal administration. All operations of trade are conducted by a Shahbunder.

Never was such stiff formality and ceremony observed as reign here, despotically, under a republican form. In 1764, to fix the etiquette of rank, 131 articles were drawn up by the government, regulating places at table, the precedence of drinking healths, the keeping of carriages, horses, and servants. By one article, childrens' little coaches are to be painted only according to the rank of the mother. Counsellors' wives may wear jewels worth 6000 rix dollars; senior merchants' 4000; others must only shine in the proportion of stars, numbered three, two, one. Ladies of rank may walk out, or go abroad, in carriages, attended by three waiting-maids, whose ornaments are minutely described; others with only one or two. The Bengal Dutch civil servants are restricted from surpassing those at Batavia, and the director at Surat was only allowed four fans, ornamented with feathers of the bird of paradise, cow, or yak tails, and gold. Carriages were taxed downwards, till keeping one was prohibited.

The salaries allowed by the Company to their servants are small, so that many kinds of extortion, bribery, and corruption, are resorted to for the purpose of keeping up parade.

Their mode of living is a heavy breakfast, about eight o'clock, an oppressive dinner at noon, the effects of which are slept off, and a tempting supper closes the day, at which large libations are poured out to Bacchus in claret, madeira, gin, and beer. Deaths are in the proportion of one to every five Europeans annually. Most of the white women are born at Batavia. They spend their mornings among their slaves, in loose dresses, and, like their nurses, sit on the ground cross-legged, chewing betel. In the evening they go out richly decorated for exercise, having their jet black hair bespangled with diamonds and pearls, mingled with flowers of the Arabian jessamine and tuberose. Before supper the ladies put on light muslin dresses, and the gentlemen exchange their velvets and wigs for white jackets, and ornamented night-caps, in which they sit smoking till the hour of rest. Females are at maturity in their eleventh year, and grow old and ugly about thirty. No attention is paid to the cultivation of the mind. Little social intercourse exists between man and woman, and as the female is incapable by delicacy and vivacity to soften the manly qualities, the male is not excited by esteem to aim at raising what he only loves for his own gratification. Both, therefore, instead of being mutually conducive to improvement, contribute to barbarise each other. The men are rude, and the women languid and insipid.

Nearly all their slaves are from Celebes and Sumatra. These unfortunate forlorn creatures are so often maddened by cruelty to desperation, that running the muck is common. This is done when reduced to desperation by melancholy, by rousing the energies to insanity with a dose of opium or bang. A rush is then made by the naked slave, on friend and foe, with a creese, and it generally happens that he wallows in the blood of vengeance, flowing from the ghastly wounds of innocent passers by, before he is cut down, or taken to undergo a refinement of torture, which exceeds description; but which has never been found to check the crime, not any more than the sanguinary codes in other countries. Some generous men, when returning to Europe with fortunes, manumit their slaves; and others, when at the point of death, strive to propitiate heaven, by giving up a possession which they can no longer retain.

The profits of the Dutch East India Company have generally been above ten per cent. Their stock was at first about 600,000*l.*, subscribed by nearly 2000 adventurers. It laid the foundation, in Europe, for the various frauds committed in the sale of public securities. We have completely overthrown their power in the East. The Hollanders have sunk as the English rose. "When will you return?" said a Dutch officer to a Portuguese, as he was embarking, after the surrender of a strong fort. "When your crimes are greater than ours," was the instructive reply. The latter might now return with fair hope of as good a reception as the Dutch.

THE FRENCH EAST INDIA COMPANY.

During the reign of Philip the Fair, France began to recover from the tyranny of the feudal system. Agriculture, manufacture, and commerce were revived; but it was not till Catherine of

Medicis had crossed the Alps that the taste of this lively nation for elegance was completely formed. The productions of the East were received from the Portuguese at first, after the trade of Venice fell into their hands; but so early as 1503 an attempt was made to get round the Cape of Good Hope, which was unsuccessful. In 1601 a small commercial society was formed in Bretagne, and the vessels sent out reached the Maldives. But Pyrard, who conducted the undertaking, was very unfortunate in his navigation, and did not return home for ten years. In 1616 another society was formed, which did not succeed well; and it was not till 1642 that a settlement was made on the island of Madagascar, preparatory to others contemplated in India. This large island, separated from Africa by the Mozambique channel, was covered with forests and morasses. It had been neglected by the Portuguese, on account of its supposed unhealthiness; but the French finding that although the coasts were barren sands, yet that inland the country was fertile and the air salubrious, a factory was established upon it. The French, however, were unhappy in not propitiating the natives. Such a spirit of hatred was at length excited in their breasts, that in repeated attacks nearly all the early settlers were destroyed, and their houses consumed.

The national energies being roused by the misfortunes of these private societies, Colbert, in 1664, established an East India Company on the model of Holland, supported by the French government, with a charter for fifty years. It was invested with very great privileges, and the stock, amounting to 625,000*l.*, was raised partly by a loan in the mother country. Accordingly four ships reached Madagascar in 1665, and a permanent settlement was made; but the French finding it impossible to construct a safe harbour, never went to much expense, and their unproductive colony was at length abandoned.

Surat was at this time the centre of Indian commerce. The French, in common with the other European Companies, established their principal factory there, and derived much assistance from the Parsees, who had settled on this coast so early as the seventh century, to escape from the persecution of the Mohammedans, who conquered Persia. These mild and industrious followers of Zoroaster had conducted themselves with great prudence, keeping clear of all political parties, and being in India what the Quakers are in Europe, friends to the whole human race. It was in the year 1668 that the French established themselves in this ancient and populous city under the direction of one Caron, who had long served the Dutch; but being disgusted with ill-treatment, he came over to his own countrymen, and did them signal service by his experience and prudent conduct.

Anxious to secure for the Company a fortified

post of consequence that might become the capital of that empire, which the French, from their first arrival, panted to establish by conquest over India, Caron surveyed the coasts, and fixed upon Trincomalee, having one of the finest harbours in the world on the rich island of Ceylon. Assisted by a French squadron, under La Haye, it was taken possession of; but this occasioned a war between the Dutch and French Companies, which proved disastrous to the latter; for after losing great numbers of brave men by sickness, in this ill-concerted expedition, the fort surrendered to the Dutch. La Haye then sailed for the Coromandel coast, and attacked St. Thomé, which had been built one hundred years before by the Portuguese, and which the Dutch claimed as their conquerors. From this also they were driven two years after; and the prospects of the Company would have been ruined had not Mr. Martin, a merchant of talent, purchased a small village, and some territory from the king of Bejapoor, near which Pondicherry was built, and became the capital of their trade and conquests. It bears the same name as the little village which was called Pudicheri.

Here the French continued to improve from 1672, the year in which the settlement was made. They formed connections with China, Siam, and some other places in the East, and established factories in the province of Bengal. War in Europe, however, enabled the Dutch in 1693 to attack the French capital in India. Pondicherry was taken in that year, and not restored till the peace of Ryswick in 1697.

Meanwhile, 1688 persons had been placed on the island of Madagascar, who, instead of the prosperity which they had expected, found graves, or such dissensions as paralysed all hope of success. Trade was carried on in such a way, and made so subservient to views of ambition and conquest, that instead of creeping cautiously along the shore, they launched into the ocean, before experience had taught them the best method of protecting the European bark against Indian waves. The Frenchmen of those days were all soldiers instead of sailors or merchants. A warlike disposition marches directly to its object, too often with rashness, while the commercial spirit imitates the fox, in accomplishing the same end by safe and slow encroachments. Reynard patiently takes his tail in his mouth, to try a stratagem, when he cannot mount the roost without the risk of breaking his neck; but the cock jumps into the water that drowns him, to get at the image of what tempts his avidity. The French Company, therefore, instead of being enriched by trade, were always poor, and had often to subscribe for losses; while their rivals, the Dutch and English, were sharing dividends of thirty per cent on adventures.

This course of ill-success was at length arrested

by Orry, the celebrated financier of the mother country. He sent his brother out to Pondicherry to execute his plans; and circumstances at length began to conspire in favour of France. Dumas was so fortunate as to obtain from the court of Delhi permission to coin money at the French capital in India, which proved to be a grant worth 21,000*l.* per annum, and by purchase or cession from the Tanjore government, districts were in a short time secured, containing 113 villages, yielding a revenue of more than 20,000*l.* yearly. The town of Karical then became a place of importance, and it was accordingly strongly fortified by the French. Their neighbour, the Nabob of Arcot, was attacked by the Mahrattas, and being vanquished and slain, his family found a place of refuge at Pondicherry. The Mahratta general demanded the surrender of his enemies, and the payment of tribute by the French, to the amount of 50,000*l.* per annum; but Dumas laughed at the Indian, and behaved with such firmness and prudence that peace ensued, and the Nabob of Arcot became the friend and ally of the French.

La Bourdonnais, during these successes, was sent on discoveries, and inspected the isles of Mascarenhas, Cerne, and Rodrique, which the Portuguese had discovered to the east of Madagascar, in the 19th degree of south latitude, but neglected. He made such a report upon their natural advantages, that it was immediately attempted to colonise the two largest, now called the Isles of France and Bourbon. The unfortunate remnant of the settlement in Madagascar here found an asylum, and these islands proved to be the most permanent possessions of the French in the East. A delightful climate and a fertile soil soon induced numerous adventurers to take up their abode where health and plenty appeared to smile on industry. The coffee tree was transplanted from Arabia: the Isle of France, which had been uninhabited before the French settled in Bourbon, under the management of the sagacious Bourdonnais, soon began to glow with yellow harvests of wheat, rice, and cassava, which latter grain he brought from Brazil for the slaves: a flourishing town was founded, the harbour of Port Louis fortified and improved, docks were constructed, and ships built and equipped which swept the Indian seas.

While these islands rose to importance under Bourdonnais, Chandernagor, the French colony on the river Hooghly, in the province of Bengal, was superintended by Dupleix, whose talents elevated it from almost nothing to a state of grandeur that excited admiration and envy. He was called to Pondicherry in 1742, and during his administration of the Company's affairs, their revenue rose to the highest point it ever gained, and their prospect was the brightest.

The English, of course, saw this with the impatience of self-interest; and the French, with the fond hope of removing the only rival that impeded their advancement. War ensued. Bourdonnais besieged Madras, and took it in 1744, when he obtained plunder to the amount of 200,000*l.*, and agreed for a ransom of 440,000*l.*, which was not confirmed by M. Dupleix, who forced all the British inhabitants of every description to quit it; for he aimed at driving the English entirely from India. The French government rewarded Bourdonnais for his conduct in India with a dungeon upon his return, great discord having arisen between him and Dupleix; and the British having received reinforcements from Europe, Admiral Boscawen besieged Pondicherry with 3720 Europeans, 300 topasses, and 2000 sepoys in 1748. In a month and eleven days he was compelled to raise the siege, after losing 1065 Britons in repeated struggles, all of which were baffled by the conduct of Dupleix, who had a garrison of 1800 Frenchmen and 3000 sepoys; but the fortifications were of course equal to an army, and his artillery was served with great skill.

Under a belief that Madras would never be restored to England, the French greatly improved it: at the peace of Aix-la-Chapelle, in 1749, it was returned. But the restless spirit of Dupleix could not remain within the bounds of moderation. He pushed his system of aggrandizement along the coasts of India for 600 miles; disposed of the soubahship of the Deccan in favour of a creature of his own, and sent an army under M. Bussy to place him in power at Aurungabad. Another creature, subservient to the interests of France, was proclaimed Nabob of Arcot, which secured for Dupleix cessions, as a valuable consideration, on the banks of the Cavery, so situated as to command the water required to irrigate the lands of Tanjore, which necessarily placed that kingdom at his disposal. He was honoured with high marks of favour by his king, and invested with the dignity of a nabob by the Emperor of Delhi, that he might influence the minds and imaginations of the natives by the utmost display of Asiatic pomp. Seated upon a tall elephant, glittering with trappings of gold and silver, followed and preceded by others in slow imposing procession, he received the prostrations of a slavish multitude with all the exultation of unbounded vanity. He sat in his durbar like the Great Mogul, and by acting the despot soon learned to be one in reality. The rights of the natives were trampled upon. Their customs and ceremonies were ridiculed and insulted. They were forced to act contrary to the rules of their castes, and their tears, lamentations, and curses spread hatred and roused vengeance. Dupleix became inflated with his own lightness; and at a time when he should have cautiously insinuated that he could scarcely walk, he trumpeted to the world that he was pluming his wings for majestic flights.

The English now saw that one of the two rival states must fall; and all the energies of the Company were directed to arrest the glaring encroachments of Dupleix, whose inordinate ambition at last bringing him under suspicion at the court of Versailles, he was replaced by M. Lally in 1758, just when a bloody war was commencing between England and France. Both parties strained every nerve to meet the coming storm, which was seen black and portentous over the continent of America. Though Great Britain was not at leisure to send out a large force to India, yet the abilities of Colonels Clive, Lawrence, and Coote supplied the place of troops. Never were harmony and emulation more conspicuous,—never were valour and self-devotion carried to a more romantic length than in those struggles between the English and French Companies for empire in the plains of Hindostan. Valour was always common to both nations; but self-devotion can only be claimed by the victorious party, and it must be restricted to the period in question; for discord as often prevails in our councils, as in those of almost any other country.

Dupleix and Bourdonnais, unquestionably the greatest men the French Company ever had in their service in India, could not agree; for, in fact, they were not magnanimous enough to sacrifice their own passions to the interests of their country; and Lally, who succeeded, had nothing but the impetuous courage of an Irishman to redeem him from the contempt of an historian. He was ungovernably passionate, gloomy, and irregular; so that there was an eternal inconsistency between his words and his actions. Suspicious and jealous, he roused in the breasts of others most dangerous commotions, hostile to the ends he had in view, by not knowing how to keep them suppressed within himself. In common with his predecessors, however, he aimed at the destruction of his foes; and, having received strong reinforcements from Europe, he attacked Madras, while the English were engaged in a most dangerous war in Bengal with the natives. This invasion of the French terminated in the capture of Chandernagor, and the overthrow of every hope the French entertained of increase on the banks of the Hooghly.

The siege of Madras by Lally will ever be considered memorable for skill and bravery on both sides. It was commenced on the 17th December, 1758, and terminated on the 17th of February following, by the precipitate retreat of the French army, who left fifty-two pieces of cannon and one hundred and fifty barrels of gunpowder behind them.

All their territories were now wrested from the French Company; and in 1761, beaten both by land and sea, Pondicherry surrendered, after a long and brave defence, to Colonel Coote. It was restored at the peace of 1763, taken again by Sir

Hector Munro in 1778, returned in 1783, captured again in 1793, and given up once more at the peace of Amiens with 25,000 inhabitants and a revenue of 18,000*l.*, arising from the town and territory which extended five miles along the coast. Bonaparte intended to avail himself of this nest to hatch a dangerous brood, and he sent out seven generals, a great number of other officers, and 1400 regular troops, with a military chest containing 100,000*l.* All his plans were frustrated by the recommencement of war, and the place was again reoccupied in 1803, but Admiral Linois carried the troops off in his ships, in proper time, to the Isle of France; for Pondicherry was then an open town, the fortifications having been destroyed by the English, in return for a similar act when the French captured Fort St. David.

At the peace of Paris, Chandernagor was restored to the French, but they are not permitted to fortify it. Pondicherry and Chandernagor are the only settlements they have now in India; for the Isles of France and Bourbon were captured by an expedition sent against them by Lord Minto in 1811. They now belong to Great Britain by treaty.

Pondicherry, which was once a beautiful city, is hastening fast to ruins. The descendants of the French in it, like those of the Portuguese and Dutch in other places, are very poor, and even ladies support themselves by various modes of industry.

Since the decline of the French in India, which commenced with the brilliant career of Lord Clive, that active and restless people have never lost sight of any opportunity to recover their influence. Upon the return of Lally to Europe, after the surrender of Pondicherry in 1761, he was arrested, tried on several charges, and sentenced to lose his head, not, it appears, for any crime he had committed, but to allay the popular indignation, which was excited by the overthrow of hopes, formed with the most sanguine fondness. Like our Byng, he was the victim of prejudice and blind fury; for he was not answerable for what he could not control, and the punishment ought to have fallen upon those who placed him in a situation where conciliating qualities were required. To an intolerant, overbearing spirit, the decline of the French must be attributed; and the elevation of the British to a contrary system.

Ever since, the trade of France with India has languished, with the exception of one short period of five years. In 1769, the charter of the French East India Company was suspended, and a free trade opened for all the subjects of that nation, under certain conditions. And in 1770, the Company made over all their property to the king, except an interest in the shares. It still exists as a body, but the trade is very trifling.

During the rise and progress of Hyder Alli, and his son Tippo, the French were indefatigable in disciplining the armies of Mysore; and in like manner, when the Mahrattas combined against the power of Great Britain in the East, one of the most adroit manœuvres of the Marquis Wellesley was the disarming of the French at Hyderabad, and their separation from the service of Scindea.

Pondicherry is in lat. 11° 56′ N. long. 79° 58′ E. Distant from Calcutta 1130 miles. It contained, when taken from Lally, about 70,000 inhabitants, and several magnificent buildings. The streets were broad, and planted on each side with a row of green trees, the shade of which was particularly grateful. Though the fortifications were destroyed, the public buildings neglected, and the native inhabitants scattered over India, yet the French restored it to beauty again, and fortified it strongly. In subsequent attacks, however, these were once more demolished, and this charming city is now doomed to appear to the contemplative traveller, like the ghost of a lovely thing that has been, and passed away, leaving but a wreck behind.

THE DANISH EAST INDIA COMPANY.

Christianity having overthrown the barbarising system of Woden, one of whose tenets was, that the regions of bliss were only open to a warrior, the Danes, forsaking their cruel and rapacious life, mixed in commercial intercourse with other nations, and became polished by imperceptible degrees.

Christiern the Fourth of Denmark, about the year 1612, was anxious to share in the Indian trade, and accident was friendly to his wishes. Boschower, a Dutchman, possessed of influence from long residence on the island of Ceylon, was disgusted with some slight he had received from his own government, and offered his services to king Christiern. A society was accordingly formed for purposes of trade at Copenhagen, and six vessels sailed under Boschower for India. Unfortunately he died during the voyage, and his second in command, Ove Guidde de Tommerup, being coldly received at Ceylon, sailed for Tanjore, where he found more encouragement. In return for some handsome presents, and the promise of an annual tribute of seven hundred pounds sterling, a cession of territory was made, upon which the Danes built Tranquebar, and the fortress of Dansburg. The Portuguese, Dutch, and English were all too much engaged at the time to prevent what they afterwards no doubt regretted. For the Dutch in 1689, although the Danish Company was not in so flourishing a state as it had been, attacked Tranquebar, and the place was only saved by an alliance with the English.

This, however, did not much retard the decline of the Danish Society, for it became bankrupt in 1730.

A new East India Company was, however, formed by the government, with very great privileges and advantages. Their capital consisted only of 135,000*l.* divided into 84*l.* shares. With this fund and the profits, they in forty years fitted out 800 ships, and nearly trebled their original stock. On the west bank of the Hooghly river about sixteen miles above Calcutta, the Danish Company built the handsome little town of Serampore, extending a mile along a beautiful sheet of water, not more than half a mile inland, and without territory, the adjacent country being British property. During the last long war the Danish settlements were in our possession. They have been restored to the mother country, under the same restrictions as the settlements of France, Holland, and Portugal. At this place the Baptist missionaries* carry on their plans for converting the Hindoos; they have been very successful in translating the Scriptures into different native dialects. Here also the debtors of Calcutta find refuge from a jail, when unable to satisfy their creditors; for even in time of war it is considered out of the jurisdiction of the supreme court, and in time of peace the flag of a foreign state enables them to enjoy liberty in poverty.

Tranquebar is situated in lat. 11° N. long. 79° 55′ E. Distant from Madras, 145 miles, S. by W. While Denmark continued neutral, the inhabitants

* Vide Appendix, note 10.

here made large sums by lending their names to cover British property, but in 1807 it was taken possession of by the British government, and was restored at the peace of Paris. The Danes are a quiet, unmeddling people. Their missionaries have been very successful in converting the Tanjorians to Christianity, and in teaching them to be happy after the loss of caste, by finding the means of subsistence in a new society; the simplicity and beauty of which have been much commended by different observers.

The Danes are certainly held in great respect by the natives in the vicinity of their two settlements, which of course they owe entirely to their just and proper conduct, their unambitious deportment, and their delicate attention to the rights of their fellow creatures, whose manners and customs they do not arrogantly insult and ridicule, because they happen to be different from their own.

THE EAST INDIA COMPANY OF OSTEND.

Austria, from its situation, its poverty, and pride, was not in a state to cope with the commercial parts of Europe in trade. Every thing connected with manufacture languished in a country where industry was not supported by the countenance of power.

This state of things was seen by Prince Eugene,

who, with all the fine qualities of a soldier, possessed those of a statesman. Having received a proposal from the merchants of Ostend, for the formation of an East India Company, he lent his whole energy to the measure. In 1717, the first ships sent out by the Ostend Company reached India. From that period for a considerable time their affairs flourished. Two settlements were made, one at Coblom, near Madras, and the other at Bankibazar on the Ganges. Their capital was at first 450,000*l.* and on this they gained 15*l.* per cent. for many years; but the policy of Austria was adverse to commerce generally, and the competition of the English in India, with other minor causes, at length drove the Ostend Company out of the market. Being neglected by the government, it sunk into oblivion. The stock was sold off, and many of the proprietors turned their views towards Sweden, for the purpose of participating in the Indian trade.

THE SWEDISH EAST INDIA COMPANY.

Sweden began to hold a respectable station among the nations of Europe from the time of Gustavus Adolphus; but it was not till the year 1731, that a rich merchant of Stockholm procured from the king a charter for the formation of an East India Company. Their success was at first very great, and upwards of 54 per cent was cleared.

upon their adventures, but in time their privileges were encroached upon by a necessitous and short-sighted government, and they were never able to increase their stock much, which was at first about 250,000*l.*, nor to form permanent establishments in India. The seat of their commerce with India was fixed at Gottenburgh, which communicates by artificial navigation with Stockholm, and their factors reside at the principal stations of the other Europeans trading with the East, but their speculations are now on a small scale.

ON THE PRUSSIAN, SPANISH, AND RUSSIAN EAST INDIA TRADE.

When the good fortune of Frederick the Great gave him possession of East Friesland in 1744, the advantageous situation of its capital, Embden, for trade, induced him to establish an East India Company, which was effected in 1751, with a capital of nearly 165,000*l.*, divided into two thousand shares. Their speculations were, however, very unsuccessful; and in 1763 a dissolution of the Company was the consequence.

The Spaniards, satisfied with their conquests in America, and prevented from turning their ambition to the East by the Pope's bull, which had vested that quarter of the globe in the Portuguese, reaped no advantage from their discovery of the

Philippines, which Magellan had visited in 1521, being then in the service of the emperor Charles the Fifth. But in 1564, Philip the Second began to establish a settlement in this distant quarter, and gave his name to the discoveries of Magellan, which had been previously called the Manillas. In 1571 the dominion of Spain was established over nine of those volcanic isles, and the foundation of the city of Manilla laid, which was strongly fortified in 1590 by Gomes Peres de las Marignas. It is situated between two volcanos, which are in a constant state of fermentation. This settlement was placed under a governor, subordinate to the viceroy of Mexico; and over the unfortunate islanders the Spaniards have always exercised the most cruel oppression, having converted the whole of them within their reach to Christianity by terror. From Manilla the Spanish galleons sailed annually to Mexico, with the various productions of India, which were paid for in cochineal and piastres. Now that revolution has deprived the mother country of Mexico, it is probable that the Philippines will be seized upon by some more commercial state than Spain, or continue an unproductive correspondence with America.

Like Portugal, Spain carried on trade with India, only on account of the king. The Philippines furnished for export tobacco, rice, canes, wax, oils, cowries, ebony, dried fish, japan wood, birds' nests, and sea dogs; but agents were stationed at the chief European settlements in India, who purchased all the valuable articles esteemed in the mother country.

The Russians, from continuing longer in a state of barbarism than other nations in Europe, had no communication with India till after the conquest of Siberia, towards the end of the sixteenth century. Having then approached the confines of China through Tartary, sharp contests arose in those frightful regions, which were at last settled by negotiations in 1689, that fixed the Russian limits at the river Kerbechi, about three hundred leagues from the Great Wall. By this treaty the Chinese permitted the Russians to send a caravan annually to Pekin ; but such infringements of manners and customs occurred by this intercourse, that in 1721 it was arranged that all transactions between the two nations should be carried on near the frontiers. Accordingly, two large magazines were established at Kiatcha, and commissaries appointed to superintend the exchange of merchandise, for specie was seldom used in this traffic. In this way Russia received tea, and many other luxuries, at the commencement of the reign of Peter the Great. But that sagacious prince, foreseeing the great advantage of commerce with India, established a communication through Astracan and Bucharia, by which the commodities of Hindostan were transported to Petersburgh. He subsequently also had important objects in view in pushing his conquests towards the Caspian Sea, and the confines of Persia. Had the English adventurer Elton not gone over to Kouli Khan, it is probably that the trade of Russia with India would have been firmly settled in that direction.

Viewing Russia as the most growing state in the world, it is impossible not to contemplate her future universal sway over Asia, if not prevented by wise precautions. Her situation is such, communicating by open roads prepared by the hand of nature, with three great quarters of the earth, that it is no wonder so many statesmen look upon the present actions of the warlike Alexander with suspicion and apprehension. In the mighty revolutions which futurity has within her womb, it is most likely that Russia and America are destined to perform great parts on the stage of the world, and that the plains of Hindostan will be the scene of mighty struggles for empire.

CHAPTER IV.

ON THE SETTLEMENTS AND CONQUESTS OF GREAT BRITAIN IN INDIA, TILL THE END OF MARQUIS WELLESLEY'S ADMINISTRATION.

England, as a commercial nation, had risen to an important station in the reign of queen Elizabeth. Her bold navigators, Drake, Stephens, and Cavendish, had extended the marine knowledge of their country; and in the year 1600 the enterprising merchants of London established an East India Company, under a charter for fifteen years, with privileges similar to those enjoyed by the other societies of Europe, then trading with the concurrence of their governments to India. Sir Thomas Roe, our ambassador to the court of the Great Mogul, was favourably received, and the moderate pretensions of the adventurers seemed at first to meet with success. Small factories were soon established at Surat, in Bengal, and on the Coromandel coast, and forts built in the islands of Java, Poleron, Amboyna, and Banda. But the Dutch, looking upon the settlements of the English with the greatest jealousy, a bloody war soon ensued between the two Companies, which nearly terminated in the ruin of the infant stations. The English were massacred on the islands of Java and Amboyna, and being neglected by the ministry of James the First, were left in a great measure to struggle with difficulties, that nothing but admirable wisdom and perseverance could overcome.

Captain Thomas Best had established a flourishing factory at Surat, about the year 1612, but the Portuguese, unwilling to admit such a rival, evinced the most rancorous spirit of hostility; and their plans for the destruction of the British settlement were only frustrated by the superiority of our naval force, which beat the armaments from Goa in three furious engagements. These successes raised the glory of the English name in India, and several advantageous connections were soon formed with native powers, ever willing to side with the strongest. The king of Persia opened the trade of his dominions to our merchants, and during the active reign of Cromwell, the Dutch were every where beaten, and their settlements taken. But Charles the Second, induced by his necessities to sell the interests of his country, permitted a rival company, for a valuable consideration, to be established, whose interests being opposed to the other commercial body, nearly led to the ruin of both. The Dutch at this time made the most formidable attacks upon the English, and in 1680 drove them ignominiously from Bantam. When, with the spirit of Britons, the old Company determined upon retaliation, King Charles sacrificed their interests for 93,749*l*., which he received from Holland. However, the credit of their name for integrity and fair dealing in India, had placed such powerful means at the disposal of the local authorities, that unsupported by the government at home, they withstood the utmost fury of their enemies. After escaping imminent perils, not only from the treachery of their king, but from the rancour and animosity with which the two companies pursued each other, the good sense of England prevailed; they were taken under the protection of parliament, and at length in 1702, the two East India Companies of England united their funds and became friends, since which the most signal success has attended their proceedings.

Meanwhile the French were beginning to push their ambitious projects forward with all the activity of hope. It was soon found that one of the two powers, England or France, must fall. A bloody war commenced in 1744, both in Europe and India, which was carried on almost without intermission till the death of George the Second, in the year 1760, by which time the French had lost all their settlements in India. The English were established in firm power, not only along the coasts of Coromandel, Malabar, and Bengal, but also in Arabia, the Persian Gulf, and throughout the Eastern Isles.

This amazing success is in a great measure to

be attributed to the uncommon genius of Lord Clive, who had commenced his career as a writer on the Madras establishment; but finding himself better calculated for the military than the civil department, he joined the army, and soon distinguished himself by acts of the most extraordinary valour. He was at length raised to rank, that gave him command. After several campaigns, distinguished by consummate skill and most daring enterprise, he placed the Nabob of Arcot, opposed by the French, on his throne, where he was supported by the English in power. He completely cleared the province of the French forces. Being then called away to Bengal to punish the Soubah of that province, the French who were considerably reinforced, attacked Fort St. David, under Lally, and beseiged Madras. But they were bravely resisted, and at last Colonel Coote, having beaten the French general in the field, besieged Pondicherry, and took his last strong-hold.

It appears that this wonderful prosperity completely changed the policy of the East India Company Hitherto their government had acted seemingly without any view to conquest or aggrandisement, and the good faith of England was respected by the natives. In the unassuming character of merchants they had been seen struggling with difficulties which excited compassion; and by industry and perseverance overcoming obstacles that created for them in the breast of every observer sympathy and esteem.

Surajah-Dowla, who had so inhumanly immured the garrison of Calcutta in the black hole*, from which out of 146 persons only 23 escaped with life, had been deposed by Colonel Clive, and put to death by his successor Meer-Jaffier Ally-Khan. This revolution and the battle of Plassey, by which it was brought about, had raised Colonel Clive's former bright character to such splendour, that honours were heaped upon him both in England and in India. By the emperor of Hindostan he was created an omrah, and by the court of directors on the 23d of June, 1758, nominated governor-general. In 1760, he returned to Europe, and was succeeded by Mr. Vansittart, who pursued a different line of policy, though aiming at the same end, the advantage of the Company.

He, however, instead of continuing hostile to Shah Allum, the Mogul Emperor, formed a treaty with him, and deposed Meer-Jaffier, whom Colonel Clive had elevated, placing Cossim Ally-Khan his son-in-law in the soubahship of Bengal. The hypocrisy and dissimulation with which this revolution was effected are truly disgusting. Mr. Vansittart said to Meer-Jaffier, "I solemnly declare, I have no other views but your good," while he was deposing him; and he held the same

* Vide Addenda, XXXIII.

language to Cossim, while stripping him of a large portion of those territories, to the sovereignty of which he professed to be raising him. Although he also received from Cossim nearly 100,000*l.*, as a present or bribe, which was reported by some of the members in council to the court of directors, yet that body, in consideration of the vast improvement of their revenue, highly applauded the conduct of their governor-general, and allowed him a handsome per centage on the increase.

However, the event proved that no confidence can be placed in a creature elevated to power on selfish principles. Cossim soon displayed the most rancorous hatred against those to whom he owed his elevation. He endeavoured to remunerate himself for what he considered he had lost, by the plunder and oppression of the subjects over whom he was permitted to tyrannise; and at length many acts of hostility were committed against the very power by whom he was supported. Among these may be mentioned the barbarous murder of Mr. Amyatt and his suite. War was, therefore, declared against him, and his army was beaten on the plains of Geriah; but he escaped into the dominions of Sujah-ul-Dowla, having first massacred about 200 English prisoners, belonging to the factories in his territories. The fate of these unfortunate men deserves a sigh. When the British army was approaching Moorshedabad, Cossim, according to the barbarous customs of

India, threatened to put all his prisoners to death, if the force advanced. Major Adams who commanded, was a man of humanity, and anxious to prevent such a sad catastrophe, found means of conveying advice to Mr. Ellis and the other prisoners of their danger, and offering the means of bribing the guards for their escape. But their magnanimous reply was "Let no attention be given to us; we are ready to submit to our fate."

By this revolution Meer-Jaffier was again raised to his former station, and Cossim being supported by Sujah-ul-Dowla, who held the power and person of the Great Mogul, a battle was soon fought at Buxar, which placed the emperor of Delhi, Shah Allum, in the hands of the English, to whom he had before voluntarily surrendered himself.

Such important events, and the confusion into which the politics of India fell during the administration of Mr. Vansittart, induced the court of directors to dispatch Lord Clive as the only man who could re-establish their affairs, and consolidate their conquests. He reached Calcutta in 1765, invested with supreme military and civil authority. His second career was commenced by professing in council that he came to reform the anarchy, confusion, and corruption which pervaded every department of the government. He, however, while professing the most disinterested motives, pursued a course of conquest, on the principle, which he made known in his public dispatches, that the princes of Hindostan were now so well convinced of our boundless views of ambition, there was no safety but in taking what, if not taken, would be turned to our own destruction. "The very nabobs," said he, "whom we might support, would be watching to destroy us; we must indeed become nabobs ourselves, in fact, if not in name. In short, if riches and security are the objects of the Company, this is the only method for securing them."

Accordingly about 600,000*l.* were extorted from Sujah-ul-Dowla, as the price of his safety; and the emperor made over for ever to the Company, the collection of the revenue of the provinces of Bengal, Bahar, and Orissa, with all legal formality, which cessions, after the payment of all expenses, yielded a clear revenue of 1,650,000*l.* Upon this the governor and council styled themselves "The magnificent merchants of the East India Company, the dewans of the magnificent provinces of Bengal, Bahar, and Orissa, servants of the magnanimous emperor Shah Allum." It is excusable to indulge a smile at this title. The ridicule it excites becomes painful, when we reflect how soon talent and genius are absorbed in the vices of ambition; and how quickly prosperity leads a conqueror to trample on the rights of mankind. Lord Clive, while he was thus consistent in enriching himself and the Company with the spoils of others, could make the nicest distinctions on points of morality, and talk like an angel about the self-destroying effects of luxury, corruption, avarice, and rapacity.

Upon this great accession of territories and riches, the proprietors of East India stock began to be clamorous for a higher dividend than six per cent, which had been the average for some time. At a numerous meeting it was fixed at twelve and a half; but parliament, remembering the South Sea bubble, rescinded their resolution, and established ten per cent as the maximum, obliging the Company, moreover, to pay 400,000*l.* annually to the British government, in lieu of the territories conquered in India, the possession of which, it was asserted, belonged of right to the crown. Soon after, however, when the charter was renewed, the dividends were increased to twelve and a half per cent, and an agreement made, that should they decrease, the stipulated sum of 400,000*l.* a year should be proportionally diminished, and cease altogether, if ever the profits should be so low as six per cent. It appears, indeed, that both at home and abroad, a universal thirst was felt to share in the vast wealth of the Company, which was soon found to be more imaginary than real. The Company's servants formed a project of enriching themselves by a monopoly of the inland trade, in salt, betel nut, and tobacco, and immense fortunes were made by individuals, at the expence of justice and British character. These articles are necessaries of life in India; it may be easily conceived what hatred, disgust, and oppression were occasioned when the prices rose enormously, and when no native was permitted to participate in the profits. In short, it appeared, that Lord Clive, instead of having returned to Hindostan for the purpose of reforming abuses, came out armed with superior power, only to inflict greater evil. Perhaps, from a concurrence of circumstances, no country ever endured more complicated misery than some parts of India in the latter part of his administration. The great landholders, finding that their tenures were declared void, left the lands untilled. A most cruel famine ensued, the frightful effects of which were increased by the horrors of a bloody war with Hyder Alli and the Nizam of the Deccan, which nearly ruined the credit of the East India Company.

Meanwhile, about the year 1767, Lord Clive returned home. The affairs of India were managed by Mr. Verelst and Mr. Cartier, till 1772, when Mr. Hastings commenced his long career. It may be easily conceived with what painful feelings Lord Clive viewed the proceedings in parliament, after his return. To find that after the most brilliant successes and accessions of territory, which had been pronounced most valuable acquisitions, the Company he had served were involved in distress, and forced to call upon a jealous people, for a loan of 1,500,000*l.*, to pay off their current debts, must have filled a mind like his, with chagrin and grief. It was proved at the bar of the House of Commons, that if the Company had not increased their territories between the years 1765 and 1768, that their dividends would have been twelve and a half per cent by trade alone, whereas the expences of their civil and military establishments had risen so much above the revenue, that they only shared six per cent, and consequently lost instead of gaining by their conquests. The loan was granted by parliament on very severe conditions. Such was the indignation excited by the oppressions which had taken place in the East, that a bill was passed for the better regulation of the affairs of the East India Company, as well in India as in Europe, by which a supreme court was established in Calcutta, and a considerable share in the government of Hindostan vested in the crown. But this was not all, for heavy charges were preferred against Lord Clive, of corruption, avarice, and oppression. He defended himself, however, with great ability; and although it was not denied, that about the time of the deposition of Surajah-Dowla, he received 234,000*l.*, under the name of private donation, an amendment was moved upon the censure, "that Lord Clive did at the same time render great and meritorious services to this country."

The remaining part of this great man's life was spent in retirement and solitude. Though he was acquitted by a public tribunal, the memory of the past tortured him, till existence became insupportable. He languished in all the horrors of melancholy and despair, amidst inexhaustible wealth, which he was unable to enjoy, and at length put a voluntary period to his life, proclaiming to the world, what has been so often proclaimed in vain, that the highest gratification of human wishes are insufficient to secure earthly happiness, if at variance with virtue and religion.

It was fully expected, that on the arrival of Mr. Hastings in India, the British character would be redeemed from the detestation in which it was held by the natives. His virtue and wisdom were in high estimation, both at home and abroad. He had passed through the ordeal of a public life with unsullied reputation. But the difficulties of his situation forced him to pursue that crooked policy which Machiavelian cunning has denominated wisdom. The qualities of his excellent heart were sometimes sacrificed at the shrine of ambition. His imagination persuaded his understanding into a conscientious belief, that he was acting in obedience to his pulse, whilst he was in some instances only consulting the cold maxims of his brain.

The first act of his government was an endeavour to improve the revenue, which he found in a most declining state, by appointing a Committee of Circuit, empowered to sell all the lands in the newly acquired provinces, by auction, to the highest bidder. Mr. Hastings' intentions in this delegation of power were fair and well intended. It is unjust to attribute to him the corruptions of agents, or the consequences of failures. In five years an alarming deficiency in the public receipts was discovered, instead of that improvement which had been fondly contemplated. One violent act often generates another. To make up the exhausted treasury with the spoils of war was next attempted. The vizier Sujah-ul-Dowla, nabob of Oude, was assisted with troops in a destructive campaign against the Rohillas, for which he paid vast sums to the British government. Fresh encroachments were found necessary to be made on the emperor of Hindostan, who had thrown himself into the arms of the Mahrattas. In a short time the flames of war were kindled up in all parts of India. But it is quite unfair to accuse Mr. Hastings of producing a general war. The ambitious views of the Mahrattas were the real causes. It was well known to them that Mr. Hastings was struggling with great difficulties, and they aimed at driving the English from the shores of India. The utmost dissension prevailed in the councils of Calcutta. General Clavering, Colonel Monson, and Mr. Francis, being in nearly all cases adverse to the projects of the governor-general. They made public representations to the court of directors against his proceedings, and hearkened to several calumnious charges from rajah Nund Comar, and other natives. A noble minded man scorns to be reduced to take refuge in defence. Conscious of his own worth, he thinks the world should give him the credit he deserves. It is probable, I humbly think, that Mr. Hastings acted on this principle. Instead of permitting his conduct to be investigated, he had the rajah arraigned before Sir Elijah Impey, chief judge of the supreme court, for forgery. He was condemned and executed, by the sentence of English law, for a crime which, according to his own code, is only a misdemeanor. This Hindoo was of the Brahman caste, held so sacred, that life is not forfeited by the commission of any crime; therefore his fate produced a sensation of the most general indignation in India, and nothing but inability prevented the native population from instantaneous revenge. It is true, his conviction was legal. True, he was subject to the jurisdiction of the supreme court. But strict law is sometimes great injustice. It is deeply to be regretted, that this native was executed.

Mr. Hastings was not long troubled with opposition from General Clavering and Colonel Monson, who both fell victims to the climate. Mr. Francis, seeing the hopelessness of opposition, returned to England, to make fruitless representations to the court of directors and His Majesty's ministers, who were equally dazzled with the gigantic plans of Mr. Hastings, for the extension of empire in the East.

The Mahratta war, therefore, which had been going on, for some time, in the west of India, was now pursued with increased spirit. The Bombay government had attempted to march a military force to Poonah, the capital of the Peishwa, who was considered the head of the Mahratta confederacy. Their general was beaten by Nana Furnese, and forced to sign a disgraceful capitulation. But when this occurred, a division of the Bengal army had penetrated through the whole extent of Hindostan, and was in full co-operation with Bombay. The government of that presidency refused, therefore, to ratify the treaty agreed to by their general. Our affairs, at this period, were in a most critical and alarming state. No man then in India, but Mr. Hastings, could have commanded fortune. The Mahrattas had formed a most formidable confederacy among themselves, and combined with the French, who were then endeavouring to regain political influence at Pondicherry. This powerful attack on us, with the avowed intention of driving us into the sea, had been joined by the Nizam of the Deccan, and also by Hyder Alli, the powerful and warlike usurper of Mysore; so that Mr. Hastings saw all the most dangerous governments of India, Hindoo, Mohammedan, and European, in arms against him, flushed with the confident hope that an end would speedily be put to British domination. Undismayed by this state of things, clearly perceiving that the native powers were only to be attached to the Company's interest by fear; consequently that it would be expedient to deprive them as far as possible of the means of destruction, he suddenly seized upon the resources of Oude and Benares, and replenished his empty treasury from their abundant wealth.

By this time, 1780, Hyder Alli had invaded the Carnatic, and in September his son Tippo, assisted by a French detachment, surrounded Colonel Baillie, and completely destroyed the division of the Madras army under his command. But upon the arrival of the gallant veteran Sir Eyre Coote, to command on the Coromandel coast, the dreadful ravages of the crafty Hyder were arrested, and he was beaten in every direction. General Goddard had attacked the Mahrattas in Guzerat. The different divisions of the Bombay army were so successful that the Mahrattas and the Nizam were soon glad to negotiate a separate peace for themselves, and to enter into an offensive and defensive alliance with the English. It is impossible not to admire the consummate ability displayed by Mr. Hastings, in thus turning the very arms that were opposed to him, against the power of Hyder, with whom they were so lately in league. Hyder Alli continued to fight with various success. Though unable to stand before the science and enterprize of Sir Eyre Coote, he was formidable in other places. His son Tippo had not only destroyed Colonel Baillie, but totally routed a strong detachment of the Company's troops under Colonel Braithwaite, on the banks of the Coleroon. It was found expedient to send General Mathews, with the disposable troops of Bombay, to invade the Mysore dominions from Malabar.

Meanwhile Hyder paid the debt of nature. Tippo, leaving the army of his father, under the command of his lieutenants, in the Carnatic, marched with a light force rapidly through Mysore, and got possession of the ghauts behind General Mathews, whom he attacked, and forced to surrender with the whole division under his command; when, contrary to the terms of capitulation, he and his officers were thrown into the dungeons of Seringapatam, loaded with chains, and tortured to death. Animated by this success, and cheered by the death of Sir Eyre Coote, whose military talents had frustrated many a deep-laid plan of his father and their French allies, Tippo was pursuing his good fortune, with the exultation of hope, when peace between France and England deprived him of French co-operation. Finding that he was threatened by the Mahrattas, he readily listened to reason, and concluded a treaty with the Company's government on advantageous terms.

Mr. Hastings resigned the government of India in 1785, at which time, although the Company had acquired considerable accessions of territories in Bengal, in the Carnatic, in Malabar, and Guzerat, yet the prospect was clouded in a most threatening manner. The Mahrattas had encroached upon the dominions of the court of Delhi, stripped the Mogul of power, and seemed by their ambitious projects to aim at universal empire in the East; while Tippo, the warlike sultan of Mysore, was known to be the inveterate foe of Britain *, whose rancour was stimulated by the French. The character of Mr. Hastings has been long the subject of panegyric and censure. By one set of men he has been raised to the most magnanimous standard; by another his virtues have been forgotten, and his vices have sunk him below the rank of humanity. Truth must admit that he possessed splendid talents. He aimed at glorious things, but in accomplishing his views he resorted, in a few instances, to expedients which every candid heart must condemn. Whilst he conscientiously believed that he was pursuing plans which had the happiness of those he governed in view, he was precipitated into measures that produced misery to many. It was the proud recollection of good motives that supported him under the laborious investigation which his conduct underwent after his return, and enabled him to look down with superiority upon those who arraigned the purity of his intentions. No man can attentively consider the public acts of his brilliant administration, without sighing over the disregard to human rights, in a few cases, which characterise them. If he attacked the

* Vide Addenda, XXXIV.

princes of India, were they not all ready to attack him? He merely anticipated them. Experience led him to know, that those who are bound only by the bond of fear, cannot love; and he conceived that in depriving the Mohammedan princes of usurped power over the Hindoos, he was so far from injuring them, that he was conferring on them and their posterity a blessing.

Meanwhile the affairs of India had occupied the serious attention of parliament. It was evident that the extension of empire in Asia was considered by the nation at large, as a sort of recompence for the loss of America. Mr. Hastings was properly styled the saviour of India; and the glory of our arms in the East shed a sort of redemption over defeat in the West. It was, however, considered hazardous to leave entirely to the East India Company the government of such an empire as chance had placed in their hands. Mr. Fox accordingly introduced a bill into the house of commons, which aimed at depriving them of even the management of their commercial concerns, but as this was thought little short of downright robbery, it was rejected in the house of lords, and soon after Mr. Pitt framed his famous India bill, which was carried into law on the 9th of August, 1784.

By the provisions of this bill, the management of their commercial affairs was left to the Company, but they were deprived of political and civil power, which was placed in the hands of a board of control, composed of privy counsellors, who were to be appointed by the king, and removable at his pleasure. The civil and military government of the country, and the revenue of the Company, were to be checked and superintended by this body. All dispatches from the court of directors were subjected to their inspection and authenticated by their signature. His Majesty's decision in council on any disputed point was to be considered final. The appointment to the office of governor-general, president, or counsellor, in the different presidencies, was made subject to the approbation and recall of the king. An enquiry was directed to take place respecting the hereditary landholders of India, who had been dispossessed of their property; and a court was established for the trial of Indian delinquents, with power to award fine and imprisonment, and to dismiss, without appeal, from the Company's service. This high tribunal consists of a judge from each of three of the courts of law, four members of the house of lords, and six of the house of commons. This memorable and important bill was further confirmed in 1787, by a declaratory act of parliament, which had become necessary by the frequent misunderstanding that occurred between the board of control and the court of directors. At this time the Company, so far from having benefited by their conquests, were embarrassed, and obliged to borrow 1,200,000*l.*, although their sales of tea in Europe had risen from six to 14,000,000*l.* annually.

Under this new arrangement, the greatest attention was paid to Indian affairs, and the prosperity which followed proved the complete success of the plan. Lord Cornwallis, to whom was intrusted the arduous task of restoring the British character in India to an honourable place in the native mind, reached his destination in 1787, and in two years raised the revenues, by wise and just measures, in Bengal, from 1,800,000*l*. to 2,150,000*l*. He leased out all the lands in perpetuity at an equitable valuation to the actual occupants, by which he gave security to property and possession, and incited labour and industry. A code of regulations were enacted in the revenue department, and for the guidance of all civil and military ranks. The army and magistracy were new modelled; and the system of corruption and injustice which in some departments prevailed, was assailed, if not rooted out.

But the moderation of his lordship and the equity of his conduct could not produce correspondent virtues in the ambitious Tippo Sultan. He had, shortly after the peace of 1784, sent an embassy to France, and panted for an opportunity to renew the war. The opening of the French revolution soon gave him hopes of support, and he found no difficulty in picking a quarrel. Our ally, the rajah of Travancore, had purchased two forts called Cranganore and Acottah from the Dutch East India Company. But in 1789, Tippo set up a claim to them, and marched towards Travancore with a considerable army. The English, being bound by treaty, interposed, and as the claim of Tippo was evidently unjust, after a long negotiation, war commenced in 1790, the Nizam and the Mahrattas being still our allies.

His lordship finding it necessary to humble the enemy in the heart of his own country, General Meadows marched with the Madras army towards Mysore, from the Carnatic, whilst General Abercrombie with the Bombay army invaded it from Malabar. General Meadows experienced a very warm reception. After a considerable advance into the enemy's country, he found it necessary to retire on his supplies; for the monsoon was approaching. Lord Cornwallis having arrived at Madras in December 1790, and assumed the command, the armies again advanced into the dominions of Mysore. In March 1791, Bangalore was taken by storm, and on the 13th of May following, his lordship encamped in sight of Seringapatam, near which, on the following day, a battle was fought that obliged Tippo to cross the Cavery. The monsoon now commenced with great fury, and the army being much in want of provisions, his lordship also found it necessary to retreat on his commissariat to Bangalore.

In February 1792, the Madras and Bombay armies formed a junction under the walls of Tippo's capital. By a night attack soon after they forced the Sultan from his camp on the island, and closely invested Seringapatam. Being at last reduced to a hopeless condition, Tippo was obliged to sue for peace, by which he was deprived of one half of his territories, and upwards of four millions sterling.

Soon after, the war of the French revolution commenced, and all the settlements belonging to that nation on the continent of India were captured by the English. In 1794, such was the flourishing state of the Company's affairs, that their charter was renewed, by a bill introduced by Mr. Dundas, and speedily passed through both houses of parliament, for twenty years, with all those exclusive privileges which the Company had heretofore enjoyed.

At this period India was blessed with profound repose. The British character had not only been redeemed by the virtues of Lord Cornwallis, but elevated in the eyes of eastern philosophy by the celebrated Sir William Jones* one of the judges of the supreme court in Bengal, from 1783 till his lamented death in April 1794. Lord Cornwallis had now returned home to reap the fruit of a wise administration, in the thanks of his king and country. He was succeeded by Sir John Shore, now Lord Teignmouth, who continued to pursue the same equitable and conciliating steps as his predecessor, in the government of the extensive

* Vide Addenda, XXXV.

possessions which Great Britain, through the instrumentality of a company of her merchants, had acquired in the finest provinces of Asia.

During this long period, from 1788 till 1795, the memorable trial of Warren Hastings was going on, under a prosecution of the house of commons, before the house of lords. Twenty-nine of the peers, however, only thought themselves competent to vote on the question before the court; for they were distracted by the length of time the trial had been pending, and the declamation of Mr. Burke, whose flowery language was more calculated to bewilder the understanding, than to promote the interests of simple truth. Eight of these peers gave a verdict of guilty; but he was acquitted by a majority of twenty-one, and left to enjoy the remainder of his life, which he did for many years, in elegant ease and social retirement, cheered to the last by a conscientious persuasion that all his actions proceeded from laudable motives.

Meanwhile, nearly all the possessions of the Dutch, and other European powers, in India, had fallen into the hands of the English. But in the interior of Hindostan, a most formidable conspiracy was going on, and threatened the most serious consequences in the beginning of 1798, when the Marquis Wellesley, then Earl of Mornington, reached Calcutta to arrest its progress, and display a combination of talent which has seldom been surpassed. The French, deprived of their settlements in India, had never ceased to regret their loss, and to hope that favourable circumstances would enable them to establish an empire in Asia, of which our arms alone had deprived them. By the possession of the Isles of France and Bourbon, they were enabled, at all times, to correspond with Tippo. Great numbers of their scientific officers were now in his service, also with different chiefs of the Mahrattas, and at the court of the Nizam, organising the native armies on European principles, ready to co-operate with Bonaparte, whom they expected every moment to approach from Egypt. This deep and daring scheme had been long in embryo. It was now upon the point of dangerous maturity.

By the intrigues of the French and the negotiations of Tippo Sultan, nearly the whole of the independent princes, both Hindoo and Mohammedan, were in combination against us; Persia and Turkey had been invited to join the confederacy. It was believed that Shah Allum had ceded Agra and Delhi to the French. Monsieur Perron's brigade under Scindea amounted to 40,000 men with 400 pieces of artillery. The Mahrattas, with a population of 40,000,000 of souls, a revenue of 17,000,000 sterling, and a territory of 1000 square miles, were ready to attack us; the five chiefs who composed that empire were directed by French councils, and animated by republican hopes. One of them, the warlike Holkar, had a formidable body of infantry disciplined and appointed like our sepoys, with an immense park of artillery. When all this is naturally considered, the mighty services rendered to the East India Company in particular, and to Great Britain in general, by the Marquis Wellesley during his administration, will appear.

The transactions of this period, in an historical point of view, are extremely interesting. Tippo's grand object was to destroy the English by means of the French. In an embassy which he sent to General Malartic, governor of the Mauritius, he speaks thus: "What do you wait for? I am ready to afford you succours. Show yourselves in India. The unbounded violence and oppression of the English have rendered all the princes of India their enemies: they are enfeebled on every side; and from the great extent of territory which they have acquired by artifice, they are dispersed in all quarters. Look upon the present time as a most fortunate opportunity. Send a large army, and an extensive train of artillery, to my assistance, and effectually chastising our mutual enemies, drive them out of India." But in soliciting the aid of his majesty the king of Cabul, he uses other language: "A hundred thousand of the followers of the faith," says he, "assemble every Friday in the mosques of the capital, and, after the prescribed forms of prayers, supplicate the Bestower of all things according to the words of Scripture,

—'Grant thy aid, O God, to those who aid the religion of Mohammed, and let us be of that number at the last day. Destroy those, O God, who destroy the religion of Mohammed, and let us not be of that number at the last day.' Your majesty must, doubtless, have been informed that my exalted ambition has for its object a holy war."

It was clearly the secret intention of Tippo Sultan, first to make the French instrumental in destroying the English; secondly, to raise up a native power sufficiently strong to overcome the conquering Europeans; and thirdly, to preserve such an ascendancy over all, that he might, in the end, secure universal empire in India to himself. The object of the French was, to come in upon the downfall of the English; and the aim of the Mahrattas was, to let the Mohammedans and Europeans expire in the struggle, while they secured the spoil by caution and management.

Amidst such conflicting interests, the prompt and decided character of Lord Mornington carried away the standard of victory. The cunning of Tippo was unable to meet the wisdom of his lordship. Though the sultan attempted to cajole our governor-general with the deepest hypocrisy, professing the most ardent friendship, whilst he meditated the foulest treachery, yet his schemes were all seen through, and a declaration of war was made against him by the Company's government, at a time when he thought he lay entrenched behind the deepest dissimulation. It was followed up with such effect, that Seringapatam was invested by General Harris on the 5th of April 1799, and taken by storm on the following 4th of May; in which operation Tippo met death with heroic fortitude, fighting till the last for glory and independence, such as they were pictured in his vain mind. Sir David Baird led the troops to the storm of that fortress, in which he had been long confined.* The conquest of Mysore placed the affairs of India in such a state as enabled the governor-general to send a considerable division of the forces up the Red Sea under Sir David Baird, to assist in driving the French out of Egypt. By successful negotiations with the court of Persia, the king of Cabul was confined to his own dominions. The Mahrattas had become our allies by successful negotiation, and seemed to view the destruction of the Mohammedan power in Mysore with apathy, though they were not very active in contributing to it.

The family and relatives of Tippo Sultan were removed from Mysore to the fortress of Vellore in the Carnatic; and the ancient Hindoo line of princes, whose power Hyder Alli had usurped, was restored to comfortable dependence on British generosity, with nearly all the extent of territory which the Mysore rajah originally possessed. The

* Vide Appendix, note 11.

remainder of Tippo's dominions was divided amongst the conquerors and the Mahrattas.

Until the reign of Aurengzebe, the history of the Mahrattas is involved in great obscurity. Sevajee, a military adventurer, who served with credit under the powerful king of Bejapoor, was the first who combined their discordant chiefs. He was born in 1626, and died in 1680. During his life the foundation was laid for a powerful empire, and a strong hill-fort, called Sattara, gave him title and security. It continued to rise, on the fall of the Moguls, till 1761, when its progress received a decisive check from Ahmed Shah Abdalli, king of Cabul, who, on the 7th of January, gained the memorable battle of Paniput, in which Ballajee-row, the head of the Mahratta states, was entirely defeated. He was the son of Bajee-row, prime minister, or peishwa, to the Sattara rajah, the legitimate successor of Sevajee, and had, in conjunction with Ragajee, the paymaster-general, or buckshee, usurped the authority of that prince, whose person he confined in the fort of Sattara, while he removed the seat of government to Poonah, and permitted Ragajee to establish himself at Nagpoor.

This usurpation laid the foundation for others; and the Mahratta state became at length divided among five chiefs, the Peishwa, Scindea, the rajah of Nagpoor, Holkar, and the Guickwar. United by no powerful head, these sovereigns often made war upon each other. When at peace, they directed their watchful attention to the state of our government at Bombay. They had officered a considerable part of their army with French and English adventurers, and disciplined native regiments in the same way as our sepoys. The distrust which they had entertained of the ambitious views of Tippo Sultan, prevented them from rendering active assistance to that prince. But as they had placed themselves in a very formidable attitude, and were now in possession of all the power belonging to the court of Delhi, whose emperor Scindea had as a sort of state prisoner, it became necessary to arrest the progress of their dangerous machinations.

Dowlut Row Scindea had gained such an ascendancy in 1795, that, upon the death of Madhurow, the young peishwa, he usurped the principal share of power; but, in October 1802, his army was defeated, near Poonah, by Jeswunt Row Holkar, and Badjeerow, the peishwa, was forced to fly to Bassein, where he concluded a treaty of perpetual friendship with the British government, and agreed to receive a subsidiary force into his dominions. He was, therefore, in 1803, replaced in authority by a British army, under the present Duke of Wellington, then General Sir Arthur Wellesley, to whom the subsequent operations afforded an opportunity of displaying those military talents which have since baffled the efforts of the greatest captains of France.

To detail the glorious particulars of this war would be a pleasing task, but we must restrict ourselves to a very brief notice. Lord Lake defeated the army of Dowlut Row Scindea, near the city of Delhi, in September 1803, while, a few days after, the battle of Assay, gained by Sir Arthur Wellesley, raised his own glory, and that of the British name, to the highest elevation. This was followed by the victory of Argaum, in the month of November following, which, for that time, destroyed the power of the rajah of Berar, and forced him to accept of such terms as Sir Arthur was instructed to offer. The warlike Holkar, after fighting with great obstinacy, was completely defeated by Lord Lake at Deeg, and obliged to throw himself, with the shattered remains of his army, into the strong fortress of Bhurtpore, from which he was subsequently driven, after the British army had sustained, in various unsuccessful assaults on that place, a greater loss than ever was experienced in killed and wounded in any three great pitched battles fought in India. In the beginning of 1805, the crafty Holkar was glad to sue for peace on any terms. On the 20th of August in that year, the Marquis Wellesley embarked at Madras for England, leaving the British empire established in India on the most firm basis, the French factions every where destroyed, and the authority of the Company acknowledged over an extent of territory as great as all Europe, with a revenue of about 17,000,000*l.* sterling.

We shall, therefore, conclude this chapter with the following state of India at this period, most accurately given by Sir John Malcolm.

The emperor of Delhi was under the British protection. Secunder Jay, the subahdar of the Deccan, was completely confirmed in our alliance, and maintained a British subsidiary force. The Mahrattas were entirely conquered, the government of Tippo annihilated, and that of the Mysore family established. All the Carnatic belonged to the Company. The conquest of Cuttack had connected the territories of Madras and Bengal, and the cessions of Guzerat and Malabar combined almost the whole coast from the Ganges to the Indus. All the Douab was in our possession, and the right banks of the Jumna, with a line of petty states, from the mountains of Kemaoon to Bundlecund.

CHAPTER V.

FROM THE ADMINISTRATION OF MARQUIS WELLESLEY IN INDIA, UNTIL THE RETURN OF THE MARQUIS OF HASTINGS IN 1823.

NOTWITHSTANDING the brilliant administration of Lord Wellesley, the mighty wars in which he had been engaged ever since his arrival in India had increased the Company's debts so prodigiously, that the directors at home became greatly alarmed; and the Marquis Cornwallis was despatched with the olive branch in 1805, and reached Calcutta in July of that year. The second administration of this nobleman was not destined to be of long duration. He died at Ghazipoor, near Benares, in the month of October following. Sir George H. Barlow remained at the head of the supreme government until the arival of Lord Minto, in July 1807.

During this period the whole of India enjoyed profound repose; but in such an extensive country, where there are so many petty chiefs, all aspiring at independence, frequent wars must occur.

The rajah of Travancore, whose territories lie in the southern part of Malabar, had been forced, by treaty, to receive a subsidiary force, and deprived of all political power by the government of Madras. Soon after the arrival of Lord Minto, a disposition was manifested by the authorities there to shake off all dependence on the Company; and it being found impossible to arrange existing differences by negotiation, a part of the Madras army entered Travancore in the early part of 1809, stormed the fortified lines of the rajah, and forced him, or rather his prime minister, who had usurped the power of his master, to make peace on any terms.

This service was scarcely performed when a very alarming rebellion, which had been for some time in embryo, broke out in the native part of the Madras army, occasioned by the discontents of the European officers, at retrenchments which were carried into effect by the governor Sir George H. Barlow, certainly in a most irritating and ungracious manner. It would answer no good end to enter into such unpleasant particulars; it may be sufficient to observe, that a judicious display of sound wisdom on the part of the government of Madras, and the commander in chief, would have entirely prevented an occurrence which must ever be deeply regretted. To such a dangerous extent was this rebellion carried, that the King's troops had to be drawn out against the Company's, and some blood was shed before its progress was arrested.

During the short peace of 1802, the French had received back their settlements of Pondicherry and Chandernagor, which upon the recommencement of hostilities were retaken by the British government in India without opposition, the very considerable military force which Bonaparte had sent out, escaping in their ships of war to the Mauritius. The possession of these islands enabled the French government to infest the Indian seas with privateers, whose daring operations were most destructive to the private trade carried on in the East. It had long been an important object, to deprive them of their nests, both there and at Batavia, on the island of Java, which they now garrisoned for Holland. Accordingly, expeditions were projected from Calcutta, Madras, and Bombay, and the Isles of France and Bourbon were captured in 1811, by General Abercromby and Colonel Keating, whilst in the same year Sir Samuel Achmuty established the British power in the island of Java.

These were the principal transactions of Lord Minto's administration, which was otherwise of a most pacific character. His policy was to temporise with the native powers. During the period of his government, the Nepaulese and Mahrattas began to display a spirit of encroachment, which ought to have been punished by the sword, instead of being compromised by unavailing negotiations.

The Marquis of Hastings assumed the government of India on the 14th October, 1813. He was received at Calcutta with the most lively demonstrations of joy, and immediately directed all his attention to the political state of the country.

In the eastern parts of the British empire, his lordship found, that the Nepaulese had actually possessed themselves of a considerable portion of the Company's frontiers, whilst in the west, prodigious numbers of Mahratta plunderers, under the name of Pindarries, carried desolation into all parts of the Deccan. The province of Guzerat was also infested by the ferocious Wagurs of Cutch, a race of plunderers, daring in their excursions, and merciless in their exactions. His lordship, therefore, finding no security in negotiation, had immediate recourse to arms, and the principal operations of his brilliant administration are detailed under the following heads.

NEPAUL WAR.

The interesting campaigns connected with the Nepaul war, commenced soon after the arrival of Marquis Hastings in India, but his lordship's declaration was not made till the 6th January, 1815.

This document, which comprises the origin of the war, sets out with stating that the Nepaulese conquests had approximated their frontier to that of the British, their ally the Newaub Vizier, and the protected Seik chiefs, from the borders of Morung to the banks of the Sutleje. In all this extent, it appears these encroaching and rapacious warriors had appropriated to themselves our possessions, and that their government had lent a deaf ear to repeated remonstrances. There is proof that the Goorcas proceeded in a premeditated system of conquest; and not only seized the parts of Mocwanpore that had been reduced by Major Kinlock, but also several other districts, containing twenty-two villages. To these provinces, below the range of hills that separate Bengal from Nepaul, the government of Catmandoo set up a claim that they had once formed the Terrai, or lowlands of the mountainous parts. But these territories had belonged to the dominions of Oude, long before the Goorcas had conquered Nepaul, and, therefore, there was not the shadow of justice in such a demand. To settle the disputes, Major Bradshaw had been sent on the part of the Company; and the negotiations were continued with commissioners from Catmandoo, till at length it was necessary to appeal to arms, for the purpose of dispossessing them of the strong-holds which they had now established within our frontier; for such was their insolence, that at length Major Bradshaw was ordered to quit the place within our own provinces, at which the conferences were carried on. The commencement of the rainy season had forced our troops to retire into cantonments, soon after the expulsion of the Goorcas from the disputed lands; upon which they returned, massacred the police left to collect the revenues, and re-occupied the districts. Requisite atonement for this new outrage having been withheld, the British government had no choice left, and therefore now resorted to arms in defence of their just rights. The proclamation stated that these arms should never be laid down, until the enemy shall be forced to make ample submission and atonement for his outrageous conduct, to indemnify the British government of India for the expence of the war, and to afford full security for the future maintenance of those relations which he has so shamefully violated.

Of such importance was this war considered, that the Marquis of Hastings left the presidency of Fort William under a vice government, and repaired to the upper provinces, for the purpose of being in the immediate neighbourhood of the scene of action. On the breaking up of the monsoon in 1814, divisions of the British army and their auxiliaries poured towards the passes into Nepaul, dispossessed the Goorcas of all the territories which had been seized by them below the hills, and took some of their strong forts. In one of these assaults, made by the division under Major General Sir Robert Rollo Gillespie, K. B., our troops were driven back by repeated charges of the enemy, who poured down from the heights in superior numbers, and with most overwhelming courage, upon which the gallant general led on the advance in person, and fell in his noble professional efforts. His death cast a gloom over the whole army in India, for among the brave British officers in the

East, not one was more highly esteemed for every virtue that constitutes the character of a gentleman, a soldier, and a scientific commander. His great merit was fully appreciated by the Marquis of Hastings, who had bestowed upon him his entire confidence.

Major General Sir Robert Rollo Gillespie was an Irishman descended from an ancient Scotch family, who settled in County Down, in the reign of James the Second. He was born at Innishargie in 1769, so that his valuable life was lost in the forty-sixth year of his age. But, "blood of the brave, thou art not shed in vain," his memory will live inscribed on the roll of fame. In person he was elegantly formed, so that a poetical imagination would compare him to the ancient heroes, who in youth were so lovely as to resemble the fair sex. But his composition was all fibre and elasticity. Every movement indicated the activity of his soul and body. His manly chest and square shoulders at once proclaimed his capability of enduring the warrior's toil. His countenance was fine and open, its lines marked with the finger of thought, and its eye beaming with the lustre of a highly polished mind. Like lightning it excited admiration and terror in his enemies; but there was a mildness in its rays that produced only the former sensation, mixed with love, in the bosoms of his friends, companions, and fellow soldiers. He had been educated for the bar, and entered at Emanuel college, Cambridge, but disliking the wig and gown, his predilection for the army appeared at an early age. He became a cornet in the 3d dragoons, from which he was promoted to a troop in the 20th dragoons, and served a considerable time with that fine corps in the West Indies, where his ability procured for him a vote of thanks from the house of assembly at Jamaica, and a superb sword as a mark of esteem. In 1802, he was promoted to the rank of Lieutenant Colonel, and returned to England. In 1805, he travelled over land to India, spending some time with the Russian and Austrian armies, and passing through Constantinople and Bagdad to Bombay. At the time of the dreadful massacre at Vellore, he commanded at Arcot, and on the day preceding it, he was to have dined with the commandant of Vellore, but fortunately he was prevented, and the next morning he received the dreadful intelligence, that the officers and European soldiers were butchered. He immediately proceeded thither, and retook the place. He afterwards served against the Seiks in the Punjab. When the expedition against Java was arranged, he was selected for one of the distinguished commands under Sir Samuel Achmuty, whose entire confidence and friendship he enjoyed. On the 26th August 1811, he stormed the lines of Cornelis, and terminated the subjection of the whole island, having distinguished himself so preeminently, that he was left in command upon the departure of Sir

Samuel, when another opportunity occurred, by which he added fresh laurels to the wreath that already surrounded his brow. The sultan of Palambang, in a fit of most wanton cruelty, had massacred the Dutch residents in his territories, and retired to a strong-hold with his treasures, leaving orders with his troops to put every foreigner to death. Colonel Gillespie reached Palambang at night during a frightful storm, and anxious to prevent the effusion of blood, pushed on with a small force, through an immense body of the ferocious Malays to the palace, which was yet streaming with gore, where he narrowly escaped the blow of a creese aimed at his heart, for a flash of lightning fell upon the weapon just in time to enable him to avoid it. Here, with a handful of troops, he kept the population in awe, till a sufficient force arrived, and saved the lives and properties of thousands of his fellow creatures. Shortly after he was equally successful in preventing the projected massacre of all Europeans at Djocjocarta. The sultan of Mataran had fortified his palace with 92 pieces of cannon, and drawn together 100,000 partizans. Colonel Gillespie boldly and unexpectedly arriving, stormed the place, and took the sultan prisoner. For these eminent services he received the highest thanks of the constituted authorities, and the honour of knighthood with superior rank in the army. Upon his return to India from Java, he joined the army, when organising for the Nepaul war, and found a glorious grave where his friends hoped he would reap further honour and distinction.

Our army consisted of about 20,000 men, auxiliaries included, formed under Sir David Ochterlony into divisions, commanded separately by Major Generals Wood, Marley, and Martindell. The campaign was opened under very unfavourable auspices, for the losses sustained both in officers and men were alarmingly great. The valley of the Dhoon was at last taken possession of, but not without a brave defence; fourteen European and seven native officers, with 488 men, having been killed and wounded in the operations from the 25th November to the 2d December 1814. After this the divisions continued to advance, and experienced the most formidable obstacles, not only from the nature of the country being one of the strongest in the world, but from the daring bravery of the Goorcas, who rushed upon our bayonets sword in hand.

Major Ludlow, after considerable success in attacking stoccades, was repulsed with great loss. Major General Wood's division suffered very severely in an attack on the fortified post of Intgurh. It appears that this officer was led under the guns of this place by one Konckanaddee Sewaree, a native of Nepaul, on whose report and fidelity he had reason to depend, before he had time to reconnoitre. The villain escaped in the confusion which followed, a heavy fire being opened upon the head of the column, many lives were lost in a few moments. His Majesty's 17th foot, led on by their brave commander, Colonel Hardyman, and supported by two native regiments, advanced upon the works, while a detachment was sent up the hill under Captain Croker, who, after driving the enemy before him with spirit and perseverance, discovered that the heights behind the post were filled with troops. Upon this a retreat was sounded, and it is probable that if the enemy had poured down at this critical moment, the loss in the division would have been enormous; it was very considerable notwithstanding, and the enemy suffered also severely. Captain Blackney commanding the left wing of the 22d regiment, Bengal native infantry, was attacked at Summonpore by about 2000 Goorcas, who after repeated charges, all the officers except Lieutenant Strettell being killed or wounded, forced the Sepoys to fly, and captured a commissariat depôt, and the baggage of the detachment. A post at Persa Ghurrie under Captain Sibley on the same day was also attacked by an overwhelming force, and taken sword in hand, after that brave officer had lost his life. In these unfortunate affairs we had 386 officers and soldiers killed, wounded, and missing. The division under Major General Marley was also successfully resisted in its endeavours to advance, and suffered severely.

But these disasters were more than counterbalanced by the continued successes of Sir David Ochterlony and Colonel Nicolls, to whose judgment and skill the speedy termination of this bloody war is justly to be attributed. The general orders issued at Futtyghur on the 3d May 1815, in praise of these excellent officers, by the Marquis of Hastings, are very flattering to them; and apparently convey an oblique censure to others.

The success of Colonel Nicolls (and the observation will be supported by the brilliant consequences which have attended similar exertions on the part of Major General Ochterlony), under the complicated difficulties presented by the quality of the country, the fortifications by which its natural strength was assisted, and the obstinate resistance of a courageous enemy, should prove the superiority conferred by military service, and the certainty that a strenuous application of its principles must entail honourable distinction on a commander. Warfare in a mountainous region offers embarrassments which, when viewed at a distance, appear insurmountable, but which dwindle into comparative insignificance under the grasp of valour and genius. It is only in unusual situations, demanding readiness of resource and animated efforts, that the difference between officer and officer can be displayed; and it ought to be always present to the mind of every military man, that he who in circumstances of perplexity tries and fails, has to plead those chances from which no operation in war can be secured; his pretensions to the character of zeal and energy being in the mean time maintained: while he who contents himself with urging difficulties as an excuse for doing nothing, voluntarily registers his own insufficiency.

Sir David Ochterlony had continued to advance on the capital, and after various contests and difficulties in getting the battering train forward, his division was encamped before Nehn on the 27th December 1814, where the enemy's main army was so strongly stoccaded, that his operations had been directed chiefly against their supplies, which were received from Billaspore. With such skill did he seize, by night attacks, certain positions around them, that he at length completely succeeded in forcing them to an action, and driving them to another chain of hills called Mungoo-ka-Dhar, where they assembled in great force, their right being covered by strong stoccades, and their left resting on the fort of Tarraghur. In this achievement Lieutenant Colonel Thompson, who conducted the night attack on the 27th December, that forced the Goorcas to abandon their position, gained great and well earned praise, and his report of the affair is interesting.

Colonel Thompson had with him a force of about 2600 men, with four light guns of the mountain train, but 1200 of this force were irregulars, armed with matchlocks. He marched immediately after dusk in the evening, but such was the impracticability of the intervening space, which as to distance he could have marched over in three hours, that the guns were only got up to the point of attack at eight o'clock next morning. He then advanced up the Diboo-ka-Tebba, to gain a position near the stone stoccade, which he had first to storm. It was situated on the highest peak of four ridges of granite, and presented a formidable breastwork of loose rocks. The enemy came down to the lowest approach, to receive our force with a galling fire of matchlocks. But one ascent after another was scaled, till at length the guns opened upon the post, from the only spot where artillery could be placed effectually without artificial works. This, however, was at the distance of 500 yards, and it was found that a six pound shot was too light to make an impression. During the night, therefore, the pioneers were employed in making fascines and gabions, to push nearer on the ensuing morning, but a little before sun-rise, an immense body of the enemy came down from the Mungoo-ka-Dhar, another strongly fortified height, still more lofty, with the intention of surrounding and overwhelming him. The struggle was long and obstinate, the enemy lost such immense numbers, that they were at last forced to retire, but their attacks were so furious, and such persevering courage was evinced, that Colonel Thompson thought it advisable to throw up works around him during the night. He was, however, reinforced by Lieutenant Colonel Lyons, and next morning the enemy abandoned the position. When our picquets took possession, it was found to be very strong. The wall was ten feet high outside, and four feet thick, composed of loose stones, extremely well built. It was surrounded by a high bamboo fence, and within there was a sort of citadel of solid masonry. The enemy in his attack lost about 400 men in killed and wounded, and our casualties were also very considerable.

In this daring way did Sir David Ochterlony proceed, seizing one point after another, and continually driving the enemy's army back, till on the 14th and 15th April 1815, a general engagement was forced on Ummer Sing Thappa, the Goorca commander in chief, in whom now merged the civil and military authority of the government of Nepaul, which terminated in the establishment of our army on the heights of Malown, and in his total defeat on the day following. But these operations were conducted in such a manner, and the consequences were so glorious, that they deserve to be noticed at some length.

On the night of the 14th of April, 1815, a strong detachment marched from the village of Purijur, and occupied a post under the centre of the enemy's position. This post was made the head of a column of attack, that followed next morning, upon a preconcerted signal being given.

The different divisions diverging from this to the right and left, gained the several points laid down in the brigadiers' instructions, and Lieutenant Colonel Thompson and Major Lawrie, being well supported, advanced up the Malown in gallant style, under a heavy and well directed fire of cannon and musketry: but before these officers could establish themselves on the ridge, they were charged sword in hand by the Goorcas, and, after a severe struggle, forced down to the main body. To gain this practicable part of the hills, therefore, became the object on our side, and successfully to oppose us was the aim of the enemy. During the whole day, the contest continued with unabated ardour, the enemy receiving continual reinforcements, in proportion to the pressure experienced by them; and such was the resolution with which they defended the ridge, that it was with difficulty, Lieutenant Colonel Thompson maintained his position on the side of the hill during the night, with the assistance of temporary works thrown up by the pioneers. Next morning the attack was renewed at day-break. Indeed, it had not ceased during the whole night, and the continual blaze of war, the crash of rolling rocks hurled from the summits of the range of steep hills, the whiz of rockets forming curves in the air, and the roar of artillery re-echoed by the various repeats of the mountains, exceeded any thing that can be conceived. The first light of day on the 15th discovered Ummer Sing, on a projecting cliff, within musket shot, holding a standard in one hand, and in the other his hatchet sword, encouraging his men, and pointing to the weakest parts of our position. Immediately after the heads of his columns appeared; and forming in excellent order, they rushed impetuously on our batteries. Notwithstanding the destructive shower of grape that fell upon their front from our well served guns, they charged, and cut down every man at them. The enemy was only repulsed by repeated conflicts with the bayonet, in which Boughtee Thappa and several chiefs were killed. After several hours' hard fighting, the enemy retired slowly up the range of the Malown, having lost immensely, and inflicted much destruction on our force. Their acts of individual valour could not be exceeded by any troops in the world. Had they been all armed with muskets and bayonets, instead of swords and matchlocks, it is hard to say how the struggle would have terminated. Many of them seized our soldiers' bayonets with one hand, and pushing the point aside, buried their swords, which were heavy and formidable, in the breasts that opposed them. But Colonel Thompson was continually reinforced by Sir David Ochterlony, who had foreseen every thing, and provided for all with consummate skill. He moreover formed a fine column of diversion, under Captain Showers, who fell in a daring attack that he made upon the enemy's flank, in which he was nobly seconded by the column under Colonel Arnold, at a critical moment, when our Seik auxiliaries had shamefully abandoned their post. After fighting the whole of this day, and maintaining our several stations during the night, which was one of the utmost privation, we gained the summit of the Malown on the 16th, and in the course of that day completed the rout and dispersion of the enemy's army. This victory was not achieved without severe loss, six officers and 400 soldiers being killed and wounded, but in its consequences it led to the most glorious results; for, shortly after, Ummer Sing Thappa surrendered himself to Sir David Ochterlony, and accepted such terms as the British government thought proper to dictate. These comprised all the objects announced in the declaration of war. A free passage through Nepaul to Tartary and China was also established by treaty, with several important advantages as to trade and intercourse.

Thus terminated the Nepaul war, in a manner most honourable to the British arms and interests, notwithstanding the disasters which marked its commencement. The high value set upon the conduct of Sir David Ochterlony and the army by which it was achieved, appears in the energetic orders issued by the Marquis of Hastings on the announcement of its final issue. "So complete a fulfilment of his instructions, under difficulties known beforehand to be of no common amount, would alone have been sufficient to establish a high rate for General Ochterlony's reputation as a commander. But there are details in the arduous service so ably conducted by him, which must meet from the mind of every one a more particular attention. The unremitting zeal, the sagacious foresight, and the admirable decision which he has had the opportunity of displaying, should make him feel himself indebted to the embarrassments he has had to encounter. They have only served to mark in brighter colours the extent of his claim to applause. The patience, the ardour, and the intrepidity of all the officers, non-commissioned officers, and soldiers of the division, must be justly appreciated and admired by all who have contemplated their conduct. The governor-general offers to General Ochterlony, and all who acted under him, his warm applause: sensible as his excellency believes they will bé to that acknowledgement of their merits from government, a still more elevating consideration attends them; they have to reflect, with honest pride, on the further lesson which they have held forth to every power in India. The British government is too satisfactorily conscious of its own superior strength, ever to abuse it by trespassing wantonly on any of its neighbours; but if its forbearance be insulted, and its patience outraged by aggression, it will always prove, that whatsoever obstacles may retard its earlier efforts, its perseverance will not fail ultimately to crush the assailants."

I shall next pursue the course of events that occurred during my further stay in India, which I earnestly hope will be found sufficiently interesting.

MAHRATTA WAR, &c.

The Nepaul war, whose principal features have been briefly described, was the first great public service which the Marquis of Hastings was called upon to achieve in India, and the ability with which it was arranged and conducted ought to have assured the native princes, hostile to British interest, that all the measures of his administration would but add to the glory of England. In traversing the vast regions of Hindostan, which lie between Fort William and the northern frontier, his lordship travelled in great splendour. He had a corps of 150 elephants and 400 camels, glittering in gold and silver howdahs, and frequently 100 native chiefs in his train, whose followers alone formed a congregation of 200,000 souls, while the followers of his own personal army were 45,000 in number: the account of 500 persons dying in his camp sometimes daily, of cholera morbus, was no exaggeration. But all this display was sound policy, for he who aims at governing foreigners, must, to do so with effect, conform to their prejudices with respect to external things, which have wonderful influence in India. Political treaties were accomplished by his lordship on the line of progression with several petty chiefs. While the war with the Goorcas was going on, negotiations were in course with Scindea and Holkar for the suppression of the Pindarries.

When the war against the Nepaulese had terminated, and his lordship found that treaties could not bind these public robbers, he made arrangements for attacking them and all their supporters and abettors.

Previous to this, his lordship had assisted His Majesty's government in Ceylon, with troops from the presidency of Madras, for the purpose of completing the conquest of that fine island. The king of Candy had for some time exercised the utmost cruelty over his unfortunate subjects, and treated the English with such dissimulation and treachery, that no longer could confidence be placed in him. His chiefs were in open rebellion against his authority ; and Lieutenant General Sir R. Brownrigg, being implored by them to end the tyranny under which they groaned, marched to Candy, which he entered without the loss of a man, and assumed the government of the whole of Ceylon.

It was a melancholy sight to behold the capital surrounded by the traces of the most cruel executions. Numbers of the natives, who had been impaled alive, were fixed on high poles by the road sides. The king had escaped to the mountains; but, being pursued, he was abandoned, surrounded and taken prisoner, his people manifesting towards him, when divested of the terrors of despotism, no other feelings than those of hatred and contempt. But it was a deplorable sight to see the misery of several of his wives and female relations. They were all, however, treated with delicacy and tenderness by General Brownrigg, and soon after his capture, the king and his household were sent to Madras on a pension. Thus has a large accession been made to the British empire in the East, and a conquest effected without bloodshed, which baffled the Portuguese and Dutch, and cost the English in former attempts a vast sacrifice of human life. The garrison left in Candy under Major Davie, when it was taken in 1803 by the British, suffered prodigiously, sixteen officers and 172 European soldiers having been assassinated in a short time, and a total loss of above 600 men sustained. But such was now the change in the feelings of the Candians' public opinion, that our troops were hailed as deliverers. What a study for tyranny and oppression!

His lordship had also directed an expedition, at the suggestion of Sir Evan Nepean, governor of Bombay, to invade the territories of the rajah of Cutch, to punish the predatory Wagurs, who had, like the Pindarries, carried fire and sword into our provinces, and this important service was successfully performed by Colonel East of the Bombay army.

No British force had previously invaded this province, which lies immediately north of Guzerat, but a friendly intercourse was kept up by treaty between our ally the Guickwar and the rajah of Cutch-Booge. British interference had happily arrested the progress of female infanticide *, which horrible custom prevailed in this quarter from the most early records of time. From the warlike habits of the inhabitants, a spirited defence was expected; but Colonel East, contrary to expectation, approached the capital without much opposition, and forced the rajah to comply with such terms as he dictated.

Cutch is naturally a strong mountainous country, and, during a great part of the year, lies in an isolated form from the overflowing of the rivers Indus and Puddar, in the angle of which this region is situated. The country is thinly inhabited, and the towns generally in ruins, but the capital, named Booge, situated at the foot of a fortified hill, is a walled city of considerable extent and great antiquity, surrounded by many curious monuments and mosques. Amongst the most magnificent of these is the mausoleum of Row Lacka, the grandfather of the present rajah. It was raised to per-

* Vide Appendix, note 12.

petuate the memory of fifteen of his ladies, who performed the ceremony of suttee, or burning with his dead body.

The interior building, on which a great dome rests, is a fifteen-sided figure, and in each angle stands a full-length marble statue, which I have myself seen, of one of the fair victims to this barbarous custom.* They are represented in the bloom of life and beauty, richly decorated, with instruments of music in their hands. Around this inner building runs a magnificent viranda, which gives it externally the appearance of a square, and at each angle there is a great entrance, with a large marble elephant, facing the flight of stone steps leading up to the grand portico. Tigers, lions, elephants, monkeys, and an endless variety of fanciful objects, cut out of stone, ornament this fabric. In the erection of their modern buildings, the Moorish and Egyptian style of architecture is blended, and the mixture of the wild pagoda with the Grecian dome forms a very beautiful whole. For many interesting particulars respecting the expedition to Cutch, we beg to refer the curious reader to a late work, intituled "Fifteen Years in India," while we confine ourselves more particularly to the subject at the head of this section.

Marquis Wellesley had humbled but not destroyed

* Vide Appendix, note 13.

the Mahratta states. The ambitious chiefs who now composed the confederacy had, in secret, cherished hopes, during the pacific administrations which followed, that they would one day resume their power on our downfall. Under the deep and artful conduct of the Peishwa, they had entered into private treaties of mutual support, fostered the organisation and discipline which had been introduced into their armies by the French, founded prodigious parks of artillery, collected immense arsenals of military stores, enlisted large bodies of Arabs, and encouraged the Pindarries, who were actually in their pay, to take annual plundering excursions as exercises in war. The Marquis of Hastings was aware of these proceedings, and, while he professed the object only of reducing the Pindarries to such a state as to respect the rights of their fellow-creatures, he aimed at the future tranquillity of India, by placing the whole of central Hindostan upon the system which had been ably sketched out by the Marquis Wellesley.* As the Mahrattas, in a state of combination, were capable of bringing into the field a very large army, and 300 pieces of cannon, he put the powers at his disposal in motion, and took the field with the most magnificent British army that had ever been collected on the plains of Hindostan, formed into

* Vide Appendix, note 14.

divisions of unequal force, but proportioned to the service, each under a general officer, and, in the whole, amounting to one hundred thousand fighting men. The main body, commanded by the noble Marquis, being in number 13,000, with 60 pieces of cannon, approached the territories of Scindea, who, seeing himself upon the point of being attacked before the other chiefs were prepared to support the cause, signed a treaty for himself, and agreed to aid the British army in the accomplishment of the object in view, together with other conditions which tended to secure his co-operation in future. The Peishwa was likewise bound by treaty; but, while the advanced divisions of the army were marching from various points towards the Nerbudda, upon the banks of which river the Pindarry forts were situated, this treacherous chief attacked part of the Poonah subsidiary force near that city, on the 5th of November, 1817, with 8000 infantry and 15,000 cavalry, in the hope of destroying it; but he was nobly repulsed by Colonel Burr *, of the Bombay army, who, with only 2000 fighting men, maintained his position till the arrival of General Smith with the remainder of the subsidiary force. This action was sanguinary on the part of the Peishwa, who lost above 500 men in the attack, though the casualties were, on Colonel Burr's side, only one officer and fifty soldiers.

* Vide Addenda, XXXVI.

The Peishwa, though repulsed, was still able to remain encamped near Poonah, and to prevent all communication between General Smith, who was on the northern frontier of his command, and the force under Colonel Burr. General Smith, therefore, received the first intimation of the attack made on Colonel Burr from rumour. Finding that the Bombay post was stopped, he suspected that all was not right at Poonah, and proceeded by forced marches towards it, where he arrived, and formed a junction with Colonel Burr on the evening of the 13th of November, 1817 *, notwithstanding the efforts of large bodies of the enemy's cavalry to prevent it. The united British force now amounted to about 5000 fighting men. The Peishwa's army was encamped in a very strong position, defended by a formidable line of batteries. It required some time to prepare for attacking him. On the evening of the 16th of November, Colonel Milnes, of the 65th regiment, forded a little river that separated the two armies, and took up a position on the enemy's side with two brigades of infantry, under a heavy cannonade, and in the face of repeated charges from the flower of the Peishwa's best troops. It was arranged by General Smith that our line should charge the enemy's batteries at daylight next morning, and, for that purpose, during the night the whole forces passed over, and formed on the right of Colonel Milnes' division, but the

* Vide Addenda, XXXVII.

Peishwa had retreated under the cover of darkness with all his guns, and made good a most difficult passage across a chain of mountains in his rear, through which there was only one practicable road, so that when morning dawned the distant hills were covered with the remains of his army. A great part of his camp was left standing.

General Smith's operations called forth the most flattering expressions of approbation from his immediate superior, Sir Thomas Hislop; and arrangements being speedily made for the military government of the city of Poonah, Mr. Elphinstone, the political resident, accompanied by General Smith and the field force, proceeded southward in pursuit of the Peishwa, and continued to follow him with unsurpassed perseverance, till that chief was fairly hunted down, and glad to retire into obscurity at Benares on a pension. But the operations which led to this event will occupy their proper place after the relation of other matters prior in date, amongst the first of which is the treacherous attack made by the rajah of Berar, in co-operation with the government of Poonah, on the subsidary force, near his capital of Nagpoor.

On the 26th of November, 1817, Colonel Scott took post on the heights of Seetabalee, which overlooked the city of Nagpoor and the British residency. At the bottom there was an Arab village, which, during the day, had been filled with troops and guns, and, in the evening, pouring from the cover of the houses, 8000 infantry, 3500 of whom were Arabs, with thirty-five guns, supported by 12,000 cavalry in the distance, made a furious charge against the post on all sides. The struggle continued during the whole of the night and till noon next day, the Arabs making repeated desperate charges. Early in the morning, having by overwhelming numbers and persevering courage gained possession of part of the heights, the defence was confined to the top of the right, which was strengthened by a breastwork composed of bags of rice. At this perilous moment Captain Fitzgerald, with a small body of Madras cavalry, charged a mass of the enemy's horse, and captured several guns, which he turned against them, as well as against those parts of the heights in their possession, and the explosion of a tumbril having created some confusion, Colonel Scott seized the crisis, charged along the summit with the bayonet, and, after one of the most severe struggles, succeeded in clearing the hill, at the same time his cavalry wheeled round the base, and cut the enemy up to such a degree, that they lost all hope of success and retired with precipitation, having lost six guns, and about 2000 officers and men. But the loss on our part was also very severe, amounting to fourteen officers, and 333 of all other ranks, killed and wounded. Nothing could exceed the chivalrous conduct of every individual. The officers had to fight with the musket and bayonet, and, as it was a struggle for life against immense numbers, the valour which saved the position can scarcely be conceived. Major M'Kenzie, Captains Lloyd, Fitzgerald, Macan, and M'Donald, Mr. Jenkins, the resident, Lieutenants M'Donald, Watson, and Campbell, and Cornet Smith, distinguished themselves. The names, indeed, of every officer and soldier in this gallant defence deserve to be engraved on something more durable than brass. The assistant resident, Mr. Sotheby, was killed, fighting bravely among the brave.

Soon after this Sir Thomas Hislop, with the Madras army, reached the Nerbudda, and attacked the Pindarries, who, being unprepared for meeting a regular force, fled, and were intercepted by the other divisions approaching on all sides, as to a common centre. Sir Thomas Hislop, having a more important enemy before him, did not rest till he came in sight of the army of Mulhar Row Holkar, encamped in a strong position near Maheidpore, on the river Sipoora, about twenty miles north of Oojain. During the advance, Sir John Malcolm had been negotiating with Holkar's ministers in vain. On the 20th of December, 1817, the British army approached Maheidpore, and the picquets were attacked by bodies of cavalry. The next morning Sir Thomas Hislop moved towards the river Sipoora, and, having beaten off several attempts of Holkar's cavalry to interrupt his line of march, he found the main body, consisting of about eighteen battalions of infantry, organised and appointed like our sepoys, with 100 guns in batteries, and supported by an immense irregular force of horse, that covered the surrounding plains, advantageously posted on the opposite bank, their left flank protected by the bed of the river, and the right by a very deep ravine; while their line, which could be approached only by one ford, practicable for guns, was protected by several ruined villages.* It was Sir Thomas's intention, upon reconnoitring this strong position, to attack in flank, but, to do so, it would have been necessary to make a long detour, he therefore determined to ford the river, the bank of which afforded some cover, and charge the line exactly in front.

The divisions of the army were formed into columns of attack for this purpose, and the artillery having cleared the bank of the Sipoora, in the immediate front of Holkar's army, the Madras rifle corps, supported by several light companies and a strong battery of horse artillery, crossed the ford under the protection of an enfilading fire from the foot artillery, stationed on their right. The Sipoora is a considerable branch of the Nerbudda, but, like nearly all the other inferior Indian rivers, it is almost dry during the summer, though it rolls with impetuosity over its rocky bed in the monsoon. On the sands lodged under the rugged

* Vide Sir Thomas Hislop's Report, dated Dec. 23, 1817.

bank on the enemy's side, the infantry formed; and the cavalry having also crossed, at a preconcerted signal the whole rushed to the storm of the enemy's left, where several batteries had opened upon the ford with most destructive effect. During this awful period, the light troops who covered the formation of the line suffered severely, and nearly all the rifle officers were either killed or wounded. But the moment every thing was ready, the troops pressed forward with such steady valour, that no pause ensued, till the men were bayoneted who served the enemy's batteries, which continued to pour a torrent of grape till the moment our soldiers reached the muzzles of the guns. At the same time the line was overwhelmed in every part by the shock of contact, and the cavalry charging during the confusion that ensued, completed their total route. Having, however, several batteries in reserve near their camp, these opened a heavy fire upon our advancing line. This led Sir Thomas Hislop to suppose that a re-formation had taken place. Upon pushing forward, however, the whole camp was deserted, and our cavalry and light troops continued the pursuit till exhausted.

This well-contested action continued from noon till three o'clock, during which time the enemy's cavalry pressed upon the reserve, and several times attacked the baggage, but the Mysore auxiliaries behaved with great spirit, and met their charges in every direction. Seventy pieces of cannon were taken, together with the whole of the enemy's camp equipage, and the plain was strewed with upwards of 3000 of their killed and wounded. The success of this battle was, in a great measure, owing to the chivalrous conduct of Sir John Malcolm, who led the most desperate of the attacks on the left, and cheered the troops by the most fearless personal exposure. His noble and commanding figure was seen by the whole line to outstride their ardour, and his lofty plume, often waved by his right hand, was a banner of union to the line. Great in his political character, and renowned as an elegant writer, this scientific soldier has, on various occasions, displayed an unsurpassed intrepidity, and a coolness of judgment in the hour of danger, which promise future increase of glory, if opportunity be afforded to the exercise of the great talents which he possesses as a statesman, philosopher, and warrior. Our loss was very severe in this battle, being thirty-eight European officers, and 806 of all other ranks, killed and wounded, but the advantages were great and permanent.

General Doveton, who commanded the second division of the army, hearing of the treacherous attack made upon Colonel Scott, proceeded by forced marches to Nagpoor, where he arrived on the 12th of December, and the next morning having drawn up in line of battle before the enemy's batteries, the rajah came over and surrendered himself to the resident, but his orders for the delivery of the cannon and the dispersion of the troops were not obeyed by the chiefs; for upon General Doveton's approach at the head of his column, a heavy fire was opened from the Sucker Durry gardens. The whole of the hostile line was instantly charged, and 75 guns, all their camp equipage, and forty elephants taken. General Doveton did not achieve this brilliant exploit without considerable loss; his killed and wounded amounting to nearly 200 of all ranks, and as the Arabs retired to the palaces and fortified posts of the city, an arduous duty was still before this gallant division.

The Arabs were strongly posted in the city, to the number of 3000, supported by a considerable body of Indian irregulars. From the want of heavy battering guns, it was the 24th of December before such an impression was made upon the gateway, as to warrant the storm of the palace with hopes of success and little loss. The place was, however, defended with such obstinacy, that all the repeated attacks, made with undaunted bravery and skill, were repulsed; and a serious loss sustained of ten European officers, and 104 of other ranks, together with upwards of 200 native officers and sepoys. But an impression was made upon the Arab chiefs, and they agreed soon after to evacuate the city, upon being permitted to march away with the honours of war under certain conditions.

The consummate ability with which the Marquis

of Hastings, who was the soul of all, had planned the field movements in this war, was now developed. Different divisions and strong detachments of the army successively in all directions met the Pindarry chiefs, who had escaped to the north of the Nerbudda on the approach of the Madras force. Generals Donkin, Marshal, Sir William Grant Keir, Brown, Hardyman, Sir John Malcolm, and Colonel Adams surprised them on different occasions, cut them up in cavalry attacks, and captured their baggage. They had no resting-place in the territories of Scindea, and when they approached Holkar, they found that he had been forced to throw himself upon the mercy of his conqueror, yield a considerable portion of his dominions, disband his forces, and place himself under the protection of a British subsidiary force. His sister Bheema Bhye, an intriguing woman, was still at the head of a body of troops, but Sir William G. Keir induced her to come over to him by private negotiation, and dispersed the force she commanded. Another of his sisters who had been friendly to the British interests; and adverse to the battle of Maheidpore, was publicly beheaded by the decree of a council of war shortly before that event. The remains of the Nagpoor army had rallied under Suddoo Baba and Munddow Row, but they were dispersed and cut up by Colonel M'Morine; and the rajah of Berar was reduced to subjection, similar to what had been imposed on Holkar.

All these successes followed each other so rapidly, that by the month of March 1818, nearly the whole of the Pindarry chiefs were overcome, and several of them had accepted grants of land from the British government.

Meanwhile, General Smith pursued the Peishwa southward with the greatest perseverance, marching for a long time at the average rate of twenty miles a day, in the face of thirty thousand Mahratta cavalry, who did every thing, in the power of such an irregular and ill appointed mass, to impede his progress. For several months, this harassing mode of warfare continued, which was exceedingly sanguinary on the part of the enemy, though the loss in the division under General Smith was comparatively trifling. During this arduous campaign, one of the Company's native regiments had an opportunity of displaying the highest qualities of courage and discipline, in nobly resisting an attack made on it by the Peishwa's whole army.

The detachment of which this gallant corps formed the principal part, consisted of a detail of Madras artillery and two six pounders, 2d of 1st regiment Bombay native infantry, about 600 strong, and 300 auxiliary horse, the whole under Captain Staunton, who marched from Seroor, on the afternoon of the 31st of December, for the purpose of reinforcing the troops left at Poonah, upon which place the Peishwa's army was advancing. Poonah is only forty miles from Seroor, and it was calculated that

Captain Staunton would reach his destination in full time; but, by one of those rapid movements which baffle foresight, his army had encamped on the banks of the river Bheema, near the village of Koragaum; and Captain Staunton's detachment, upon gaining the heights overlooking that place, on the morning of the 1st of January, 1818, saw, to their surprise, 20,000 cavalry and several thousand infantry with guns encamped in the plain below. To retreat was impossible. Captain Staunton had just time to occupy part of the village, when he was attacked, in the most determined manner, by three divisions of Arabs, supported by immense bodies of horse and the fire of two guns. The enemy's troops were animated by the presence of the Peishwa on a distant height, attended by several of his sirdars or chiefs, who flattered his highness with the prospect of witnessing the destruction of this gallant handful of British troops, most of whom were Mahrattas. This memorable attack commenced about noon, and continued with unremitting fury till 9 P. M., at which period the detachment had lost nearly the whole of the European artillerymen, and about one-third of the infantry and auxiliary horse. The exertions which the European officers had been called upon to make, in leading their men to frequent charges with the bayonet, had diminished their numbers. Lieutenant Chisholm of the artillery, and Mr. Assistant Surgeon Wingate, 2d of 1st regiment, were killed, and Lieutenants Swanston, Pattinson, and Connolan were wounded; leaving only Captain Staunton, Lieutenant Jones, and Mr. Assistant Surgeon Wiley, nearly exhausted, to direct the efforts of the remaining part of the detachment, who were nearly frantic from the want of water and the unparalleled exertions they had made throughout the day without any sort of refreshment, after a fatiguing march of twenty-six miles. Doubtless, this detachment would have been entirely destroyed, had it not been for the rapid pursuit of General Smith, which forced the Peishwa to draw off, and retreat during the night of the first, upon which Captain Staunton returned to Seroor.

But General Smith continued the pursuit of the enemy with indefatigable perseverance, and at length on the 20th February, after a night march of near thirty miles, came up with his highness at a place called Ashtee*, where, being completely surprised, he was forced to throw the flower of his cavalry between himself and danger. His best general, Gockla, was killed in this brave but unsuccessful attempt to sustain the charge of our dragoons. The greatest part of his treasure and baggage fell into the hands of General Smith; together with the young rajah of Sattara, his brother and their mother. Nothing could be of more importance than this capture, for the Company's

* Vide Addenda, XXXVIII.

government having determined to depose the Peishwa and restore the ancient family, the possession of the true representative of the honoured line of Sevajee, in the person of the young rajah of Sattara, produced the highest degree of exultation.

General Smith immediately returned towards Poonah, to hand over his valuable prize to Mr. Elphinstone. The rajah being supplied with elephants, and all the external pomp of eastern grandeur, formed a gorgeous spectacle at the head of the British line.* He and his brother were, notwithstanding their splendour, mean and stupid-looking young persons; but the queen mother was an exceedingly fine, intelligent woman, with the remains of great personal attraction. Her complexion was fair; she sometimes rode on horseback, and managed her charger with skill and ease. She exhibited none of that timidity which one would naturally expect from an Asiatic female, but, on the contrary, appeared to be a most able political character.

Sir Thomas Hislop was now about returning with the Madras army, and the Marquis of Hastings had left the field for the purpose of retracing his steps to Fort William. The sensations with which his lordship reviewed the glorious course of his political and military career in India, must have been most gratifying to his great soul, and the vast

* Vide Addenda, XXXIX.

sum he had contributed to the amount of happiness enjoyed by 100,000,000 of people, every hour presented itself, no doubt, to his intellectual eye. Some of the divisions of the army had also reason to exult in the prospect of important pecuniary reward; for the booty taken at Poonah, Nagpoor, and Maheidpore was immense.

The Peishwa was now the only native chief who remained in force, and he was so completely beset on all sides, that much longer resistance was impossible. But in several parts of the country, bands of robbers, composed of disbanded soldiers and mountaineers, still gave employment to detachments, and there were several strong hill-forts in the possession of Arab garrisons, who, in the distractions of war, set conquest at defiance. General Hislop, in the route of his army returning to Madras, reduced some of these refractory chiefs to obedience. The circumstances attending the storm of Talnier, a fort ceded to us by Holkar, situated in Kandeish on the river Tuptee, were so extraordinary that they became a subject of parliamentary inquiry.

Sir Thomas, when within a march of Talnier, had received intimation that the Killedar of that place intended to resist the occupation of his fort by British troops, although he had received the order of his sovereign to surrender it, and, upon the approach of the advanced guard, some guns, and a number of matchlocks, were fired from the walls. The fort was surrounded by deep ravines, and quite inaccessible to reconnoissance by cavalry. It was, however, closely approached by the engineers covered by light infantry; and the Killedar having returned no answer to an attempt at negotiation, the field pieces were brought into position, and the defences of the gateway demolished to such a degree, that Sir Thomas determined upon storming it, in the hope of at least making a lodgment within. For this purpose a column of attack was formed and pushed forward to the gate. The Killedar, being alarmed at these preparations, sent out a flag of truce and solicited terms; upon which he was desired to open his gates and surrender himself and his garrison unconditionally. After some little delay, the two outer gates were opened and the head of the column entered. At the third gate the Killedar came out through the wicket, and surrendered himself to the adjutant-general, Colonel Conway. A party of grenadiers was then pushed forward through the wicket, and still further through another gate, but they were at length stopped by the fifth entrance being shut. The Arabs within were clamorous to have some terms mentioned, before they delivered themselves up to the mercy of Europeans; but after some delay, the wicket of this gate was also opened from within, and Lieutenant Colonel Murray, Major Gordon, and two or three other officers entered it, followed by ten or twelve grenadiers of the Royal Scots, upon which they were attacked by the Arabs, and, before aid could be afforded, cut down. Major Gordon and Captain M'Gregor were stabbed to the heart, and Colonel Murray and two other officers wounded in several places with daggers. The gates being burst open, the storming party entered the fort, and the Arabs retreated to the stone buildings, where they continued to defend themselves until all the garrison, about 300 Arabs and Hindoos, were put to the sword. "A severe example," says Sir Thomas Hislop, in his report to the governor-general, "indeed, but absolutely necessary, and one which I have no doubt will produce the most salutary effects on the future operations in this province. The Killedar I ordered to be hanged on one of the bastions, immediately after the place fell. Whether he was accessary or not to the subsequent treachery of his men, his execution was a punishment justly due to his rebellion in the first instance, particularly after the warning he had received in the morning."

The coldness of this language freezes the heart! "*Absolutely necessary!*" Who was the judge of this necessity? A military commander, flushed with victory, having nothing to dread from a little delay, destroys the existence of three hundred of his fellow-creatures for an outrage, which seems to have been produced more by the precipitate, imprudent, and haughty manner in which the wicket was entered, than in any premeditated malice; and the Killedar was hanged, although he surrendered himself on the good faith of an implied promise. What! was his disputing the order of General Hislop such a crime? Might his motive not have been excellent? Did he not know that his sovereign master had been conquered, and that his cession of the fort might have been extorted? Is it not heart-breaking to a brave man to be forced to yield? Should not such feelings be respected by the brave, and every allowance be made for passion and irritation in an enemy, when sinking beneath superior force? But I do not presume to pronounce upon the conduct of my superior. I merely venture to reason upon the feeling excited in my breast by his own words. There are military situations where horrible examples are necessary. The evidence before the public does not show that this was one of them. Sir Thomas Hislop in justice should not be rashly charged with the blood of 300 men, nor do I presume to arraign him. His own state of the case is before the reader, and a judgment may be formed thereon. His temper and forbearance on former occasions called forth the applause of the Marquis of Hastings, and far be it from me to deprive him of the benefit. "To Lieutenant General Sir Thomas Hislop," says his lordship, in the orders he issued, 21st of February, 1818, upon quitting the field army, "it might seem superfluous to offer praise; yet there are titles to applause which should not be absorbed in the lustre of victory. The temper and forbearance with which his excellency, possessing all the consciousness of superiority from the quality of his troops, endeavoured to avoid a rupture with Holkar, and the judgment with which he improved success after his conciliating efforts had failed, demand high commendation."

All the officers in command of divisions or departments received his lordship's warm approbation also, in public orders when he was leaving the field. Brigadier Generals Sir John Malcolm and Doveton, Major Generals Sir William Grant Keir, Marshall, Donkin, Sir David Ochterlony, and Brown, Brigadier Generals Hardyman, Toon, Smith, Munro, and Pritzler, and Colonel Adams, were thanked in a most dignified manner, and this fine general order concludes in the following impressive words: — "The alteration produced within three months, in the state of central India, is beneficial to the inhabitants, in a degree which the most sanguine could scarcely have ventured to hope; and to every officer who has been engaged in the undertaking, the remembrance of having had a share in effecting a change so interesting to humanity, will keep pace with that consciousness of having advanced the prosperity of the Honourable Company by efforts of zeal and courage, for which the governor-general offers his earnest thanks, however unequal that acknowledgment may be to the merit which calls it forth."

The Peishwa was now the only obstacle to the return of the whole army to quarters. He had been driven entirely out of his own dominions by the indefatigable and able pursuit of General Smith. It was his fate to receive the last blow from Colonel Adams, who intercepted his retreat on the 17th of April, 1818, killed upwards of 400 of his adherents, took his five remaining guns, and all the camels and treasure elephants he had left. The force under Colonel Adams had marched, on the previous night, upwards of thirty-one miles, and the pursuit and return made sixteen more, which was hard service under a burning sun; for the heat begins in April to be terrible in the Deccan. Not long after this the subtle Bajee-row *, finding his game lost, which he had played not without skill, surrendered his person to Sir John Malcolm; and received a princely pension, on condition that he would resign all pretensions to power, and reside quietly, for the remainder of his life, at Benares. His Arabs, his Portuguese infantry, and heavy guns were still to be conquered; for, not being able to keep up with the rapidity of his flight, they had been left at Sholapore, a strongly fortified town in the south of his late dominions. General Munro assaulted that place on the 10th of May, 1818, and

* Vide Addenda, XL.

having made a lodgment within it, a smart action was fought, and several of the guns captured, but the main body retreated. It was, however, closely pursued by General Pritzler, who cut in among them with his cavalry, and killed upwards of 800 in the route that followed, so that their total dispersion was effected. Major De Pinto, who commanded the Portuguese half caste battalion in the service of the late Peishwa, here lost his life, and nearly all the Arab chiefs shared his fate; for these ferocious soldiers of fortune think it a disgrace to ask for quarter, or to part with their arms. Such only as threw their weapons of defence away escaped into the neighbouring woods and ravines.

In the course of the following month and June, all the forts and strong-holds in the Deccan and Concan were taken, many of them by assaults. The Arabs defended themselves with desperate bravery, and in many places refused quarter. During some of these awful attacks on the fortified summits of high hills, the thermometer stood at 145°, being 49° above blood heat in Europe.

The war was now completely at an end, and the troops were placed in cantonments for the monsoon. In its effects it consolidated the British empire in the East, and increased the resources of the Honourable Company upwards of four millions in sterling money, per annum. All the extensive region from the confines of China to the eastern frontier of Persia, and from the Himalaya range to the Cape of Good Hope, are now directly or indirectly influenced by Great Britain. Since 1818, general peace has diffused the blessings of security over those fine countries which were then traversed by destructive armies. It is easy to conceive the difference. Places that were at that period scenes of desolation, now teem with domestic enjoyment. Without the security of high walls, the husbandman may now sow his rice, and plant his sugar-cane. He will no more, from his lofty loop-holes, see the produce of his fields destroyed by rapacious plunderers. His wives and his daughters may now go to their wells for water without the dread of abduction and murder. Their naked chubby offspring may sport under the plantain and cocoa, unmindful of worse enemies than the snake. To think of the satisfaction with which the Marquis of Hastings * has returned to his country, without one single aspersion on his fair fame, and how his dignified age will be cheered by the recollection of the glory of a well-spent life, which has been ever active in heaping benefits on his fellow-creatures, are delightful subjects for reflection, in which every feeling heart can participate.

The military achievements during the administration of the Marquis of Hastings did not end with the Mahratta war; for, immediately after its

* Vide Addenda, XLI.

termination, an expedition was sent up the Persian Gulf under the command of Sir William Grant Keir, who added further laurels to his own fame and that of Great Britain, by the reduction of the Joasmere pirates; and after his return, the force, which was stationed on the Arabian coast, being attacked, another expedition was sent thither under Sir Lionel Smith, which, in its operations, was equally brilliant and successful.

During the peaceful flow of happiness there are but few materials for history. To notice the numerous regulations which were framed during his lordship's administration in India, for the security and enjoyment of all ranks, would be a pleasing task, but a tedious one for the reader. One of his lordship's latest efforts of wisdom in India, was directed against the horrid practice of burning wives with the dead bodies of their husbands. That ceremony is now placed under the inspection of the police; and as permission can only be obtained by an European magistrate being made sensible that the female wishes to die, and that her expressed wish is the result of her own free will, there can be little doubt but humanity will start such difficulties, as will, in time, greatly diminish this deplorable sacrifice of life.

CHAPTER VI.

OF THE THREE PRESIDENCIES, CALCUTTA, MADRAS, AND BOMBAY.

THE area of country at present subject to the presidency of Calcutta, or Bengal, may be estimated at 200,000 square miles; and if this be divided into twenty-four parts, three will represent rivers and lakes; eight, waste, irreclaimable, and barren parts; one, sites of towns and villages, &c.; three, free lands; and nine, liable for revenue, according to the most accurate estimates.

This extent of region comprehends the whole soubahs of Bengal and Bahar, part of Orissa, Allahabad and Berar, the Morung, Cooch Bahar, and all the districts in Oude, &c. acquired since 1801. The population has been ascertained by calculation, without accurate census, to be about 40,000,000 of souls. The gross produce of the land amounts annually to 43,000,000*l.* sterling money. About a seventh of that sum comes into the Company's treasury. The whole revenue amounts to about twelve millions, and the whole charges, civil, military, &c., &c., to about seven in sterling money. In 1809 the Company's Bengal debt amounted to upwards of 20,000,000 sterling, and it has not been much diminished.

The civil and military government of this presidency is vested in a governor-general and three counsellors. For the administration of justice there are, in the civil and criminal departments, one supreme court stationed at Calcutta, six courts of appeal and circuit attached to six different divisions, and forty inferior courts stationed in so many different districts. The Mohammedan law continues to be the ground-work of criminal jurisprudence, but its administration has been greatly improved by the Company's government, the pleadings being now written in the native languages, the courts held openly at stated times, and all suitors being allowed counsellors, who are chosen from the Mohammedan college at Calcutta, and the Hindoo college at Benares.

Calcutta, the capital of British India, is situated on the eastern bank of the river Hooghly, in lat. 22° 33′ N., long. 88° 28′ E. It is about one hundred miles from the sea, by the winding of the river, which is, before the city, full a mile broad. The approach is magnificent, each bank being adorned with elegant villas and gardens. In the year 1717 this extensive city * was a petty village, and the country around it a jungle and marsh. It now extends along the river upwards of six

* Vide Addenda, XLII.

miles, and the numerous spires of churches, temples, and minarets, with the strong fortifications of Fort William *, and several imposing public edifices, such as the government house, exchange, town hall, college, writers' buildings, and the suburb called Chouringee, which is a line of Grecian palaces, render the external aspect of Calcutta perhaps equal in splendour to any capital in the world. But, upon a closer view of the houses, which are about 100,000 in number, they will be found poor mean buildings, with the exception of the European part of the city, consisting of perhaps 8000 dwellings, occupied by British, Portuguese, and Armenian † inhabitants. The whole population is estimated at 600,000 souls; and the surrounding country is so numerously inhabited, that, in an extent of twenty miles round, it is said there are 2,225,000 people.

The European society of Calcutta is numerous, their habits convivial and hospitable, their mode of living luxurious, and their appearance splendid in the extreme. Visits are paid generally in palanquins; but covered and open carriages, of all the descriptions fashionable in England, are numerous. The table is covered with vast variety, and Madeira and claret are introduced even in the houses of the middling classes every day at dinner.

There would be no great interest in describing

* Vide Addenda, XLIII.

† Vide Addenda, XLIV.

the public edifices of Calcutta, most of which are common buildings, on the usual principles of European architecture. Places of public amusement are not numerous. There is one respectable theatre, and an assembly room, but little frequented; for, although no place in the world exhibits a more numerous display of splendid private parties, yet public intercourse is unfashionable, and pride has separated general society into circles, whose centres are like the heads of castes by which they are surrounded. *

The descendants of Europeans, called half castes, are here very numerous; and seven large schools are supported by them. There are also excellent male and female orphan asylums, hospitals, and a variety of charitable institutions, which do honour to the liberality of the inhabitants of Calcutta. Since the establishment of an episcopacy in 1814, in India, consisting of a bishop and three archdeacons, &c., great attention has been paid to the education of the natives. The late Dr. Middleton, first bishop of Calcutta, was mainly instrumental in founding the Mission College, for instructing native youth in the doctrine and discipline of the church of England, in view to their becoming preachers, catechists, and school-masters, and for other general purposes connected with the extension of education and conversion. It appears

* Vide Addenda, XLV.

from the last report of the Calcutta School Society, that there are 200 schools within the precincts of its control, and that upwards of 5000 native children are studying various branches of European literature in Calcutta and the vicinity. But what proves beyond doubt that an amazing change has taken place in the prejudices of the natives is, that Hindoo females are now students at several of our institutions. At the last anniversary meeting of the Calcutta Female School Society, the committee remark, that there were pupils from the highest as well as the lowest castes; for instance, there were two Brahmans, four Kaynsthus, and seven Vishnubers, who are considered of the highest rank. In short, a learned native has published a treatise, in the Bengalee language, to prove that it was formerly customary among the Hindoos to educate their females, and that the education of women is not, as is generally supposed, disgraceful or injurious, but, if encouraged, will be productive of the most beneficial effects.

Calcutta is as yet in an infant state: — no city in the world has ever improved or grown more rapidly, and if it continue for another century to progress as it has done during the last, it will be the wonder of posterity. Some of its institutions are, however, susceptible of great improvement, particularly the supreme court, whose jurisdiction over Europeans extends to the distance of 1200 miles, and yet there is no circuit branch; so that a criminal, with all the witnesses necessary to convict him, must be brought to the presidency, where punishment is inflicted, at a distance from the scene of perpetration. Another defect is that all the natives, who are subject to the jurisdiction of the king's court, are tried by a British jury, of which they may complain with good reason. In short, executions have taken place in Calcutta for crimes, on principles of British law, which according to the Hindoo code were not capital offences. The case of rajah Nund Comar is quite in point, and as his fate has been described, an allusion to it is only necessary.

The external and internal trade of the presidency of Calcutta averages about 14,000,000 sterling annually, a great part of which is carried on by private adventurers, since the opening of the ports of Calcutta, Madras, and Bombay, to a free trade*, but the East India Company have such an advantage in a monopoly of certain articles, and in the privilege of framing local regulations, that no enterprise can compete with, and many speculators to the Indian shores have been completely ruined. Upwards of six hundred ships and vessels take their departure from Calcutta annually, with 150,000 tons of merchandise, and as the same number, on an average, yearly sail up the river, the activity of the scene may be conceived.

* Vide Appendix, note 15.

In Calcutta and its vicinity the curiosities are not numerous, but interesting. There are no great temples and mosques. The churches, chapels, and meeting-houses are not very commanding edifices, compared with the private mansions, many of which are truly magnificent. But when I was in Calcutta, the black-hole was to be seen, and the monument which commemorated its tragical story, though so much shattered by lightning, that I understand it now ceases to meet the eye. The Company's Botanic Gardens are also worthy of observation *, and the governor-general's country residence at Barrackpore, in a beautiful park, is another object, with the Danish, French, and Dutch settlements up the river Hooghly, the banks of which at all times present contrasts of natural beauty and frightful superstition.

MADRAS.

Madras is the capital of the British possessions in the Deccan, and south of India. It stands in lat. 13° 5′ N., long. 80° 25′ E., and is distant from Calcutta 1030 miles, and from Bombay 770.

The coast on which Madras stands is lashed by a raging surf, over which the city appears to great

* Vide Addenda, XLV.

advantage, and the numerous palms in its vicinity look charmingly green. All the sandy beach seems in motion with human life. The colonnaded edifices that meet the eye have the appearance of marble, from the fine shell mortar with which they are plastered and polished. Romantic boats and canoes approach the vessel, filled with gracefully formed natives, and the attention is divided between bodies rustling in silk and decorated with jewels, and others almost naked.

At Madras nearly all the civilians live in garden-houses, so that the town does not present the splendid appearance of Calcutta; but the country around, though naturally barren, is rendered artificially beautiful; and fine roads, shaded with trees, intersect it in all directions. The mode of living at Madras is much the same as in Calcutta; but provisions of every description are much dearer than in Bengal, and of course society is not so extensive as in the supreme presidency. It is, perhaps, on that account, full as pleasant, and more general. The whole population of the black town of Madras* and Fort St. George is about 350,000 souls. Accounts are kept at this presidency in star pagodas, fanams, and cash; while in Calcutta the currency is in rupees, annas, and pice. Eighty cash make one fanam, twelve fanams a rupee, and three and a half rupees a pagoda, worth eight shillings. In

* Vide Addenda, XLVI.

Calcutta twelve pice make an anna, and sixteen annas a rupee, worth two shillings and sixpence.

Justice is administered on the same plan as in Bengal; a supreme court is established at Madras on the model of that of Fort William. The revenue is about five millions sterling per annum, which is nearly all expended in paying the necessary establishments. This presidency indirectly controls about twenty millions of the native population of India, but its immediate subjects do not exceed twelve millions; for it has within its boundaries the nominally independent principalities of Mysore, Travancore, and Cochin.

In a commercial point of view this presidency is inferior to Bombay. Its export trade is chiefly in piece goods, and the whole value of its shipments out and in annually does not exceed five millions sterling.

BOMBAY.

The presidency of Bombay, which governs the whole north-west coast of India, is situated on an island formerly comprehended in the province of Aurungabad. Lat. 18° 58′ N., long. 72° 38′ E. Distant from Calcutta 1300 miles, and from Madras 770.

Bombay Island is about ten miles in length, by three in breadth, and it is joined to Salsette by a vellard or causeway. The island of Salsette communicates at low water with the continent. The rise of the tide being here, during the springs, seventeen feet, and possessing docks on a large scale, Bombay is the first place in India for ship-building; an abundance of fine timber being imported from Malabar. As a place of trade it stands high in rank; occupying the station that Ormus formerly did, being now the western mart of all India. The exports and imports of Bombay generally average six millions of sterling money annually, and above 200 ships of different nations arrive and depart yearly from the fine harbour which is formed between this island and the main.

All the marine force which the Company have, consisting of fifteen fighting vessels, belongs to Bombay; for the pilot service, which numbers ten schooners, employed in conducting vessels from the Bay of Bengal up the river Hooghly, the navigation of which is intricate and dangerous, cannot be described as a marine for offensive operations. The cruisers of Bombay are chiefly employed against pirates, who have infested the western coasts of India, since the time of Alexander the Great; and in nautical surveys.

Justice is administered on the Bombay establishment on the same principles as at Madras and Calcutta. Instead of a supreme court, there is a king's recorder*, with three barristers and eight

* Vide Addenda, XLVII.

attorneys; but such has been the extension of territory by late conquests, that no doubt this presidency will soon be placed on the same respectable scale, in point of judicature, as the other two capitals. Madras and Bombay have their own governors, and councils of three members like Calcutta, but they are subordinate to the governor-general. The inhabitants of the whole island of Bombay are computed at 220,000. In this number there are 8000 Parsees and 4000 Jews. The Portuguese inhabitants are also numerous, but, as in other parts of India, the mass of the people are Hindoos.

There are many beautiful garden-houses on the island of Bombay; and the society of the place is sufficiently diversified and agreeable, but the style of living is far less luxurious and profuse than in Bengal, though equally comfortable and elegant.

Till the termination of the late Mahratta war, the territorial possessions under the immediate jurisdiction of Bombay were small compared with those of Bengal and Madras; but by the deposition of the Peishwa, a great part of whose dominions have been added to this presidency, and by cessions from Holkar and other chiefs, a most respectable extent of country, not only round the coasts to the river Indus, but in the most fertile parts of the Deccan, now belongs to Bombay, with a revenue which it is supposed will average five millions sterling per annum. The native population, directly controlled by the Bombay presidency, does not perhaps exceed eight millions of souls. The authorities upon which these calculations are made, are not set forth as accurate, being merely an approximation to what cannot be ascertained but by a careful census.

We have been intentionally brief* in our notice of the three presidencies of India, because in every common gazetteer, their particular history is given at large. Bombay owes its consequence to the Portuguese, to whom it was ceded in 1530, but the vicinity of their chief settlement, Goa, prevented it from becoming the western emporium, though it was strongly fortified, and always considered as an important post. It was received by king Charles the Second, in June 1661, as part of his queen's marriage portion, from Portugal, and continued as an acquisition of the crown till March 1668, when it was transferred to the East India Company, who found themselves greatly injured by the trade carried on by the king's servants. In 1686, the seat of the Company's government was transferred from Surat to Bombay, and it has since continued to rule the western coast of India.

The harbour of Bombay is safe and commodious, and the scenery sublime and romantic. In external appearance Bombay bears no resemblance to either Calcutta or Madras. The style of architecture at

* Vide Addenda, XLVIII.

the two latter places is Grecian, the houses in and about Madras being generally one story high, with beautiful colonnaded fronts and terraced roofs, while in Calcutta they are two or three stories high, the lower apartments being thought unhealthy; but at Bombay the houses are constructed with wooden pillars, supporting wooden verandas, sometimes three stories high, and the roofs slated.

Calcutta and Madras owe their consequence entirely to the East India Company, having been both insignificant villages when factories were first established at them. But Bombay and its vicinity appear to have been places of vast importance to the ancient Hindoos; for the numerous magnificent caves on the islands of Elephanta and Salsette are amongst the most remarkable antiquities of India.

The caves of Kenneri on Salsette are so numerous, that they seem at one time to have formed a subterraneous city. One of the largest was formerly fitted up as a Portuguese church, and the great idols were defaced that had belonged to Paganism. At the sides of the great portico there are yet two gigantic figures, twenty-five feet high, standing erect. The inhabitants of this subterraneous city were supplied with water by fine reservoirs cut out of the living rock, many of which are still full of cool and delicious water.

These caves, however, magnificent as they certainly must appear to every visitor from Europe, are infinitely surpassed by those in the mountain of

Elora near Dowlutabad, for an exact description of which, I refer the curious reader to the sixth volume of the Asiatic Researches; and to the splendid publications of Mr. Daniels.*

Some of the other curiosities on the island of Bombay have been already noticed, and we shall now conclude this book in humble hope that its contents have not disappointed the expectation of the reader.

* Vide Addenda, XLIX.

MEMOIRS OF INDIA.

BOOK III.

THIS portion of our work will be found to contain such miscellaneous remarks as a long residence in different parts of the British possessions in India have suggested. Our plan is first to make such general and particular observations on India, as may occur, and then to accompany a young adventurer, from his preparation till he have been some time in that country, and shall return to the place of his birth, either from debility, or with such independence as he may think suitable to his future happiness. As we conceive his thoughts and calculations must in a great measure be similar to what our own were, we shall endeavour to guide him by our experience.

CHAPTER I.

MISCELLANEOUS REMARKS ON INDIA, FOR THE BENEFIT OF YOUNG ADVENTURERS.

THE area of the British empire in the East is nearly equal to all Europe. There is such an interesting variety every where, that in travelling from West to East, or from South to North, the understanding is continually roused to reflection. To appreciate properly the character of the Hindoos, it is necessary to enter deeply into the constitution of their castes, which produce their habits and motives to action. They are certainly gifted with talents in different degrees, in no way below the standard of other men. All the virtues that adorn our nature are found in Hindostan, as well as the vices which degrade us. If men are estimable for valour and fidelity to their king, the warriors of India are behind no class on earth. Innumerable instances of their self-devotion in the service of their country might be adduced. The Khetris resisted invasion till death — for in all those parts of India conquered by the Moguls, it is said, that not one of that unadulterated caste remains in existence. Victory or death was their aim in fighting, and to this day it is customary with some of the tribes that imitate them, to put an end to the lives of their families, when unsuccessful in defending their independence, and die sword in hand, with as much determination as those exhibited who fought round Leonidas at Thermopylæ. An instance of this occurred at the storm of Bobilee, a fort in the northern Sircars, by the French, in 1767. There had long existed a feud between Rangaru, the chief of this place, and the head of a neighbouring state, named Viseram Rauze, who induced Monsieur Bussy to besiege it. These forts, throughout India, are very like old British fortifications before the general use of artillery, consisting of a strong rampart of earth or stone, with a parapet, towers, and flanked gates, through all which, numerous loop-holes enable the besieged to hurl their weapons, or fire their small arms at the approaching enemy.

M. Bussy invested it with a battalion of French infantry, 550 strong, 250 cavalry, four field pieces, and the whole of Viseram's irregulars. The artillery soon destroyed the battlements, and the force assailed it by escalade in four divisions, but every man who attempted to mount the parapet was cut down. This repulse only inflamed the ardour of the soldiers; and the artillery having made a breach in the wall, the storm was renewed, but after fighting with perseverance for several hours, not a man could enter the breach. Great numbers of Rangaru's soldiers had now fallen about him, and while the French were forming their shattered column for a fresh attack, he addressed his officers and the remnant of the garrison. "Noble souls," said he, "no hope remains. You know your duty. Preserve our wives and children from the violation of Europeans, and the still more ignominious authority of Viseram Rauze." Upon which the oldest man was despatched to tell the females their fate, and to set fire to the sepulchral habitation, in the form of a funeral pile, in which they were with their children ready for the event. This temporary building, composed of straw, brimstone, and other combustible matters, was erected in the centre of the square, and a match being applied to it, the whole was instantly in a blaze. In the meantime, quarter had been offered to Rangaru and his brave companions by the French, who admired such courage, but it was rejected with disdain; and after a most horrible struggle, in which M. Bussy lost a great number of men, the fort was entered, every one of its defenders opposing himself to an antagonist, while he was able to wield his poniard. Four only escaped with ghastly wounds; and a few days after two of these crept into the tent of Viseram Rauze, and despatched him with thirty-two wounds. Had they failed, the other two were bound by an oath to revenge their master. Surely such conduct was equal to that of the Roman, who thrust his hand into the fire for missing the life of

Porsenna; and although I am far from holding up such barbarous acts as worthy of imitation, yet men who can behave thus, would, if civilised, possess all the generous traits that belong to chivalry. Nor are the women less determined than the men in devoting their lives, when called upon by what they conceive to be duty or affection. Thousands annually consume themselves with their husbands' bodies, in the hope of inheriting future bliss. Amiable credulity! Nay, they have often voluntarily died with brothers and fathers whom they tenderly loved.

We besieged Adjighur, a strong fort in Bundlecund, in 1809. After a very brave resistance it was evacuated by the garrison. Lutchman Dowah, the chief, was unable to protect his wives, who remained in the place, and it was necessary to remove them. For this purpose, an old man, the father of one of the ladies, was sent to prepare them with assurances of the most delicate treatment, but he was implored to end their existence, as they had heard that Lutchman was slain. Accordingly the old man cut all their throats, and his own immediately after, for they were all found lifeless when the house was entered. *

The bravery of the Honourable Company's sepoys might also be adduced as a proof of Hindoo courage. During the siege of Cudalore,

* I relate this on both written and oral authority.

in a desperate sally made by the French, our sepoys foiled some of their veteran troops with the bayonet.

It is therefore not for want of animal courage, and a proper love of king and country, that the Hindoos have been for ages subject to foreigners. This must be attributed to their institution of castes, which weakened the whole national fabric by infinite division and individual interest. Instead of depending upon the physical strength of the state, which is always found in the peasantry, kept in activity of body and mind by necessary toil, this hardy race was commanded never to aim at glory, and by this radical defect their country sunk into dependence. Science is necessary to direct the multitude, and noblemen are requisite to command the population, but it is to the resources of the commonalty that every state must look for its security. The poet has then justly called a bold peasantry "their country's pride." In Hindostan, however, there is no such thing. The whole Brahmanical fabric is founded upon exclusion and slavery, therefore those over whom it exercises its influence must be unaspiring slaves. Yet horrible as this is, it is better than no religion. On its promises a poor tottering human being depends, through all the inconsistencies of his nature. In obedience to the dictates of Brahma, he lays down his head under the wheels of the great procession car, pierces his back with an iron hook, and hangs thus, whirled round by a high wheel, lies bleeding on thorns, and at last drowns himself in a sacred river to feed crocodiles; yet he hopes all this will procure for him salvation, when fleeting life shall have passed away; and in this world he abstains from the gratification of wicked desires, in compliance with the moral laws of his caste.

The Hindoo subahdar of Barwa, a town in Bundlecund, in 1790, was an accomplished scholar, and deeply versed in the sciences of Europe. At the age of sixty he was studying the Encyclopædia Britannica, in the English language, yet sometime after, feeling his end approaching, he repaired, according to the custom of his tribe, to Benares, and drowned himself in the Ganges.

Near Mangee, a town in Bahar, at the confluence of the Ganges and Goggrah, there is a banyan tree, consisting of about sixty stems, which occupy an area of more than half a mile in circumference. Under this huge shade a naked devotee sat in one posture twenty-five years, except during the four cold months, when, as a further punishment, in compliance with his vow, he sat up to his neck in the sacred river.

Yet the Brahmans who control the minds of the Hindoos, commit the most atrocious crimes before their eyes. At Amran, a town in Kattywar, held by Hirjee Khowas, there is a monument to perpetuate the memory of a Rajghur Brahman, who cut his own mother's head off, at the great gate of the fort, to prevent Hirjee Khowas from depriving him of some disputed property. The victim on these occasions glories in death, and consents to its infliction; and while the innocent cause of the catastrophe is doomed to damnation, by general opinion, the matricide is honoured by his caste, and feels no remorse. That this superstition should not have been long ago destroyed by the seeds of death within itself, seems to me most astonishing. The Hindoos are an intelligent, acute people, in the common concerns of life. Their natural intellectual faculties appear no way inferior to other men's. I have talked to many of them possessed of different degrees of information, from the peasant that turned the clod to the learned pundit who expounded the laws; and on any subject out of the sphere of their prejudices, I found them as much disciples of Descartes as myself: that is, they seemed to doubt whatever struck their senses as requiring proof, and took nothing on the bare assertion of others, without the concurrence of their understandings; yet whenever I touched upon their particular creed, all was wildness and a chaos, which not one I ever met could reduce to any thing more than imaginary comprehension. The learned Brahmans can speak on the subject with uncommon beauty. Some of them have acquired a considerable knowledge of our language, and to hear them explain the charming morality of their sacred code, the sublime duties enjoined, and the axioms and maxims by which they allege that their lives are governed, would almost persuade Agrippa to believe Paul. Yet the wildness of every system which the Vedas and Sastras prescribe, is such, that any well-informed European would suppose the absurdity obvious; and I generally examined the face to see whether the heart was in tune with the tongue, but except in the professed sceptical classes, I believe all the Hindoos have perfect faith in the Brahmanical doctrines.

Their wild notions with respect to chronology and mythology have been long themes for wonder and speculation. The same runs through all the arts and sciences cultivated among them. Every thing obscure is rendered incomprehensible, and when involved in perplexity it is left as the utmost length which human intellect can go. These circumstances of the mind have of course kept its faculties within the same small circle for ages, which would have been the case in Europe, but for those great luminaries who formed tangents from the sphere of received opinion. But in India, the poet, mathematician, astronomer, and musician, are all bound in chains by sacred rules that no man can understand; and which, therefore, are pronounced divine, as if the Almighty would instruct mankind by lessons above his comprehension. In music, they were restricted to 36 sacred melodies, and the hours by night and day for their performance laid down. Their ancient instrument, called Dwitantri, had only two strings, which, tuned in fifths, produced the heptachord. Like ourselves they had seven notes, *sa, ri, gu, ma, pa, dha, ni.* They have our major and minor modes, but here simplicity ends, for their scale is divided into three parts. First, from the navel to the chest; second, from the chest to the throat; and third, from the throat to the brain.* Besides the 36 sacred pieces, in many of which only two wild notes are used, they have 48 lighter melodies for dancing, which were invented by one of their gods after morality had become corrupted. In this state music now stands, the popular airs in India being generally Persian. Poetry has greater intricacy. It is divided into 21 classes. In the first of six syllables, 64 combinations are composed on the syllables of each verse; 4096 on those of the half stanza; and 16,777,216 on the 24 syllables which constitute the complete stanza. These classes all rise progressively in difficulty, so that in the last 67,108,864 combinations are composed on 26 syllables, within each verse; nearly 4,503,621, 000,000,000 on 52 syllables, and more than 20,282,388,000,000,000,000,000,000,000,000 on a hundred and four syllables which form the stanza.

The Brahmanical fabric is altogether so extraordinary, than when I reflect upon its ceremonies,

* Vide Asiatic Researches, vol. ix.

festivals, processions, and images, I can only account for the principles upon which it keeps possession of the minds of rational creatures by referring it to the old maxim, "Custom is second nature." What we behold daily we cease to think strange. This has produced such harmony between the Hindoos and Mohammedans in India, that the latter have ceased to persecute the former, and, indeed, many of them have now adopted the modes which they behold from infancy, instead of those brought from beyond the Indus by their forefathers. The aborigines, in the vicinity of British and Mogul stations, have lost their purity as ancient Hindoos, and embraced many foreign opinions and habits. Indeed, nothing but familiarity could reconcile men to the monstrous objects that are every where worshipped in India. In one place is seen a huge form resembling a human creature, but with three glaring eyes and sixteen hands; in another, the heads of elephants and hogs fixed to the trunks of men. Here, indecent figures quite naked, resembling Priapus; there, monkeys and many-headed horses. In one sacred temple, a great fish with a man projecting from its mouth; in another, disgusting shapes of men with numerous hands all armed with weapons, and many faces besmeared with oil and paint. But for the innumerable hideous forms held in veneration by 100,000,000 of men, I refer the reader to Moor's Hindoo Pantheon. Many of the stories attached to those monsters are equally disgusting, and, one would suppose, more calculated to excite hatred and horror, than respect and love, yet such is the amazing delusion under which a rational creature may labour that idols are actually adored as living gods by men in a state of such mental refinement, that many of them cannot only argue most acutely against those parts of our holy scriptures which have produced great difference of opinion among Christians, but arraign others upon which our sects have never yet disagreed. I might here repeat several ingenious objections which Hindoos, with whom I conversed, made to Christianity, but to show their refinement of thinking I refer to Baldæus, a Dutch clergyman, who wrote on India from personal observation in 1671. "A certain Indian," says he, "asked me once, whether, when John baptised Christ, he did so in the name of the Father, Son, and Holy Ghost. I answered yes. He replied that Jesus was thus baptised in his own name, which he thought an absurdity. I told him there was nothing absurd in the matter, since Christ was not baptised upon his own account, or as God alone, nor as a bare man, but as being endowed both with the divine and human nature. That the Son of God could not be baptised otherwise than in the name of God; and that under the word God, were comprehended the Father, the Son, and the Holy Ghost; that Jesus was the same in essence with the Father and the

Holy Ghost; and that there were no degrees in the Deity, for though the Father was the first, yet the Son was as truly God as the Father and Holy Ghost: wherewith he was well satisfied. For the Indians being generally very ingenious, they ask many acute questions concerning the creation and end of the world, the immortality of the soul, hell, and such like." Yet the incredible things they believe concerning their own deities, without ever doubting their truth, might be supposed to render them pervious to the creeds of other nations. I shall instance this by reference to interesting known facts.

The followers of Gunputty believe that he is now incarnate in the person of Chintamun Deo, who resides at Chinchore, near Poonah. It is also credited, that at the death of eight Deos, who have preceded the present one, an image of the god miraculously arose from the ashes. To this image, or to the large statue of Gunputty, the incarnation performs pooja, or worship, for the Brahmans say that the image is the greatest, his power not being affected by the avater, or flesh. They also think that Deo is so full of the divinity, that his senses are absorbed, and therefore he acts the fool all his life; that is, he appears to possess only sufficient sense to ask and answer in a childish manner. But he eats, drinks, and marries several wives, like other Brahmans. The former Deos are buried in small temples near the river Moota, which passes the palace in which the present one resides, with flights of steps down to the sacred water, for daily ablutions and ceremonies. Women and priests may be here seen constantly bathing and perfuming the idols, while children are decking them with flowers, and pilgrims and devotees making their rich offerings; priests chaunting sacred pieces, musicians and bards, dancing girls and jugglers, necromancers and buffoons, all striving by gesture and action to increase the revenues of the Deo, who sits cross-legged in listless indolence and apathy. It is also amazing how they venerate a statue of stone or wood, into which it is believed a certain god has been incanted. Long pilgrimages are made to some of these images, which were stolen from particular temples, or whose place of residence was changed as they suppose by a miracle, on account of some insult or neglect.

At Weerawow, in the district of Parkur, a sandy tract to the south of Cutch-Booge, there is an image of Goreecha, or Goreeka, so ancient that it is believed to have once occupied a Banyan temple in the renowned city of Gour, one of the great capitals of India in remote times. This idol is of marble, two feet high, sitting with his legs across. It was for a long time, after the decline of Gour, in Pareenaghur, another ancient town, which was destroyed during the invasion of the Moguls, but Goreecha, or Goreeka, fell into the hands of a Rajpoot chief, from whom he was stolen, or escaped by a miracle to Weerawow. Seventy thousand Banyans annually visit him at Morwarra, where the ceremony is performed of producing him with great mystery, as described in the first volume of the Transactions of the Literary Society of Bombay, by Captain M'Murdo, who says that the rajah occasionally mortgages the income he produces for 18,750*l*. Besides this large sum levied at Morwarra, all the adjacent towns and chiefs extort contributions from the caravans of pilgrims, who also suffer great hardships in the desert regions around this remote spot, and numbers of them perish every year in the same way as at Juggernaut. At Daccour, in Guzerat, is the original idol of the famous temple of Dwarka. It came thither no one pretends to know how, about 600 years ago, since which time that place has been held in esteem.

Dwarka * was the residence of an incarnation of Chrishna, under the name of Runchor, and at it there is one of the most celebrated pagodas in India, but the Brahmans have been thrown into dejection by the escape of their god twice; for after great trouble, when he fled to Daccour, they incanted his essence into another statue, which crossed over about 130 years ago to the island of Bate, and they suppose that if their present one should take offence, an end would be put to his worship at the Goomty's sacred waters. To this wild and re-

* Vide Addenda, L.

mote corner of Guzerat, about 20,000 Hindoo sectaries repair annually, for purposes of devotion; and at this beautiful temple, and two others on the island of Bate, separated only by a narrow arm of the sea, a revenue of 30,000*l.* per annum is produced by voluntary offerings. The chief of Bate, who is high priest of his own temple, receives the dresses and sweetmeats presented to the god, and retails them out again to the devotees at low prices, so that imposition is there practised openly, and yet the delusion is so strong, that all appears divine. At Aramra, situated a few miles from Dwarka, Vishnu performed the exploit of cutting open the large conch shell in which the demon Shunkudwar concealed himself and the Vedas which he had stolen. He excused himself for the theft by saying that he hoped to have been put to death by Vishnu, which would have secured him future happiness.

In short, statues of wood and stone are absolutely believed to be real gods, and worshipped accordingly. Their table is laid every day, and their beds made at night. They are bathed and perfumed with most scrupulous regularity. At the great pagodas of Ramisseram *, Seringham, Conjeveram, Chillambaram, and Tripetty, in the south of India, though nearly two thousand miles from the source of the Ganges, the idols are bathed every day with water carried by pilgrims from Gangoutra, or the sacred junctions. This is sold again to the devotees, and

* Vide Addenda, LI.

produces a revenue. In many of their magnificent temples, Europeans are permitted to approach near the idols, taking off their shoes; the Brahmans encourage curiosity. But in some places the images are shown with great mystery, and they are often kept in dark recesses, far from the entrance, so that the gloom and magnificence, the wild sounds of shrill instruments of music, and the roar of great drums and conch shells, with the disfigured faces of the worshippers, and the abstracted appearance of the Brahmans really bewilder the senses.

Tripetty, in the Carnatic, is so sacred, that it is said no European or Mohammedan ever saw its interior. An incarnation of Vishnu is worshipped here. The natives say that the pagodas are built of great carved stones, like those which excite our wonder at Chillambaram, Dwarka, &c., and covered with plates of gilt copper so curiously ornamented with figures, that they are pronounced the works of superior beings. At the famous pagoda of Mallacargee and Brahma Rumbo, situated on the south bank of the Krishna, in a desert, 113 miles from Hyderabad, the idols are only shewn by the flashes of a brass speculum, that fall upon them so as to leave imagination to form a sublime picture, from a faint outline of something which cannot be described. These temples are enclosed by a great wall, forming a square, 600 feet long by 510, and covered with curious sculptures. But to enter into the description of such fabrics in India, would fill volumes. They are nearly all in the Egyptian style of architecture, and so massy that they have endured amidst the wrecks of matter around them, from times of which there is now no trace. By what powers of mechanism they were constructed, is a curious enquiry for the antiquarian.

At this day the only method the natives have of raising great bodies to any desired elevation is by forming an inclined plane of earth, as their building proceeds, which answers the purpose of our scaffoldings and cranes. Up this mighty stones are moved by the application of manual labour, aided merely by the powers of the lever. In many places the domes which ornament the mosques and the pagodas in northern India, where the Hindoo architecture is now of a mixed kind, between the Egyptian and Grecian, are formed on a mound or ball of baked clay, after which the earth is removed and the inside polished, Simple as those methods are, all the fabrics in India might have been constructed in this way, and the caves excavated by the repeated applications of the chisel alone. Sculpture never attained very high perfection in Hindostan. The execution of the rarest specimens is not to be compared to our school, though some of the airy statues of females in the caves of Elora and Elephanta are exquisite as to the finest proportions of form; but in painting and sculpture a good outline is the first advancement towards perfection which a scholar makes. To cause the canvas or marble to glow with living expression, to teach passion how to speak in stone, and to produce by light and shade an alto relievo on a flat surface, with an imitation of grief, joy, hope, anguish, despair, so natural as to impose upon judgment, are points which nothing I ever saw in my extensive travels in India supports. The black marble bull in the beautiful pagoda of Tanjore is perhaps a specimen of the highest degree to which the art of sculpture was carried. In ancient times Tanjore was the Benares of the south, and it still retains that character, many of the Brahmans being literary men. The rajah of Tanjore is a learned, ingenious, and liberal minded man, having been educated by the Danish missionaries, and carefully instructed in European learning, yet he continues firmly attached to the Brahmanical faith. The whole of Tanjore is like a garden, and a perfect contrast to many other parts of the coast similar as to soil and local advantages. Fine canals conduct the water of the Cavery, secured by prodigious mounds, across the whole country and irrigate every field.

Indeed the whole southern quarter of India bears traces of having been once cultivated to a high degree; but two thousand years seem to have made scarcely any difference in the manners of its peasantry. In customs, food, houses, and clothing, the poor Hindoo is nearly the same now as his forefathers were then. There are, however, admirable forms of village government remaining among them, which are strong testimonies of ancient civilisation. Those of the same caste live in many places like a great family, having a community of rights, the oldest man being the chief magistrate of the association, with a committee under him to settle all litigated matters on principles of equity. Such is the beautiful simplicity of many communities at present in India, that far advanced as we undoubtedly are in arts and sciences, yet from Hindoo rural felicity our politicians might derive important information; and as they have encouraged a system of education improved on Indian suggestion, so, by adopting what is admirable in the remnant of Hindoo policy, they may still further advantage the interests of their country.

Many of the small villages in the Carnatic, &c., consist of a row of houses on each side of a wide street with a range of cocoa nut and plantain trees before the doors. Some of the larger villages have streets which cross at right angles, forming a fine square in the centre. Here the choultry, or house appointed for travellers, stands. If no river passes near, artificial reservoirs, faced with stone, preserve a plentiful supply of rain water. The dwelling-houses have in general an open viranda running along the whole front, and under the trees before the doors, the inhabitants both men and women occasionally sit, which has a cheerful effect. This description applies properly to the south of India, for in Hindostan Proper, where the hot winds prevail, the houses are constructed so as to exclude the air, and they appear externally of an unprepossessing form.

In the Carnatic, the washerman of the village will be seen in one place making his collection; the schoolmaster in another, teaching the children to write in the sand; the smith busy at his anvil; and the barber seated crosslegged under a tree, operating on the head, and addressing the hearing with that loquacious rattle for which his calling is famous all over the world; while the shrill tones of music are heard in a neighbouring pagoda mixed with the loud voice of the great drum. At the same time, perhaps, a party of jugglers will be playing off their tricks for the amusement of the idle, and fantastically dressed fakiers strutting about to extort money by the extravagance of their stories and gestures. The cutwal or magistrate will be found administering justice and promoting harmony, surrounded by his aged advisers, who with gravity and wisdom admonish the young to imitate the old, and place before their eyes a bright example in their own conduct. No female exclusion is here observed. The women, ornamented with trinkets, are seen nursing their little ones, or employed in their household affairs, while the young girls, whose black hair is generally braided up and ornamented with flowers, are drawing water from the wells.

The Brahmans, who control opinion, are, like the other three great original castes, subdivided into numerous sects and professions, and in the clerical order they have no supreme head. In every pagoda the high priest is an independent sovereign, supporting all his inferiors attached to the institution out of its revenues, and contracting with the civil power for military aid or forbearance. He is, in short, every thing that an abbot is, except in owing obedience to the Pope; for his submission to the colleges at Benares is merely matter of choice. His Brahmans are like monks, and the only chain of subjection, by which the various pagodas of each sect are combined, consists in the reverence paid to antiquity, and the pilgrimages and offerings to great idols at particular places. In this way a constant intercourse is kept up between the remote parts of India and Benares; and a correspondence, maintained for the general interests of the particular worship, carried on at every temple throughout Hindostan. But there is no doubt, in my mind, that at one time the whole Brahmanical institution was combined under a supreme head, whose great pagoda was perhaps at Palibothra on the sacred Ganges. The manner in which the Brahmans live is an interesting subject for meditation. Many of them, when ambition or hope courts them forward, are as active and enterprising as Jesuits; while others dose away their lives in listless indolence, apparently abstracted from all the concerns of this world. At Malabar Point, on the island of Bombay, there is a cleft in a rock of such sanctity, that it attracts pilgrims from all parts of India for regeneration by passing through it, which is a work of great difficulty. Near this was a celebrated ancient pagoda now in ruins. It was polluted, like the other temples and caves near Bombay, by the Portuguese: there is a modern one near its ruins, dedicated to Sacksimi, the goddess of plenty, which is held in great veneration. The aperture in the rock and this temple support a beautiful village of Brahmans built round a delightful tank. Under the shade of trees planted around this fine sheet of water, the Brahmans perform their religious ceremonies and bathe in the sacred pond, to which there are on all sides magnificent flights of stone steps. Many of these learned and religious men have lived here from childhood without having ever felt the desire of gratifying curiosity by a visit to Bombay. Such is the extraordinary nature of man, when stimulated, his activity knows no bounds, yet under relaxation he falls into the opposite extreme. Many of the Brahmans are exceedingly immoral; bands of dancing girls are attached to their pagodas for purposes of prostitution. They aim not at power, being devoted to pleasure. But, on the other hand, the activity and art with which they pursue their objects are well known. Cromwell did not usurp with more address than Bajee-row, the first of the ruling Peishwas of Poonah. Tallyrand did not change sides with more talent than Purneu, who preserved his influence with Tippo till the last, and after his death secured the friendship of the East India Company, and turned the reverses of his late master to the advantage of his present. In beholding the stupendous works which he projected for the embellishment of Mysore, and the improvement of agriculture, I clearly saw the genius that had executed those fabrics in old times, with perhaps as simple means, which are now attributed to the gods.

Between Ceylon and the continent is the famous bay of Condatchy, which contains a pearl fishery that yields government an average revenue of 40,000*l.* per annum. The pearls are of a beautiful whiteness, yet not so much esteemed by the natives of India as the yellow ones of Ormus. About every seven years the banks are fished, being laid off so as to come annually round. In this time the pearls are supposed to attain maturity; but it is believed, that if left much longer, they become so troublesome, from their size, to the fish, that they are thrown into the sea. Most of the divers are trained up from children on the island. The usual time they remain under water is two minutes, during which period the oysters are collected in a net tied round the neck, from which is a signal cord communicating with the boat, by which they are assisted in regaining the surface. Some of those unfortunate creatures perish in attempts at remaining long under water, which is an object of great emulation. Four minutes are occasionally spent under the fluid, and one man remained, in 1797, six minutes below. They are paid according to the number of oysters they catch; and such is their perseverance, that sixty-seven returns have been made by one diver in a fore-noon, with from 50 to 100 oysters in his net every time. Many lose their lives, and others are horribly lacerated occasionally, by ground sharks; but the divers are so superstitious that they still believe their conjurors and priests can save them, and government, as well as the farmers of the pearl fishery, pay several of that description of impostors for removing their fears. It is quite a lottery in what oyster a pearl may be found; for there are numerous blanks to a prize, and the latter is often so small as not to exceed the size of a mustard seed. The oysters are, therefore, often disposed of unopened to the highest bidder. When the pearls are found they are instantly drilled by men who are very expert in this way; and sometimes a valuable prize is got for a mere trifle.

It has been supposed, that at some remote period, the Carnatic and Coromandel formed a splendid seat of extensive empire over part of India, and the ruins of Travicarry perhaps now mark the site of government. Here several large streets can be traced, and the gateway of a gorgeous pagoda eight stories high. It is now, however, only remarkable for extensive petrifactions of trees into flint, or a kind of stone, nearly as beautiful as cornelian, and a very large tank which covers several acres. Many of the hill-forts, both below and above the ghauts, are places of great strength. All the principal ones are now occupied by British garrisons; but impregnable as they are by nature, they add but little to the real strength of the country; for, whatever force is sufficient to traverse the plains, may soon reduce the hills by starvation. Few traces of Mohammedan splendour meet the eye in the south of India; but in Hindostan Proper, and even in the Deccan, there are numerous edifices which, though now in ruins, lend romantic beauty to the scene.

In modern times the south of India was subject to the government of Visiapoor, now called Bejapoor, situated not far from the Krishna. Aurengzebe conquered it in 1689, at which time the native historians say it contained 984,000 inhabited houses. It is now greatly in ruins, and exhibits a spectacle of the Mogul fallen glory; for some of the mosques remaining are magnificent structures. The mausoleum of Ibrahim Adal Shah is about 400 feet long and 150 broad, covered with an immense dome, supported by square pillars, carried to a great height. Some of the other domes are 120 feet in diameter. The fort was eight miles in circumference, built of massy stone; and the ruins all round this extend to such a distance, that it is like a mere point in the centre of a great circle. To immortalise the capture of this strong place, Aurengzebe caused an immense cannon to be cast. This great gun is still to be seen at Bejapoor. It is of brass, fourteen feet long, and nearly the same in circumference, and it would receive an iron ball of 2,646 pounds weight.

In the centre of the Deccan, to the extent of 420 miles by 220, lie the dominions of the Nizam, with a population of 8,000,000 of souls, not more than a million of whom are Moslems, although the government has been Mohammedan since A. D. 1585. When Aurengzebe completed the conquest of this region in 1687, he fixed the capital of the Deccan at Aurungabad, from which the royal residence was transferred to Hyderabad, by the late Nizam Ali, which has reduced the magnificence of that once splendid city, Aurungabad, to ruin. At the new capital, which is now a very considerable town, containing about 12,000 inhabitants and some fine mosques and palaces, the Mogul character appears in more variety than in any other part of India; for the court of Delhi is now a mere cipher. A numerous retinue of noblemen surround the throne, who spend their fortunes in ostentatious display, or profligate profusion. Their palaces glitter with costly articles of plate, while their lofty rooms are hung with the lustres of Europe. Many of them dress in English broad cloth, for the weather here is cold, though in 17°

north; yet its elevation is such that, for three months in the year, Fahrenheit's thermometer is often as low as 35°, and seldom ranges higher than 45°; but, immediately before the monsoon, the sun is exceedingly powerful. These luxurious nobles live in a free manner, and some of them cultivate the society of Europeans. They are educated generally for the military profession. Their complexions are fair, and sometimes ruddy. They are fond of showing their children to the English, and they are, when young, very pretty. Our ladies, who visited their wives, gave us almost as favourable a description of the charms of the females, and the decorations of their apartments, as Lady Mary Wortley Montague did of the Kahya's fair Fatima. Their dresses were of the finest gold Dacca muslin, flowing in rich profusion, exposing the fine swell of their bosoms, and the delicacy of their arms, while their ready smiles spoke good-humour and happiness. Under their gowns they wore silver muslin drawers, and their silk slippers were embroidered with gold. Their hair was decorated with pearls and flowers, and they exhibited a profusion of costly trinkets. Numerous maids richly attired waited their commands, and sweetmeats and perfumes were brought in, with delightfully cool sherbets and ices. They had musicians, dancers, and story-tellers to entertain them, and their little ones were brought in to be shown with exultation. When they pay visits, it is in great state; and their carriages glitter with costly ornaments of silver and gold. It does not appear that many men of rank have more than one favourite wife. When they avail themselves of the right of having a plurality, the ladies live in separate houses, and have distinct establishments. The Mohammedan nobles and gentry drink wine, and dine reclined on low couches; but when entertaining Europeans they sit at table, and have various courses of delicately dressed dishes, with a very splendid dessert. Dancing, recitation, and story-telling are their favourite amusements, while they loll on their low velvet sofas, and enjoy their hookas. The stories are generally of the extravagant description, told in the Arabian Nights; but their recitations are often beautiful pieces from the Persian and Hindoo poets. Many of the pictures in those fine tales are real copies from life of oriental customs and manners, which are common in India. During the flourishing state of the Mogul empire, the court of the Khalif al Rashid, in Bagdad, was scarcely so gorgeous as that of Delhi. The shadow of its shadow only remains at Hyderabad, but even still it is worthy of admiration. At the courts of many of the rajahs the ancient customs and manners of India are preserved; but all the public ceremonies have been often described.

Many of the Hindoo ladies of high rank enter into the schemes of government and the intrigues of state, with spirit and ability. They are not so much confined as the wives of Mohammedans; and it is supposed, on good grounds, that previous to the invasion of Mahmood of Ghizni, no such thing as the seclusion of females existed in Hindostan. Certainly at this day there is no more of it among some of the lower orders, than in Europe; but, agreeably to custom, women hide their faces from strangers with part of their garment. Many of those whom I saw seemed to me as intelligent, as domineering over their husbands, and as perfectly free in their habits, taking their local prejudices into account, as our females of the same rank. In the historical part of this work is described the unembarrassed manner of the queen of Sattara, and also, in the same, mention is made of two of Holkar's sisters, one of whom was beheaded by her chiefs, for interference with state affairs, and the other commanded a division of troops, when she surrendered to Sir W. Grant Keir. In short, we are not sufficiently acquainted yet with the rights of women in Hindostan. Material exceptions are to be made to any general description of female life in the East. The peculiar customs respecting women in Malabar have been noticed; and even among the Mohammedans, females have in some places extraordinary privileges. In the province of Jutwar, contiguous to Cutch, the Jut women can, when they choose, leave their husbands and marry other men. When this is determined upon, the wife collects all her acquaintances, breaks her husband's furniture, and persecutes him till he agrees to a separation. The females are held in such respect, that a traveller cannot have a better protector than a woman in passing through hordes of these robbers. In Afghanistan, ladies have also great influence over men. I have mentioned the consequence of a veil being sent to a chief there by a distressed female. Many instances of sincere attachment came to my knowledge among the middle orders in India, and it certainly is but fair to extend what exists in part to the whole. I consider the custom which enjoins a woman to die with her husband, as a recognition of love in the Brahmanical code, for, although it springs from selfishness to call upon a beloved object to perform a sacrifice repugnant to the feelings of nature, yet it proves that the introduction of it contemplated man as unhappy in death, without the objects that contributed to his felicity in life. The Mohammedans erect splendid monuments in memory of their wives, and the Tauje Mahal, near Agra, is one worthy of particular notice. This mausoleum was erected by the emperor Shah Jehan, to commemorate the celebrated and beautiful Noor Jehan Begum. It is about 190 yards square, in a superb enclosure of 300. A dome rises from the centre, which is seventy feet in diameter. At Noorabad, in the same province, there is another gorgeous monument situated in a fine garden, laid out by Aurengzebe to perpetuate the personal and mental accomplishments of Goona Begum, a princess celebrated for many pathetic pieces of poetry written in Hindostannee. Her shrine bears this simple but affectionate tribute in Persian; "Alas! Alas! Goona Begum."

The province of Aurungabad, in which a great part of the Nizam's territory lies, contains many curious ruins in its former capitals, Dowlutabad, Aurungabad, and Ahmednuggur. * Dowlutabad was taken about the year 1293, by Allah-ud-Deen, and reduced to permanent subjection by Mallik Naib, the emperor of Delhi's general, in 1306. It became in the 14th century such a favourite with the emperor Mohammed, that he injured Delhi by his endeavours to establish his capital in this central situation. But it is now a heap of ruins, and all the glories of the Moguls in the west of India, are absorbed by Bombay, the British capital in this quarter, of which particular mention has been made.

Surat, which for a long time continued the principal station of the East India Company's government, is still a very populous city, containing full 200,000 souls. It is situated on the south side of the Tuptee river, about twenty miles from its junction with the sea. This city is one of the most ancient in India, and, it is said, still bears the same

* Vide Addenda, LII.

name it did, when the Ramayuna, a Hindoo poem of great antiquity, was written. It was called by the Mohammedans of India, "The gate of Mecca," because the pilgrims embarked here for Arabia. At this place the Parsees established themselves at an early period. They are mentioned by Abul Fazel as very numerous in his time. At present their number amounts to about 15,000. In 1807 a census was taken, and there were 1200 of the mobid or sacerdotal class, and 12,000 of the behdeen or laity. Surat is 177 miles from Bombay, 243 from Poonah, and 1238 from Calcutta, *viâ* Nagpoor, lat. 21° 13′ N., long. 73° 3′ E.

In passing through the Deccan, a traveller is struck with the different appearance of the Hindoos. When in the Carnatic he was accustomed to tall graceful figures, with narrow chests and slender bodies. As he proceeds through the Deccan and Hindostan Proper, he observes these general characteristics no more. The countenance assumes a brighter tint, the limbs are strong, the shoulders broad, and the stature that of the middle size in England, with frequently those fine, manly, tall fellows whom we so often see in Europe. The Rajpoots are a race of as fine-looking athletic men as could be produced in the world, while the mountaineers and many of the Mahrattas seldom exceed the height of five feet three inches. In the higher classes of life the complexion is often that of Spain and Portugal. Their clothing is of cotton and silk, stuffed and quilted ; with warm Cashmere shawls. The peasantry wear a coarse kind of woollen, like camlet, which is perfectly water proof, and made so as to cover the head and body. The shepherds who tend the flocks, from whose wool this stuff is manufactured, live with their families, in many parts of India, in the deserts, having moveable houses for their wives and children, like large baskets or beehives, and when exposed to the weather, the men are perfectly secured by their dress as if inside a tent.

The whole of Hindostan Proper is sacred ground. All the rivers are dedicated either to gods or goddesses, and every mountain, city, and village have been the scenes of exploits, which form the Hindoo mythological romances; but the great temples were nearly all destroyed or mutilated by Mohammedan fury. Yet such was the persevering spirit of the Indians, that they impressed many of the Moguls with a belief of their absurd opinions. Abul Fazel, who wrote a most able description of the empire of Acber in 1582, assures us that the river Sopra, near the ancient and sacred city of Oojain, sometimes flowed with milk, at which he expressed astonishment, but no doubt. In another place he gives an account of the pilgrimages made by the natives to Nagercote, a city on a mountain in the province of Lahore, where devotees imagine they obtain their wishes by cutting out their tongues. " It is most wonderful," says he, " that they grow again in the course of two or three days, and sometimes in a few hours. Physicians believe that when the tongue is cut, it will grow again; but nothing, except a miracle, can effect it so speedily as is here mentioned." The royal master of this fine writer was, however, an enthusiast himself, and of a most superstitious turn of mind; no doubt his minister was of the same bent when he credited such absurdities. Acber, it is said, made a pilgrimage on foot of 230 miles, to worship at the tomb of Khaja Moyen-ud-Deen, for the purpose of obtaining male issue; after which he had three sons; and of course this passed as another miracle, performed by the greatest Mohammedan saint ever known in India, the contributions at whose tomb still support 1100 peerzadas, or attendant priests. Here are the remains of a magnificent palace, built by Shah Jehan, in a fine garden, and near it is the celebrated lake of Pooshkur, where there are numerous Hindoo temples round its romantic shore. The ruins of one, destroyed by Aurengzebe, denote it to have been of amazing magnificence. The statue of Brahma is here, with four heads, the size of a man. Pilgrimages are made to this temple from all parts of India. But it would fill a volume to notice only a few of the curiosities in this holy land, where there are yet fine roads for several hundred miles, shaded with fruit trees. Every thing bears the traces of the country having been once cultivated like a garden, and civilised to the highest degree.

The ruins of Kanoge are situated in the province of Agra, on the west bank of the Ganges, which city is supposed once to have been the capital of a vast empire. Its mouldering remains cover an area equal to all London, but no temples of consequence remain, though the plain is covered with broken idols and remnants of Hindoo worship. Two mosques are now the only fabrics of consequence. This city was plundered and destroyed in the invasion of Mahmood of Ghizni, in the year 1018. Ferishta mentions some of its rajahs, several years before, and describes it as a city of wonderful splendour. Here the most general language in India is said to have had its origin, and it is but reasonable to suppose, that the empire which circulated this tongue so diffusely over the continent, under the name of Hindostannee, must have been very extensive. Gour, which was the great capital of Bengal, in ancient times gave rise to Bengalee, which is only current in that province. Its ruins extend fifteen miles by three or four in breadth, along the old banks of the Ganges, in Rajemal, near the town of Maulda. Many of its materials have been carried away to build palaces and mosques in Moorshedabad; only a great mosque, lined with black marble, and of exquisite workmanship, and two lofty gates of the citadel, remain in a state of preservation.

The still more ancient cities, which produced the derivations from the Sanscrit, in which the sacred records of the Brahmans, Jains, and Budhists are written, have passed away and left not a trace behind, to reconcile the wide differences of opinion of learned orientalists on the subject.

Many ingenious Europeans, in travelling over India, and beholding such marks of remote antiquity and civilisation, which seem on a superficial view to warrant the Brahmanical chronology, have been staggered in their belief of scriptural history; I have heard several officers, whose understandings were otherwise sound and acute, talk lightly of our sacred volume, merely from the mental conviction which they felt, that the time allotted for such advancement in arts, science, and civilisation, was too short for the march evidently made, till the period when we have authentic accounts of this part of Asia. I gave the subject, of course, most attentive consideration, and I am convinced that no argument can be founded upon ruins, or their non-existence; for in one hundred years, decay of buildings is so rapid in India, that cities melt away almost like snow, having been at all times built of perishable materials. The immense size of towns, whose ruins we yet behold, is also no good foundation to build any hypothesis upon: for we have observed, in modern times, with what rapidity, prodigious masses of men have been congregated to any point which became the seat of empire. Kanoge only swelled the population of Delhi, and Gour, of Moorshedabad, while perhaps Palibothra sunk as Kanoge rose; for we see the common course which events take in the East, exemplified in Calcutta, Madras, and Bombay. Nor was the advancement of the Hindoos in art, science, and civilisation ever such, as to establish a very high scale for them in the antiquity of the world. In rural economy, I admit, they seem to have excelled nearly all nations. It is true, the Hindoos in very remote times constructed amazing pyramidal pagodas of huge stones, excavated mountains, and cut down rocks by repeated strokes of the chisel to resemble the forms of men and beasts; but the sculpture does not entitle the artists to rank with ancient Greece, and it is evident that when the Vedas and Purannas were written, science was in its infancy. I must, however, draw myself away from this subject; but I beg to refer any sceptical reader to Sir William Jones's Essay in confirmation of the Mosaic records.

The ancient grandeur of India merged, in modern times, in Delhi, which was once the largest and most populous city in the world, having been the capital of the Patan, and still that of the Mogul empires. When in its most flourishing state, it is said to have contained 2,000,000 of souls, and its ruins at this day extend over a space of twenty square miles. Modern Delhi, built in

1631, by the emperor Shah Jehan, is situated on the western bank of the Jumna, 976 miles from Calcutta. It is seven miles in circumference, and has seven fine gates of free-stone. An account of the mouldering palaces, colleges, canals, and extensive gardens here, would fill volumes. Many of the mosques are still preserved in fine order, particularly the Jama Musjid, or great cathedral, which was built in six years, and must have cost an enormous sum. The royal palace is about a mile in circumference, and the gardens of Shalimar are said to have cost 1,000,000 sterling. Sensibility, in wandering over their ruins, sinks into melancholy. All their walks and arbours are now desolate, which were once full of life, beauty, and hope. Three thousand pavilions, mosques, and sepulchres, lie around in mouldering heaps. All these vast dilapidations of human splendour may be seen at once, from the top of the Cuttub minar, a celebrated pillar nine miles from Delhi. It is 242 feet high, and consists of a base of 27 sides, fluted into semicircular and angular divisions. The great shaft has four balconies, at stages up its altitude, which are gained by means of a spiral staircase, and a majestic cupola of red granite crowns the whole. It was built A.D. 1205, by Cuttub Shah, whose tomb is near it, and it has, therefore, stood 618 years. This minar is said to have been intended for a great mosque, which was begun, but not finished. About 50 miles N. E.

of Delhi, on the old banks of the Ganges, are the famous ruins of a once celebrated city called Hastinanagara which was held sacred by the Hindoos. The natives say it was entirely destroyed by white ants, and this, I suppose, has arisen from the prodigious ant-hills near it, which rise up all round in conical pyramids to a great height.

The Patans and Moguls have left behind them vast monuments of their power in India. I was at first surprised, in travelling over the country, to observe very few bridges; and those I saw in the Carnatic and Mysore were only composed of prodigious square stone pillars placed on their ends in the river, and covered with similar stones. But I soon discovered, that the great rivers of India are so liable to overflow their banks during the monsoon, that bridges over some of them could not be constructed, that would withstand the impetuosity of the rush of waters. That wonderful bridges were made in ancient times, we have evidence by the ruins of the magnificent bridge 300 yards in length, at Sivana Samudra. Rammas bridge, which is said to have united Ceylon to the continent, I do not mention, because I believe it to be, like the Giant's Causeway, a natural production. At Jionpore, in the province of Allahabad, there is a bridge of ten arches, over the Goomty river, which has stood since the reign of Acber, although our troops have, I am most credibly informed, frequently sailed over it during the monsoon, and yet though submerged for many days at a time, it has suffered no damage from the current. This bridge is so complicated in its construction, that no native architect could build, or place one like it now. There is another in the province of Lucknow, over the Sye, of fifteen arches, which is a fine specimen of Moorish architecture. Near this capital is Constantia, the palace erected by General Martin, who rose from the ranks of the Company's service. Lucknow is a very populous city, contains several splendid fabrics, and here is the magnificently lighted sepulchre of Asoph-ud-Dowlah, whose eccentricities form an era in pageantry. The ruins of ancient Oude are in this province, which city is mentioned in the Ayeen Acbery to have been once 148 coss in length and 36 in breadth, which perhaps is a satire on native exaggeration, for a coss being at least 1½ English miles, this measurement would make it exceed all belief.

Benares, the most sacred city of the Hindoos, situated on the Ganges, about 460 miles from Calcutta, is the ancient seat of learning; and continues to be to all India what Rome was once to Europe. It contains about 600,000 inhabitants, and many of the houses are six stories high. Here nearly all the rajahs and great Hindoos of India have vakeels, who perform religious ceremonies for them. The greatest pagoda was pulled down by Aurengzebe, who, with its materials, built a prodigious and magnificent mosque, from the minars of which the city and its numerous temples, and grand flights of steps down to the river, may be seen with great advantage. About 8000 houses are occupied by Brahmans, who live on charity, though many of them are extremely rich.

To notice all the objects worthy of curiosity in this quarter of the East, would considerably exceed the limits assigned to these observations. Only two or three others shall be briefly mentioned before we close this book, which it is very earnestly hoped contains a great deal of interesting matter, with much information of a useful nature for young adventurers to India.

The capital of Bahar is Patna, seated on the south side of the Ganges. It contains about 150,000 inhabitants. In the British burying ground there is a monument to commemorate the murder of all the English here in 1763, two hundred in number, by the German adventurer Somro, who was in the service of Meer Cossim. Some writers suppose this to have been the site of Palibothra; while others give the preference to Allahabad, which is seated at the junction of the Ganges and Jumna. The fort of Allahabad is one of the strongest in India, and the place is so sacred that pilgrims repair hither to be drowned. Inside the fort there is a most extraordinary excavation, of vast magnitude, supported by pillars. The natives believe it extends under ground to Delhi, for the air is so impure, that no one has been able to examine it. Another of these remarkable caverns is situated near Gayah, in Bahar. It is a room with a vaulted roof, forty-four feet in length, eighteen in breadth, and ten in height, and dug out of solid rock, with an entrance six feet high, and two and a half wide. On the interior there are several inscriptions; and in the hills around are a great many other caves, all supposed to have been dedicated to the worship of Budha. From the pilgrims who resort thither, a greater revenue is derived by government, than from the pagoda of Juggernaut, the sum received here annually being about 16,000*l.*

Dacca is such a modern city, that it is not noticed in the Ayeen Acbery, though it now contains 150,000 inhabitants, and exports the finest muslins in the whole world. These beautiful specimens of Indian manufacture are produced by the assistance of wheels, reels, and looms, of the most simple form that can be conceived. Nothing but Hindoo patience could accomplish such wonderfully elegant productions with such means. Some of the women spin with the distaff, sitting on the edge of a hole, which they make in the ground, sufficiently deep for the length of the thread, and it is amazing how even and fine they form it, with their delicately small fingers.

CHAPTER II.

PREPARATION FOR INDIA, AND PASSAGE OUT.

THE descriptions of young men who proceed to India, may be classed under the denominations of Company's civil, military, and marine servants; king's officers, and private adventurers. It is necessary that they should all be well educated, grounded in pure principles of moral and religious duty, and accustomed, by regular scholastic discipline, to notions of obedience and subordination; but it is certainly of more importance for a youth to be well acquainted with European literature, than to devote a precious portion of time in studying oriental languages at home, when he is so soon to be in a situation where he can assist theory with practice.

In the above classification, all the young men who go out as writers, curates, assistant-surgeons, cadets, midshipmen in the Bombay marine, ensigns in king's regiments, or as master's mates in the Bengal pilot service, have a good prospect before them. Certain allowances await them on arrival in the country. A proper exercise of wisdom, on their part, is not to fix their expectations too high; for the sanguine disposition of youth is pregnant with great and very often fatal disappointment. It will also be judicious for them to treasure up this truth, that their prospects are in different degrees essentially good. It depends in a great measure upon their own good conduct, to command the smiles of health * and fortune. These two fundamental principles of thought will guard the mind against the encroaches of false hope and dangerous despair. It is proper for the other description of youth, I mean private adventurers, to bear in mind that, unless they go out to some commercial establishment as free traders in the Indian seas, or to be employed in some way by established European settlers, there is not on the face of the earth a worse theatre for action. The various offices under government are filled with native clerks, and there is scarcely an avenue open to a stranger. If he be a well-educated person, he can only look for employment as an assistant in some of the schools at the presidencies, or as an editor of a newspaper, or in some other chance capacity, for which he may long look in vain. If a tradesman he may find employment; but unless he has capital, the climate forbids his successful establishment, for all laborious occupations are performed by natives; and Europeans in India soon become so exhausted, as to be quite unfit for me-

* Vide Addenda, LVII.

chanical exertion. A permission from the court of directors of the East India Company, is necessary, for a private adventurer, which is generally given in the form of a free mariner's indentures. This, however, does not prevent the local authorities from ordering the stranger out of the country if he misbehave, to do which they have absolute power. But many Europeans have smuggled themselves into India; and if an adventurer be very correct and circumspect in his conduct, he will not find much difficulty in evading the local regulations on this subject. *

It is assumed, that all young men who adventure to India, embark for that distant region to better their condition, with the hope of returning to their native land for the purpose of enjoying that *otium cum dignitate* which ought to be the reward of an actively employed manhood. For this purpose, habits of economy and care should be early formed, and from the first conception of the idea of making India the sphere of exertion for independence, a regimen of both mind and body should be commenced, and undeviatingly pursued. To preserve health in India, strict temperance in all things is indispensably necessary; to acquire wealth, a fixed practice of living under income, whatever it may be. Youth most unfortunately often imagine that they are called upon, when mixing with society,

* Vide Appendix, note 16.

to imitate the highest in extravagance of expenditure. The generous principle from which this imagination of the heart flows, is honourable to man's nature, but discreditable to his judgment; for the increase of salaries is a reward for service, and as etiquette has established a scale for expence in proportion to rank, it is an absurdity for a junior to ape seniority. It is like the dwarf foolishly attempting the stature of the giant, and generally meets the fate of the frog in the fable, that burst by over-exertion to rival the ox in size.

In fitting out for India, we would strongly advise the young adventurer to take nothing with him but what may be absolutely necessary. In this small stock, we place a few very useful books of reference. But to carry out the stores of camp-equipage, the saddles, bridles, bales of broad cloth, and varieties which many young men do, is altogether mistaken profusion. In nine cases out of ten, the stock which a young gentleman takes out is injured by want of care, or is of a different description to that which he finds necessary on arrival in India. He also discovers that he could have equipped himself there at half the expence which he did in London, and his regret and chagrin are increased by the want of those means of which he was deprived by rash anticipation. The wisest plan is to embark with only what is necessary for the voyage; and with such scientific apparatus as may be useful in all situations, either for amusement or improvement, carrying out a bill on some house of agency; or a sum of money for equipment in India. The bill is the better mode of the two, for it serves as an introduction, and provides against probable loss, for the exchange on English money varies very much in India, and a system of fraud is practised on Johnny Newcome at each of the presidencies, which it requires no common prudence to repel.

The passage to India now seldom exceeds four months and a half, but it is a period to which great importance ought to be attached. An adventurer is fortunate, who meets with a gentlemanly experienced commander of the ship, for much depends upon his temper and manner, in keeping up proper ceremony and preserving that agreeable harmony which is so very easily disturbed by selfishness and imprudence, in the narrow sphere to which the passions and inclinations of society are confined on board a vessel, where there is no such thing as avoiding daily intercourse without the most intolerable imprisonment. Indeed the situation of a set of fiery impatient young men, cooped up within the sides of a wooden house, surrounded by the ocean for four months, is so critical that it requires every possible attention and care to prevent the many unhappy consequences which may arise out of accidents. When good temper and a general disposition to please prevail, the hours fly away swiftly, and there is so little to draw away attention while scudding before the trade or monsoon, which steady weather is experienced during the greatest part of an Indian voyage, that an improving course of reading may be pursued, and the mind invigorated while the imagination is amused.

There is a roving disposition, or propensity, in human nature, which leads young men to think little of the pain of separation from the delightful associations of boyhood till after departure. It is then that the unobserved tear trickles down that cheek which, perhaps, felt but a faint flush of emotion when bidding adieu to objects, the loss of whom affection had never been taught by experience to appreciate. Even during the voyage, the painful sensations of an exile, far from all he loves, are not so keenly felt as when he lands, and meets with none of those endearments which usually awaited him upon returning home from former excursions. The mind is very highly excited during a voyage to India, and imagination is kept on the alert by the most pleasing visions of expectation. It often happens that these delightful day-dreams are found to be just as unsubstantial vapours as their nocturnal sisters, and it therefore becomes an exercise of prudence in every young man, to prepare his understanding for a situation in which he will require the full exercise of his reason to combat those yearnings for a return to joys which he is apt to imagine are fled for ever.

But he may rest assured, that such feelings will not continue to destroy his peace of mind; and that he will soon form new associations and friendships; to part with which will, at some future period, occasion no inconsiderable wound to his dearest sympathies. Let each adventurer, therefore, think seriously upon these probable changes in his mind, and he will be able to endure them without that despair which has maddened several amiable young men into acts of suicide.

CHAPTER III.

CAUTIONS TO BE OBSERVED, ON ARRIVAL IN INDIA.

Upon landing at any of the presidencies, crowds of natives, who speak tolerable English, press upon strangers, and it requires no small share of prudence to guard against imposition. They approach with the most insinuating address, and produce characters which are calculated to remove suspicion. The necessity a stranger is under of placing himself in the power of some interested person, as well from want of information as for the supply of his absolute wants, ensures employment to great numbers of the most cunning description of men in India. Their objects are, to get charge of the luggage for the purpose of conveying it to some tavern, the proprietor of which rewards them for bringing him guests; to engage such servants as the stranger may require, all of whom pay for their places; to exchange English money and purchase the refit, which every one requires after a long voyage, by which they make considerable profit. To avoid the consequences of reposing confidence in such designing knaves, I would suggest that the stranger should leave his luggage on board the ship, and go on shore with any letters of introduction he may have, or for the purpose of reporting his arrival at one of the public offices, where he will receive information that may be serviceable. Such young men as do not belong to the civil or military service, will do well to be guided by the advice of the captain of the vessel; for I can assure them, that by placing themselves at the disposal of an agent, who will offer himself at the landing-place, they may, probably, be led into folly and inconvenience, which they will long remember with deep regret. In short, I consider caution on this head of such importance, that I have known the worst misfortunes of several adventurers originate in connections which they accidentally formed with natives, on arrival in India.

The next point, to which I would advert, is the caution that ought to be exercised in the choice of companions. In general, our youth contract in public schools, from mixing with ranks in life far above them in fortune, notions of extravagance and splendour, which are agreeable to the generous and liberal feelings of that animated period of existence. But if these propensities be not checked, they inevitably lead to the formation of habits, which completely destroy that prospect of independence for which a man is adventuring his life, and spending his time in an uncongenial climate, at a distance from all the associations of childhood. If the inconsistency of human nature was not proverbially known, it would surprise any man to behold young adventurers in India living in such a state of intemperance and luxury, as if the pursuit of pleasure and the expenditure of wealth and health, were the objects for which they had left the bracing regions of Europe, to sojourn in the burning plains of Hindostan. It is a lamentable fact, that the votaries of fashion every where stimulate each other to excess, by a constant struggle to make what is to follow surpass every thing that has gone before in magnificence; but, in no part of the world, is this truth more obvious to common observation, than in India, where a rage for display seems to be a species of epidemic, that attacks every stranger, if not resisted by sound judgment and strength of understanding. I, therefore, warn every young adventurer to reflect, at the threshold of his undertaking, upon the views which he and his friends have had, in making India the scene of his operations, and to act in consistency thereto, by avoiding companions who evidently proclaim the danger of their course by not following reason as their guide, which would lead them to practise the strictest rules of self-denial, as a sure and certain means of expediting the accomplishment of their fondest hopes.

Instead of that profusion and waste of time and money which characterise the youthful, civil, and military servants of government in India, the rational aim of every one should be on his first arrival to qualify himself for promotion, by acquiring local information on all subjects, and making himself master of some of the useful native languages. The faculties of the human mind are so active, that if intellect does not find them profitable employment, they will run into useless luxuriance of their own accord, in the same way that a rich garden yields a multitude of weeds, if not supplied with proper seed to receive the benefit of its generous fertility. Is it not most necessary, therefore, for every adventurer to recollect, that if he does not, on his arrival in India, lay the foundation, or sow the seeds of industry, patience, perseverance, and care in his mind, that indolence, restlessness, imbecility, and luxury will grow up in their stead, and propagate their pernicious offspring.

But whilst I earnestly press upon the young adventurer, the necessity of being reserved in his general intercourse with strangers, I by no means insinuate that he should not cultivate the society of worthy young men of his own age and profession. He should, on the contrary, endeavour to become the centre of a well-selected circle of friends. In the choice of them he should be guided by the qualities of the heart, in preference to those of the head. It is an amiable and philanthropic disposition, to aim at improving others while we endeavour to perfect ourselves; to receive information from those who can impart it, with the generous intention of bestowing it on others, whose opportunities may not have been equally fortunate. I strongly advise every youth to shun the contagion of vice and folly, but to look upon ignorance with charity; and, wherever the desire of improvement is manifested, to encourage the young shoot that may lead to excellence, with tender attention. It was finely said of the late amiable Dr. Hunter, who died at an early age in India,

> "Though vers'd from earliest years in classic lore,
> Though rich in later times with Asia's store,
> He never knew the vanity that flies
> Association with inferior ties;
> But still with sentiments to nature warm,
> Lov'd all that trifles in a human form."

Were young men not credulous and unsuspecting, they would not be such objects of the fears, hopes, and affections of their parents. We see in our children our own green years, and whilst memory recurs to the generous confidence, which we often reposed on the smiling aspect with self-exultation, she reminds us how frequently deceit and villany lurked beneath, like vipers under a beautiful rose, and we start with apprehension for the safety of our offspring when first exposed to the treachery of the world. It is happy for the young, that they know not the dangers which surround them; like many a tall ship, they push over quicksands and shoals, in ignorant security, the knowledge of which might produce hesitation pregnant with danger.

CHAPTER IV.

REMARKS ON SUBJECTS CONNECTED WITH RESIDENCE OR SERVICE IN INDIA.

The civil and military servants of the Honourable Company are not long in India before they become important members of society; for the civilians, as soon as they pass through the college exercises, are attached to some of the departments of government as assistants, where in time they advance to distinction; and military officers, upon joining their regiments, become guardians over the happiness of their inferiors, and, therefore, are responsible for the discharge of most useful duties. Magistrates in this country have not near so much influence over the population as civilians in India have among the lower orders of the natives. They may inflict great misery, or promote the comfort and enjoyment of all around them. By oppressive conduct, either through the malevolence of their own dispositions or by inattention to the native agents, who act under them, many of whom are rapacious and merciless, they injure their own reputation, and the dearest interests of their employers; but, by watching and promoting the welfare of the poor unprotected Hindoos, they both lay up a hoard of bliss for themselves, in reflection upon the past, and materially serve the cause of their country, whose pride and glory consist in the justice and benevolence of her sons. Both civil and military adventurers, therefore, have a wide and noble field before them in India, and it should elevate their souls to reflect on the power which they have of doing good.

In journeying over the extensive and interesting regions, which young adventurers see in a few years' service in the East, it is a most delightful thing to have the mind well stored with the historical occurrences which have rendered particular places remarkable. Nothing, I believe, expands the understanding more than reflections upon the past with a view to the benefit of the future. We are thus carried away entirely from the selfish present moment, and rest upon something that raises us in our own estimation, because it is superior to our proper cares. To the military student, India offers an ample school for instruction, as well as to the civilian. The former, while viewing the scenes of battles and manœuvres, will learn to avoid those errors which led to defeat and disaster, and to imitate the particulars which commanded victory and success; whilst the civil as well as the military servant will sigh over the spot where villany was achieved, and learn to despise actions which are stamped with infamy.

The prejudices of the natives of the country should every where be respected, and their manners and customs studied, that no unintentional insult may be offered, or injury inflicted upon their minds. It is as cruel as it is ungentlemanlike to scoff or ridicule strangers for things which make them respectable in their own eyes, and respected by their friends and associates. How would we feel under the sneer of haughty proud foreigners who laughed at us, because their vanity led them to make what was familiar to themselves a universal standard? If we cautiously inquire, we shall find a reason for almost every custom which has been introduced into human society; and although Europeans are at first inclined to look upon the manners and usages of the East as absurd, yet, in time, they behold that every thing is the natural effect of institutions. They soon discover that many of the Hindoo customs are well suited to the climate and nature of Asia, and learn to doubt their own judgment of others, the use of which they find beyond their comprehension. In this temper of mind, a civil or military servant of the Company in India will behave to all the natives in such a manner as to command their respect, confidence, and esteem. It ought to be impressed upon the understanding of every European in India, that his individual conduct may be productive of good or evil; for men are every where inclined to pronounce upon the whole from the examination of a part. How often is every country disgraced by the shameful behaviour of particular members of it.

A true Christian, while serving in India, will pity the delusion of the Hindoos, at the same time that he admires their faith and constancy. Instead of considering them sunk below the level of human respectability, he will set a proper value upon their creed, and clearly perceive that their religion, bad as it is, raises them above the atheist or scoffer at divine things. He will behold them with that universal charity * which his own sacred records breathe, and, whilst he avails himself of such opportunities as occur of diffusing the light of our Gospel amongst the Hindoos, he will carefully abstain from all interference with their religious ceremonies. No man of sound judgment and enlarged capacity can doubt that Christianity will, in time, overthrow the fabric of Brahma; but the influence of our Holy Scriptures in Hindostan will not be known till education has, like a pioneer, gone before and cleared away the filth of prejudice and superstition. This is at present rapidly going forward, and I am confident that God, in his own good time, will bring about the total conversion of the Hindoos, agreeably to his revelation. The arguments raised against this by a late respectable French missionary †, and also against the circulation of the Bible,

* Vide Addenda, LIII.

† Vide Appendix, note 17.

are contrary to the promises of Christianity. The Abbé Dubois may be perfectly right in saying that the time for converting the Hindoos has not yet arrived. For government to try experiments on this subject, would be most dangerous. If our government had aimed at the conversion of the Hindoos, there is no doubt that a very numerous Christian society would have been speedily formed amongst them; but it has not been our policy; and perhaps it is wise to leave the word of truth to its own influence. The efforts which are now making in India to educate the natives, are, perhaps the most effectual towards the interests of the Christian religion of any that have yet been made. But is my humble belief, that if the British missionaries were permitted to locate the converted Hindoos upon the waste lands in our provinces, either in conformity to ancient Hindoo civilisation, or to plans found practicable in Europe for bettering the condition of the poor, such a foundation for native Christian society would be laid, as could never again be shaken by the attractions of idolatry. Round such a nucleus the native population would gradually congregate, till civilisation * extended from the mouths of the Ganges to the Indus, and from the Himalaya mountains to Ceylon.

Young men go out to India, at that period of life, when the love of pleasure and self-gratification

* Vide Appendix, note 18.

supersedes considerations of remote interests: the future, for which life is risked in a dangerous climate, is sacrificed without reflection to the present. Such is the inconsistency of our nature. Hence it is, that so many amiable youths of most respectable families form connections, by marriage in India, which blight the fond hopes of their parents; whilst others become entangled by the voluptuous charms of some sable beauty, and, before they are aware, find themselves surrounded by a numerous offspring of half caste illegitimates, the difficulty of providing for whom embitters their future lives. Both these dangers ought to be avoided by a sound exercise of wisdom and restraint; but I certainly pity the youth less who marries and becomes the father of children of his own colour, of whom he need not be ashamed, than the unfortunate man who entails disgrace upon the natural objects of his affection, and who at length has to leave them in an inferior walk of life, when he returns to his native country. The Indian beauties, while young, possess fascinations of the most bewitching description, and often fix the affections of Europeans to such a degree, that every thing is sacrificed to them. But they soon grow old and ugly, and not being linked to the heart that fondled them by mental congeniality, they are forsaken very often for some young countrywoman, who adventures to the East in search of a husband. Such is the effect of familiarity in blunting sensibility, that I have known several of these cast mistresses and their children receive very kind attention from the ladies who supplanted them in affection; whilst, in other cases, I have discovered a deep source of unhappiness in the jealousy of the wife, who viewed every tender remembrance of her husband for his illegitimate children and their mother, as a declension of her hopes, and an insult offered to her superiority. Of all things I enjoin young adventurers to form early resolutions against connections with the half caste, Hindoo, or Mohammedan women, either by marriage, or in the common way, as not only involving their own happiness and future prospects in misery and disappointment, but entailing upon others anguish and ignominy, for which the gift of life is no recompence.

Marriage, being the most important change in life, deserves in every part of the world great circumspection previous to contracting it. The chances are numerous against happy marriages in India, where young people meet, whose modes of life have been very different. The gentleman is at first sight charmed with a pleasing exterior, and in the generosity of what he terms love, invests the object of desire with every thing which his imagination suggests as necessary to felicity. When it is too late, such a precipitate wooer finds very often that the disposition, temper, education, taste and inclination of his choice are totally different from his conceptions, and he is obliged to form himself upon a new model, or to forego all his fond pictures of conjugal bliss. Happy is the young adventurer, who carries with him to India some image of loveliness from the scenes of his boyhood, whose impression and recollection will attract him back again to form a union with sentiments and habits similar to his own. Upon this principle I would strongly urge young men to form resolutions against marriage in India, during their first term, or ten years of service; at the expiration of which, they should avail themselves of the privilege of returning home on leave, as well to renew their constitutional vigour, as to form a matrimonial plan of life. Allowing that a youth goes out to India at the age of eighteen, and returns home on three years' leave when twenty-eight, he will then be in the maturity of his judgment for fixing his own happiness in the choice of a wife; he will be established in his profession, in a fair way of providing for a family, and at that period of life, when he may reasonably expect to see his children settled before the scene of this world closes upon him for ever.

Upon returning to India, he should exert every energy he possesses to secure independence, or the power of retiring from the service when he pleases. For this noble purpose, from the commencement of his career something should be saved every month, and regularly transmitted to an agent, to be invested in government securities, as an accumulating fund. It is wonderful how a small nucleus increases, by a continual roll in this manner. In short, very few fortunes are ever made in any other way, and the young adventurer may depend that if he follows this plan, he will soon command means which will ensure success, and warm the frozen regions of the north, when he feels inclined to exchange foreign heat for native cold. No man should ever calculate on becoming independent by chance. Industry, integrity, and perseverance command fortune, and economy secures her favours as a refuge, when activity fails from the inevitable wear and tear of life. In every situation it is man's best policy to be true to his trust, and faithful to his employers, never, therefore, let the adventurer to India be false to himself, when in official situations, by robbing the public, or the government, but, nobly just, return to his mother earth, enriched with consciousness of his own worth.

CHAPTER V.

ON RETURNING FROM INDIA, AND IN CONCLUSION.

With respect to the period of retiring from the service, or returning home, much must depend upon health and inclination. Numbers destroy the happiness which they have in prospect, by remaining too long, whilst others, by departing before their independence is secured, lay up for themselves subjects of chagrin and regret. The point, where contentment should rest, is of such a moveable nature, that it requires firmness of judgment to fix it. A man's mind expands, like his horizon, as he advances, and, continually opening new desires and prospects, leads him often to place enjoyment within the precincts of imagination, instead of the sober confines of reality and experience. He ought at first to fix the object of his wishes, and when he has realised it, sit down with gratitude to the protecting power that enabled him to succeed.

I leave the choice of the period of retirement to taste alone. After twenty years' service in India, there are so many links to be broken in quitting it, so many valuable old friends to be left behind, so many familiar pleasures to be sacrificed, and habits to be reformed on the prospect of returning home, that he is not an object of envy who has to endure the struggle. If he have a family to transport with him, the heavy expenses attending their passage, if his fortune be confined, will consume a considerable part of his little fund; and if he has permitted his ideas of comfort in retirement to soar beyond the bounds of simple sufficiency, he will be miserably disappointed. The real wants of life may be supplied in this country by a very moderate fortune, and much solid happiness enjoyed in social retirement, but after the experience of luxuries in India, which habit has constituted necessaries of life, it requires a considerable exertion of sound sense to bear those deprivations which the old Indian has inevitably to endure.

The European mind falls into a warmth of liberal feeling in India, which leads a man to expect much from relations and friends upon returning to his native shore, but there is no train of thought more deceitful. It would be an ungrateful task to lay open the selfishness that exists in all family circles; but I warn adventurers to secure their own independence by industry and economy, and never to trust, upon coming home, to their nearest and dearest blood for what they cannot afford to themselves.

When a man has returned to his native land, let him not idly sigh for joys of which recollection reminds him, but let him sit down with gratitude to that God who has enabled him to realise his reasonable expectations, assured that he is formed to be happy in any situation, and that as much real enjoyment and comfort may be had under the free constitution of his own country, as in any other part of the world. He is, therefore, bound, where-ever he may settle, not to become a drone, but, like the busy bee, to contribute every thing in his power to the prosperity of the hive to which he belongs, the interest of his country, and the honour of his king. In short, to crown an active life by an useful old age, cheering the poor around him, in proportion to his means. Thus he will find his last reward, a grave amidst the tears and blessings of his neighbours.

I have at length come to the close of my proposed plan. With most anxious hope that the contents of this volume may be useful in their practical effects, I bid the reader farewell. I beg to assure the British public, that I have been desirous of promulgating only what should merit the good opinion of them and their posterity.

> "Live we a longer or a shorter date,
> If wise men praise us, or if blockheads hate?
> No — but the greetings of the good impart
> Peculiar pleasure to the feeling heart:
> Cheer the dull prospect of this earthly state,
> And reconcile us to imperious fate."

APPENDIX.

Note 1.

The temple of Juggernaut is situated in Orissa, on the bay of Bengal, about 300 miles south-west of Calcutta. By late accounts from India it appears that its celebrity is upon the decline, and that such vast multitudes do not now annually press towards it as formerly. The following particulars are abridged from the Rev. Dr. Buchanan's description, in his "Christian Researches."

Such numbers of pilgrims die on their way to this pagoda, that for fifty miles around the country is covered with human bones. Hundreds of old people travel annually thousands of miles to die there. Some of the pilgrims measure the whole way they have to travel with their bodies. The dogs, jackalls, and vultures, live in the vicinity on human prey, as the bodies are not buried, but left to be devoured. When the crowds of pilgrims first see Juggernaut, they raise a tremendous shout. Around the pagoda for several miles it is like a vast encampment. Sometimes great numbers are killed by the rush of the multitude when the great outer gate of the town is opened.

The idol Juggernaut, or the Moloch of the East,

is seated on a throne in the pagoda, between his brother and sister, Boloram and Shubudra. He is made of a large block of wood, having a frightfully large visage, painted black. His arms are of gold, and his apparel is gorgeous. The other two idols, equally hideous, are of a white and yellow colour. Both sexes look with moral turpitude upon the indecent figures, cut out of stone, that surround them on the walls and gates. These idols are paraded about on their cars or pagodas of artificial framework, seventy feet high, drawn along by men with cables, during the days of the grand annual festival, or Rutt Jattra, while the wheels are often red with the blood of devotees of both sexes, that throw themselves beneath, to be crushed to death. These devotees, with clotted hair, and painted bodies and faces, are seen every where practising their various tortures. It is supposed that there is constantly a multitude of 100,000 souls in and about Juggernaut, and the wild shouts from this huge mass are appalling when the idols are brought out of the pagoda, to be placed on the triumphal car. The multitude, having green palms in their hands, fall down and worship the idol: then the procession moves forward, preceded by elephants and dancing girls. Upwards of one hundred priests are performing the ceremonies in the different stories of the pagoda. The priests sing and shout; sometimes telling the people that the god is pleased; at others that he will not move, and that no force can draw the car, unless he smiles and gives the approving nod. Their action and gesture are altogether lascivious, and the shouts of approbation in proportion to their grossness, are yells of sensual delight. The idol is said to laugh with joy when the wheels of his car drink the blood of a devotee.

Juggernaut's annual expenses are:

His table - - - - -	£4,514
Wearing apparel - - - -	339
Servants' wages, dancing girls, &c. -	1,250
Contingencies - - - -	1,373
Elephants and horses - - -	378
Rutt, or annual state carriage - -	839
	£8,693

Note 2.

The military fanatics of India make it their glory to sacrifice themselves in what they esteem a just cause, and on such occasions not a man ever flinches from his ground. An instance of their self-devotion occurred at the battle of Argaum, 29th of November 1803, in which the present Duke of Wellington routed the army of the Berar rajah. It is told in the following spirited manner by Colonel Stewart, in his "Sketches of the Highlanders of Scotland."

"The army was drawn up in one line of fifteen battalions, the cavalry forming a reserve, or second line, the 78th being on the right, and next to them the 74th; and the 94th forming the left of the line. When this regiment (which was supported by the Mysore horse) reached and formed on their proper ground, the whole moved forward, the 78th directing its march against a battery of nine guns, which supported the enemy's left. As they approached, a body of 800 infantry rushed out from behind the battery, and, at full trot, made for the intervals between the 74th and 78th. Surprised at this daring advance, the regiment obliqued their march, to close the interval, and with ported arms moved forward in quick time to meet their assailants. But a muddy deep ditch (before unperceived) intervened, and prevented an actual shock with the bayonet. The enemy, however, stood by the ditch, with a resolution almost unparalleled in Eastern troops, firing till their last man fell. The following morning upwards of five hundred dead bodies were found lying on the ground where these men had been drawn up. They were a party of desperate fanatics, who fought from a religious principle."

Vol. ii. page 197.

Note 3.

Marriage takes place in India when the parties are infants, the contract being entered into by the parents. Upon which occasions an effort is made to display all possible consequence, and the savings of many years are expended freely in ostentation. The young bride and bridegroom are paraded about in carriages, palanquins, on horseback, or on bullocks; in proportion to the circumstances of the persons concerned, so is the magnificence or penury of the exhibition; and the extent to which this vanity is carried may be conceived by the reader, from the following abridged account of the marriage of young Vizier Ally, as given in Forbes's "Oriental Memoirs."

It took place at Lucknow in 1795. The nabob Asoph-ud-Dowlah, whose adopted son the bridegroom was, had his tents pitched on the plain near the city, two of which were lined with the finest English broad cloth, and cost 50,000*l*., being each 120 feet long, sixty broad, and the poles sixty feet high, with walls cut into lattice-work, for the sable beauties of the seraglio, and those of the nobility, to see through. His highness was covered with jewels, to the amount of at least two millions sterling. "From thence," says Forbes, "we removed to the Shumeeana, which was illuminated by 200 elegant girandoles from Europe, as many glass shades with wax candles, and several hundred flambeaux; the glare and reflection were dazzling and offensive to the sight. When seated under this extensive canopy, above a hundred dancing girls, richly dressed, went through their elegant, but rather lascivious dances and motions, and sang some soft airs of the country, chiefly Persic and Hindoo-Persic."

Thence they formed a procession to a beautiful garden, and the march was grand beyond conception. "It consisted of about 1200 elephants, richly caparisoned, drawn up in line, like a regiment of soldiers. About a hundred elephants in the centre had houdahs, covered with silver; in the midst of these appeared the Nabob, mounted on an uncommonly large elephant, within a houdah covered with gold richly set with precious stones. The elephant was caparisoned with cloth of gold. On his right hand was Mr. George Johnstone, the British resident at the court of Lucknow; on his left the young bridegroom: the English gentlemen and ladies, and the native nobility, were intermixed on the right and left. On both sides of the road, from the tent to the garden, were raised artificial scenery of bamboo-work, very high, representing bastions, arches, minarets, and towers, covered with lights in glass lamps, which made a grand display. On each side of the procession, in front of the line of elephants, were dancing girls, superbly dressed (on platforms, supported and carried by bearers), who danced as we went along. These platforms consisted of 100 on each side of the procession, all covered with gold and silver cloths, with two girls and two musicians at each platform.

"The ground from the tents to the garden,

forming the road on which we moved, was inlaid with fire-works; at every step of the elephants the earth burst before us, and threw up artificial stars in the heavens to emulate those created by the hand of Providence; besides innumerable rockets, and many hundred wooden shells that burst in the air, and shot forth a thousand fiery serpents; these, winding through the atmosphere, illuminated the sky, and aided by the light of the bamboo scenery, turned a dark night into a bright day. The procession moved on very slowly, to give time for the fire-works inlaid in the ground to go off. It was further lighted by above 3000 flambeaux, carried by men hired for the occasion. In this manner we moved on in stately pomp to the garden, which, though only a mile off, we took two hours to reach. When we arrived at the garden gate, we descended from the elephants, and entered the garden, illuminated by innumerable transparent paper lamps or lanterns of various colours, suspended to the branches of the trees. In the centre of the garden was a large edifice, to which we ascended, and were introduced into a grand saloon, adorned with girandoles and pendent lustres of English manufacture, lighted with wax candles. Here we had an elegant and sumptuous collation of European and Indian dishes, with wines, fruits, and sweetmeats; at the same time about a hundred dancing girls sung their sprightly airs, and performed their native dances.

"Vizier Ally was at this time thirteen years of age, and his bride ten; they were loaded with jewels, so that they could hardly bear their weight; and the wedding ceremony was repeated for three successive nights, to the no small gratification of Asoph-ud-Dowlah's vanity."

Note 4.

Had the Marquis Wellesley continued in India to complete his plans, it is supposed that the whole system of human sacrifices would have been suppressed. His humanity and intrepid spirit stopped the murders committed at Saugur Island, where, on an average, there were twenty-three persons destroyed every month. His lordship passed a decree in council, "declaring the practice to be murder, punishable by death." The law, entitled a Regulation for Preventing the Sacrifice of Children at Saugur, and other places, is dated the 20th of August, 1802. This was a noble imitation of the Mohammedan governors, who at one time saved whom they pleased, and suffered no deluded female or other person to commit suicide. But as the practice is sanctioned by public opinion, no positive law can entirely prevent it. We know the effect of our own enactments respecting duelling.

Note 5.

The first Protestant mission to Tanjore or to India, was founded by Bartholomew Ziegenbalg, of the university of Halle in Germany. In 1707 he built a Christian church at Tranquebar, in which he is buried. He translated the Bible into the Tamul tongue in fourteen years. Our pious king, George the First, patronised this learned missionary, and with his royal hand wrote a letter to him and John Ernet Grundlerus, at Tranquebar, dated 23d of August, 1717, in terms expressive of great goodness of heart, and zeal for the cause. In this letter, his Majesty says, that in his kingdom, "a laudable zeal for the promotion of the gospel prevails," and he assigns that as a reason for the great pleasure the success of the mission gave him, by which he shows not only the ardour of his own soul for the conversion of the heathen, but the desire he felt to please his people: and in another letter written to the members of the mission, ten years afterwards, he says, "In the mean time, we pray you may enjoy strength of body and mind, for the long continuance of your labours in this grand work, to the glory of God, and the promotion of Christianity among the heathens; that its perpetuity may not fail in generations to come."

The missionaries have been ever animated to exertion, as well by the inspiring influence of God as the heart-cheering eloquence of man. They have numerous letters from the most learned men in Europe, and the archbishop of Canterbury aided the wishes of his sovereign, George the First, with all his power: — among many paragraphs of his letter, written in latin, to the Protestant mission at that time, are these beautiful words.

"Let others be pontiffs, patriarchs, or popes; let them glitter in purple, in scarlet, or in gold; let them seek the admiration of the wandering multitude, and receive obeisance on the bended knee. Ye have acquired a better name than they, and a more sacred fame. And when that day shall arrive when the chief Shepherd shall give to every man according to his work, a greater reward shall be adjudged to you. Admitted into the glorious society of the prophets, évangelists, and apostles, ye with them, shall shine like the sun among the lesser stars in the kingdom of your father, for ever.

"O happy men! who, standing before the tribunal of Christ, shall exhibit so many nations converted to his faith by your preaching: happy men! to whom it shall be given to say before the assembly of the human race, 'Behold us, O Lord, and the children whom thou hast given us:' happy men! who, being justified by the Saviour, shall receive in that day the reward of your labours, and also shall hear that glorious encomium; 'Well done, good and faithful servants, enter ye into the joy of your Lord.'"

Dr. Buchanan speaks thus of the Tanjore Christians from personal observation. "After the sermon was ended, I returned with the missionaries into the vestry or library of the church. Here I was introduced to the elders and catechists of the congregation. Among others came Sattianden, the Hindoo preacher, one of whose sermons was published in England some years ago, by the society for promoting Christian knowledge. He is now advanced in years, and his black locks have grown grey. As I returned from the church, I saw the Christian families going back in crowds to the country, and the boys looking at their ollas or leaves upon which they took notes of the sermon. What a contrast, thought I, is this to the scene at Juggernaut! Here there is becoming dress, human affections, and rational discourse. I see here no skulls, no self-torture, no self-murder, no dogs and vultures tearing human flesh! Here the Christian virtues are found in exercise by the feeble-minded Hindoo, in a vigour and purity which will surprise those who have never known the native character but under the greatest disadvantages, as in Bengal. It certainly surprised myself; and when I reflected on the moral conduct, upright dealing, decent dress, and decorous manners of the native Christians of Tanjore, I found in my breast a new evidence of the peculiar excellence and benign influence of the Christian faith."

Note 6.

The Syrian Christians of Travancore inhabit the interior of it. When Vasco de Gama arrived at Cochin, in the year 1503, they had a Christian king. At this early period there were upwards of one hundred Christian churches. For 1300 years before this, they had enjoyed a succession of bishops appointed by the patriarch of Antioch. But the Portuguese exercised great cruelty over them, and subjected them to the inquisition of Goa. It appears that their religion was the same nearly as the Protestant church of this day. Their priests married; they owned but two sacraments, baptism and the Lord's supper. They invoked no saints, nor had they any images; they did not believe in purgatory, and had no other dignitaries in their church but bishops, priests, and deacons. St. Thomas established Christianity at a very early period in Travancore, and at length suffered martyrdom near Madras.

At Muttacherry, near Cochin, the Jews have two respectable synagogues, and are divided into two classes called Jerusalem or white Jews, and ancient or black Jews.

The white Jews came to India soon after the second destruction of the temple. On their arrival the king of the country granted them a settlement at Cranganore, A. D. 490. They continued at Cranganore for nearly 1000 years under seventy-two governors, and were joined by many other Jews, but at last discord arose among them, and one of their chiefs called in the assistance of an Indian rajah with a great army and destroyed their houses, palaces, and forts, driving them from Cranganore, when they fled to Cochin and found an asylum at Muttacherry. White Jews look upon black ones as half castes. It is supposed the latter came to India many centuries before the former.

Vide Rev. Dr. Buchanan, and other authorities.

Note 7.

The Jains talk in their books of 2,000,000,000,000,000 sagaras, or oceans of years. Now a palya is an estimate of the time a vast pit, filled with chopped hair, would take to be emptied at the rate of one hair in a century; and a sagara is ten cotes of cotes of times a palya, or 1,000,000,000,000,000 palyas are equal to one sagara.

Asiatic Researches, vol. ix.

Note 8.

The Suttee Jong, or age of purity, 3,200,000 years.

The Tirtah Jong, or partial corruption, 2,400,000 years.

The Dwapour Jong, or partial depravity, 1,600,000 years.

The Kalli Jong, or depraved age, 400,000 years.

It is believed that about 5000 years of the Kalli Jong or present age have expired. In the first age men lived 100,000 years; in the second 10,000; in the third, 1,000; and in this, human life is limited to 100.

Note 9.

"During the months of November and December," says Dr. Dellon, "I heard every morning, the shrieks of the unfortunate victims who were undergoing the question. I remembered to have heard, before I was cast into prison, that the *auto da fe* was generally celebrated on the first Sunday in Advent, because on that day is read in the churches that part of the Gospel in which mention is made of the last judgment; and the inquisition pretend by the ceremony to exhibit a lively emblem of that awful event. I was likewise convinced that there were a great number of prisoners, besides myself; the profound silence, which reigned within the walls of the building, having enabled me to count the number of doors which were opened at the hours of meals. However, the first and second Sundays of Advent passed by, without my hearing of any thing, and I prepared to undergo another year of melancholy captivity, when I was aroused from my despair on the 11th of January, by the noise of the guards removing the bars from the door of my prison. The Alcaide presented me with a habit, which he ordered me to put on, and to make myself ready to attend him when he should come again. Thus saying, he left a lighted lamp in my duugeon. The guards returned about two o'clock in the morning, and led me out into a long gallery, where I found a number of the companions of my fate, drawn up in a rank against a wall; I placed myself among the rest, and several more soon joined the melancholy band. The profound silence and stillness caused them to resemble statues more than animated bodies of human creatures. The women, who were clothed in a similar manner, were placed in a neighbouring gallery, where we could not see them; but I remarked that a number of persons stood by themselves at some distance, attended by others who wore long black dresses, and who walked backwards and forwards occasionally. I did not then know who these were; but I was afterwards informed that the former were the victims who were condemned to be burned, and the others were the confessors. After we were all ranged against the wall of this gallery, we received each a large wax taper. They then brought us a number of dresses made of yellow cloth, with the cross of St. Andrew painted before and behind. This is called the san benito. The relapsed heretics wear another species of robe, called the samarra, the ground of which is grey. The portrait of the sufferer is painted upon it, placed upon burning torches with flames and demons all around. Caps were then produced called carrochas; made of pasteboard, pointed like sugar loaves, all covered with devils and flames of fire.

"The great bell of the cathedral begun to ring a little before sun-rise, which served as a signal to warn the people of Goa to come and behold the august ceremony of the *auto da fe;* and then they made us proceed from the gallery one by one. I remarked, as we passed into the great hall, that the inquisitor was sitting at the door with his secretary by him, and that he delivered every prisoner into the hands of a particular person, who is to be his guard to the place of burning. These persons are called parrains or godfathers. My godfather was the commander of a ship. I went forth with him, and as soon as we were in the street I saw that the procession was commenced by the Dominican friars, who have the honour, because Saint Dominic founded the inquisition; these are followed by the prisoners, who walk one after the other, each having his godfather by his side, and a lighted taper in his hand. The least guilty are foremost; and as I did not pass for one of them, there were many who took precedence of me. The women were mixed promiscuously with the men. We all walked barefoot, and the sharp stones of the streets of Goa wounded my tender feet and caused the blood to stream, for they made us march through the chief streets of the city; and we were regarded every where by an innumerable crowd of people, who had assembled from all parts of India to behold this spectacle; for the inquisition takes care to announce it, long before, in the most remote parishes. At length we arrived at the church of St. Francis, which was, for this time, destined for the celebration of the act of faith. On one side of the altar was the grand inquisitor and his counsellors, and on the other the viceroy of Goa and his court. All the prisoners are seated to hear a sermon. I observed that those who wore the horrible carrochas came in last in the procession. One of the Augustine monks ascended the pulpit, and preached for a quarter of an hour. The sermon being concluded, two readers went up to the pulpit, one after the other, and read the sentences of the prisoners. My joy was extreme when I heard that my sentence was not to be burnt, but to be a galley slave for five years. After the sentences were read, they summoned forth those miserable victims who were destined to be immolated by the holy inquisition. The images of the heretics who had died in prison were brought up at the same time, their bones being contained in small chests, covered with flames and demons. An officer of the secular tribunal now came forward and seized these unhappy people, after they had each received a slight blow upon the breast from the Alcaide, to intimate that they were abandoned. They were then led away to the bank of the river, where the viceroy and his court were assembled, and where the faggots had been prepared the preceding day. As soon as they arrive at this place, the condemned prisoners are asked in what religion they choose to die; and the moment they have replied to this question, the executioner seizes them, and binds them to a stake in the midst of the faggots. The day after the execution, the portraits of the dead are carried to the church of the Dominicans. The heads only are represented (which are generally very accurately drawn, for the inquisition keeps excellent limners for the purpose) surrounded by flames and demons, and underneath is the name and crime of the person who has been burned."

Note 10.

The baptist mission commenced about the year 1793. Dr. Carey is deeply learned in several of the Indian languages, and Mr. Marshman is one of the best Chinese scholars of the present day. At the press of Serampore, translations have been printed of the Scriptures in the Sanscrit, Bengalee, Orissa, Mahratta, Hindostannee, Guzeratee, Seik, Carnata, Telinga, Burman, and other eastern languages.

Note 11.

"History," says Colonel Stewart, in his "Sketches," speaking of the storm of Seringapatam, which Major General Baird commanded, "has seldom produced a more striking difference in the fortunes and circumstances of a man's life, than in the case of this officer. He now entered as a conqueror within the walls of a town where he had been led in as a prisoner, and kept in chains for three years, suffering under the most cruel treatment, *for he was wounded and taken prisoner in Baillie's defeat.* As a conqueror, he showed a bright example of the difference between ferocious and generous minds.

His revenge, when retaliation was in his power, was shown by endeavours to save the now prostrate enemy and the inhabitants from the fury of his troops, who knew what he and his brave fellow-sufferers had been made to endure, and were consequently more than usually exasperated."

Note 12.

In some tribes of Rajpoots the female children are destroyed, and wives are purchased from other tribes. This unnatural custom is supposed to have originated in pride. The Jerajahs, Jaits, and Rajkumars practise infanticide, and the mother herself is commonly the executioner, either by putting some opium into the infant's mouth, or drawing the umbilical cord over the face. Colonel Walker, political agent in Guzerat, investigated the matter by desire of Governor Duncan, whose humanity prompted him to aim at its abolition. It had been a custom there for 2000 years, and Broach or Barygaza is mentioned by very ancient authors as its chief seat. According to calculation, 300 children were murdered annually in Kattywar and Cutch. Colonel Walker's correspondence with the chiefs of those countries is extremely interesting, and fully detailed in the records of the times, but particularly in Moor's Hindoo Infanticide. He entreated many of them to let their daughters live, and at first received positive refusals and insulting letters. A curious one from Futteh Mahomed, to whom he wrote, in addressing the Row of Boogebooge, is all I can insert. " It is notorious that since the avatara of Sri Chrishna, the Serajahs, who are descended from the Jadoos, have, during a period of 4,900 years, been accustomed to kill their daughters; and it has no doubt come to your knowledge that all of God's creation, even the mighty emperors of Hindostan, besides all others the conductors of the affairs of this world, have preserved friendship with this court, and never acted in this respect unreasonably. But you, who are an *amir* of the great sircar, the Honourable Company, having written to me on this subject, I have felt much uneasiness, for it does not accord with your good character. This durbar has always maintained friendship with the Honourable Company; and notwithstanding this, you have acted so unreasonably in this respect, that I am much distressed. No one has, until this day, wantonly quarrelled with this court, who has not, in the end, suffered loss. Do not again address me on this subject." Nevertheless, Colonel Walker did persevere, and at length by publicly discussing and exposing the enormity of the practice, many of the supporters were led to abhor infanticide; and although Governor Duncan had only received a cold approval from his superiors, he had the satisfaction of saving many thousands of infants by his spirited and benevolent interference through Colonel Walker. The supreme government acknowledged that his plan was worthy of humanity; but added, "the speculative success of it cannot be considered to justify the prosecution of measures which may expose to hazard the essential interests of the state." Yet it is probable that no speculation in India ever raised the British character so high in the estimation of the natives; for many of the mothers came, some years afterwards, to Colonel Walker's tent in Kattywar, and placed their female children in his hands with all the natural marks of affection, emphatically calling their little ones his children. Public opinion, however, was still adverse to the preservation of them, for, in many instances, the little ones were disguised as boys. The innocent creatures appeared ashamed of acknowledging their sex, and assured Colonel Walker that they were not girls, calling on their fathers with infantine simplicity to corroborate their assertions. *Fifteen Years in India.*

Note 13.

It is really melancholy to think that a custom should be supported for ages by men, which deprives children of their mother when it is the will of Providence to call away the father. Can any thing be more affecting than to see a lady in the bloom of life, decked with flowers, arrayed in all her jewels, perfumed and painted, led round the funeral pile of her husband, amidst the exulting shouts of a crowd, to be consumed by blazing faggots? In some parts of the Carnatic, a pit is made, and the widow leaps into the flames, or is thrown in by the Brahmans. But in most other places, she takes the dead body in her arms, kisses it, and places the head on her bosom, as she sits down in a sort of shed erected over the funeral pile. A procession then goes round it, great shouts are raised, and it is set on fire. If the blaze spreads properly, pain is over in a few moments, for the smoke produces suffocation; but the fire is sometimes so bad, that the legs and arms are roasted before life is extinct. But what fortitude it requires on the part of the victim to see the preparations, to go through the ceremonies, to distribute presents! All which she is expected to do with ease and satisfaction. The Roman lady who showed her husband how to die, and presented him with the dagger reeking from her own heart, exhibited not an example of greater magnanimity than that of a Hindoo wife performing suttee.

The sacrifice of human life in this way is enormous, for sometimes great numbers of concubines perform suttee, in common with the widows of a deceased great man. In the year 1803, it was ascertained that two hundred and seventy-five widows were burned with their dead husbands within thirty miles of Calcutta; and in 1804, one hundred and fifteen suttees were performed near the city. Allowing two millions of Hindoos within the circle of this estimate, and seventy millions for the number of natives in India who observe that ceremony, the annual loss of lives is little short of 7000. On the 12th of September 1807, near Barnagore, three miles from Calcutta, the body of a Koolin Brahman named Kristo Deb Mookergee, who died at the age of ninety-two, was burned. He had left twelve wives, three of whom were burned with him. One was a venerable lady, having white locks. Being unable to walk from age, she was placed upon the pile by the Brahmans. The two others were young, and one of them was very beautiful. The old lady was placed on one side of the body, and the two others on the opposite side, when an old Brahman, the eldest son of the deceased, set the pile on fire, which was instantly in a blaze, amidst the shout of Brahmans, and din of tom-toms and tooteries which drowned the dying cries of the victims. "The Koolin Brahmans," says Dr. Buchanan, "are the purest, and marry as many wives as they please. Hindoos think it an honour to have a Koolin Brahman for a son-in-law. They sometimes have great numbers of wives. Rajeb Bonnerjee, of Calcutta, has forty; Raj Chunder Bonnerjee, forty-two; Ramrajee Bonnerjee, fifty; and Birjod Bookerjee of Bisrampore, now dead, had ninety."

Fifteen Years in India.

Note 14.

The plans of Marquis Wellesley for the government of India were so far beyond the grasp of common men, that they were misrepresented at the time, and ill-understood afterwards, by those whose duty it was to follow the road prescribed by his lordship's genius.

During the decline of the Mogul empire, many of the Hindoo princes usurped power which was invariably directed towards the accomplishment of ambitious views. The whole country was thus gradually involved in war, and it became a scene where every petty chief enriched himself by plunder, and acknowledged no right but that of the sword. When the British government became possessed of the power which the Mogul emperor was no longer able to use for the benefit of mankind, it became a duty to reduce those turbulent chiefs to obedience, or at least to neutrality. As extension of territory was not the policy of the Honourable Company, and therefore, the conquest of native independent princes prohibited, the local British authority in India found it a most difficult task to deprive them of external political power. The Marquis Wellesley's system comprehended a general plan of neutralising their private operations, by placing a subsidiary force in the dominions of each : a number of small well-organised bodies ready to move in any direction upon the shortest notice, composed of British troops and well-disciplined natives, at the disposal of a political agent at the different native courts, being thus in a sort of well-connected chain stationed throughout India, would be fully sufficient to secure the peace and prosperity of the country. In short, a subsidiary force has the effect of reducing a native prince almost to the level of a subject, without depriving him of the pomp or consequence, within his own dominions, of sovereignty. Nearly all the native princes are now either directly or indirectly reduced to obedience, and deprived of political power; which effect the Marquis Wellesley clearly foresaw, from the operation of his subsidising plan. Others considered it so pregnant with danger, that its practical operation to the full extent was left to be proved by the talented nobleman who has lately returned crowned with glory from the East

NOTE 15.

IN the year 1797, America was admitted to a free trade with India and China, and from that period the East India Company of England, being undersold both in the Indian and European market, sustained very serious losses.

The merchants of Great Britain, from the above period, endeavoured to participate unrestrictedly in the valuable trade to those distant countries; but the court of directors met their applications to parliament with such strong arguments, that their object was frustrated till the renewal of the charter in 1813, by Lord Castlereagh's Bill, when a free trade with India was granted to the subjects of Great Britain under certain restrictions.*

Scarcely any alteration took place in the Company's political power, except by a small increase of the influence of the crown, in regard to the nomination of governors-general. But a free entrance to the chief ports of India was granted to all British speculators, on condition that their voyage should be made in conformity to local

* Vide Addenda, LVI.

regulation, and their return restricted to such harbours as were to be fixed by a decision of the Privy Council. This free trade was to be carried on by vessels not exceeding 350 tons burden, and piece goods were only to be introduced into the port of London. The China trade, however, which is the only source of commercial emolument to the Company, is secured to them exclusively by charter

Note 16.

The government of India is in many respects armed with despotic power; and it is necessary that every adventurer should know how his right of loco-motion is circumscribed; how he may be removed from acquired property and connection without trial or condemnation before any court of justice; and how he is prohibited from publishing his free opinion upon public occurrences, by the press being under the censorship of the chief secretary to government at the three presidencies.

No European is permitted to travel in India, or to go into the interior, without a passport, excepting civil and military servants of the Company, when on route to join their stations or regiments.

Any European may be sent home from India, by an order in council, at a moment's notice, whether he has a licence to remain or not, if the government deem him a dangerous subject.

The liberty of the press does not extend to India, and as government there have power vested in them by charter, to frame such regulations as they may consider expedient, they can suppress any newspaper or public print that dares to write in opposition to their views.

Mr. Buckingham, a gentleman of great talent, who established a popular paper in Calcutta, in

1818, which obtained such circulation as to ensure to him and his family the prospect of independence, has lately been sent home for giving publicity to matter offensive to the powers in authority there; but as his case is now before the public, and likely soon to become the subject of legal investigation, I shall merely allude to it as illustrative of my text.

With respect to the right of loco-motion, I am convinced that nothing would be more injurious to the interest of Great Britain, or inhuman to the Hindoos, than to permit speculative Europeans to wander away from the presidencies at pleasure. They would every moment insult the natives by ignorance of the usages of the country; and if they happened to be designing men of talent, their ability would soon be directed to the Company's destruction. There are instances on record of European deserters in India becoming most dangerous enemies: existing circumstances, therefore, justify the first regulation. But as to the second, it appears to be a most dangerous exercise of power, and fitter for a Hindoo or Mogul government, than one deriving its functions from the British parliament, the zealous guardian of a free constitution. To tear a man away from his property, to injure him, perhaps, irreparably in his prospects, to break his mind, and to cloud his days with adversity, without the verdict of a jury, that bulwark of a Briton's birth-right, seem to me monstrous things, unjustified by any necessity. If there was no tribunal in the country, before which alleged crime could be proved and punished, exigency might apologize for an arbitrary act. It is deeply to be lamented that such a power should be given to a government that owes obedience to a king who has no such authority; and it seems to my understanding so absurd, as to deserve a place in the catalogue of human inconsistencies.

On the subject of the last right possessed by the government of India, I beg to observe, that the freedom of the press has done so much for the civilisation and improvement of the whole earth, that it is a most deplorable misconception to arrest its operation in any part of the world; to correct its abuse is another matter. Truth is the brightest object of human pursuit: and it never blazes with more effulgence than when placed in opposition to falsehood. Discussion elicits truth, therefore the free utterance of opinion serves truth. Why it should be dangerous to make the truth known every where, I cannot perceive; seeing that truth should be the delight of virtue. To deny freedom to the press is to say, "I am afraid that my motives should be examined." Happy is the man who has such a mentor! Happy is the king, or governor, who can sit alone and read what he believed was unknown to all but his own conscience! Such a person may change his course; he may be drawn away from a precipice. In short, it is the freedom of the press which has forced our kings for ages to be true friends to themselves, which has prevented revolution, and which, perhaps, is that unknown principle that invigorates the constitution of England, and restores her to health and youth periodically. I cannot clearly understand how a free press in India could do harm, if it does good in any other country. It is the will of the British parliament, and the court of directors, that the inhabitants of India should be governed equitably; civilised and enlightened by the diffusion of education. What can contribute more effectually to this than a free press? Will not every Hindoo say, when he hears that it is not permitted in India, "The Company's servants are afraid to have their actions scrutinized by competent witnesses—they dare not appear before the bar of public opinion." However, I am aware that a great deal may be said on the other side. I also know that the utmost liberality characterises the government of India on all subjects connected with literature, philosophy, and religion. It is only on political topics that the editor of any paper in India is restrained; and when I reflect upon the state of that country, and the folly of particular editors, there may be strong reasons given for the right exercised by the local authorities. In short, I doubt my own opinion on the subject.

Note 17.

"The question to be considered may be reduced to these two points," says the Abbé Dubois, late missionary in Mysore;—"First, Is there a possibility of making real converts to Christianity among the natives of India? Secondly, Are the means employed for that purpose, and above all, the translation of the Holy Scriptures into the idioms of the country, likely to conduce to this desirable object?

"To both interrogatories," continues the Abbé, "I will answer in the negative: it is my decided opinion, first, that under existing circumstances there is no human possibility of converting the Hindoos to any sect of Christianity; and, secondly, that the translation of the Holy Scriptures circulated among them, so far from conducing to this end, will, on the contrary, increase the prejudice of the natives against the Christian religion, and prove in many respects detrimental to it.

"If any of the several modes of Christian worship were calculated to make an impression, and gain ground in the country, it is no doubt the Catholic form, which you Protestants call an idolatry in disguise: it has a pooja, or sacrifice (the mass is termed by the Hindoos pooja, literally sacrifice); it has processions, images, statues, *tirtan* or holy water, fasts, tittys or feasts, and prayers for the dead, invocation of saints, &c., all which practices bear more or less resemblance to those in use among the Hindoos. Now, if even such a mode of worship is become so objectionable to the natives," (he has before said that it was hated and despised) " can it be reasonably expected that any one of the simple Protestant sects will ever prosper among them.

" The naked text of the Bible, exhibited without a long previous preparation to the Hindoos, must prove detrimental to the Christian religion, and increase their aversion to it, inasmuch as this sacred book contains in almost every page accounts which cannot fail deeply to wound their feelings, by openly hurting prejudices which are held most sacred.

" What will a well-bred native think, when, in reading over this holy book, he sees that Abraham, after receiving the visit of three angels, under human shape, entertains his guests by causing a calf to be killed, and served to them for their fare? The prejudiced Hindoo will at once judge that both Abraham and his heavenly guests were nothing but vile pariars; and without further reading he will forthwith throw away the book, containing (in his opinion) such sacrilegious accounts.

" In the mean while he will become more and more confirmed in the idea, that a religion which derives its tenets from so impure a source, is altogether detestable, and that those who profess it must be the basest and vilest of men.

"Such are the effects which, in my humble opinion, the reading of the naked text of the Bible cannot fail to produce on the unprepared minds of the prejudiced Hindoos."

Note 18.

The Marquis Wellesley founded the College of Fort William on the 4th of May, 1800. From that period till 1807, it produced about one hundred volumes in oriental literature, on subjects most interesting to mankind, and connected with the civilisation of the East. This establishment is still carrying on the diffusion of knowledge, though now on a much reduced scale. The Asiatic Society, formed by Sir William Jones, have contributed largely to information on Indian subjects; and the Bombay Literary Society also deserve the thanks of mankind for their exertions. But there is a general apathy complained of in the British public respecting their extensive empire in the East, which is deeply to be lamented. There is, in fact, no sympathy between the Western and Eastern world. In manners and customs the people of the West are a distinct race from those of the East, and it would never be suspected by a person unacquainted with history, that both originated in the same stock. Yet there is such a grand field for the expansion of benevolence and philanthropy in the consideration, that upwards of 100,000,000 of our fellow men may be eternally benefited by the interest which we take in their welfare, that the coldest heart should be warmed into a lively glow on such a subject.

ADDENDA.

On a second revision of this work, the following notes occurred to the author, not only as illustrative of the text, but as useful to young persons.

I.

In travelling from the river Burrumpooter or, more classically, Brahmapootra, which is the largest river of India, through Bootan, Nepaul, Lahore, and Cabul, to the city of Herat, on the borders of Persia, we find these regions bounded, on the north, by one continued chain of mountains. This range from its eastern extremity, in about lat. 28° and long. 93°, on to Cashmere, runs in a north-westerly direction to lat. 35°. In this course it is known by the name of Himalaya, which means *region of perpetual snow*. But from Cashmere to its western extremity it bears the name of Hindoo Coosh, which is the particular designation of one of its highest snowy peaks. The highest peak in this prodigious range of mountains is called Dhawalageri. It has been ascertained to be 27,677 feet above the level of the sea. No part of the Andes, in South America, towers to such an amazing height. It is, therefore, the highest mountain, at present known, in the world. The skeletons of horses have been found, in these mountains, so far from the plains, that they never could have existed in such a situation. It is a curious fact in geology. Along with many others of a similar nature, it tends to confirm our sacred account of the universal deluge.

II.

The shawls of Cashmere supply the whole civilised world. It is said, they are manufactured at sixteen thousand looms, each of which gives employment to two or three men. The work is so inconceivably tedious, by which the fine patterns are produced, that not more than a quarter of an inch is completed in a whole day. It is not unusual to find a loom occupied with one shawl for an entire year. When the pattern is new or very intricate, the superintendent workman describes to those under him the figures, colours, and threads, which they are to use, keeping before him the drawing from which he makes them work. His wages varies from eighteen pence to two shillings a day; while the common workmen receive from three-halfpence to sixpence daily. The wool is imported from Tibet in bales or packages of twelve pounds weight, at an expense of 1*l.* 8*s.*, or thereabouts each. It is said there are about 80,000 shawls manufactured, on an average, annually in Cashmere; which would be five for each loom, for although a very fine one would occupy a loom perhaps a year, yet ten or twelve of the inferior sort may be fabricated in that period.

III.

The beautiful vale of Cashmere, the happy valley, as it is called, is nearly one hundred miles in length, and surrounded by high mountains which enclose it on every side. Its soil is fertile, and watered with innumerable streams, which flow down the mountains and serve to supply the several lakes that are situated in the valley. The climate is delightful, and, what is most singular, it abounds in the various fruits and flowers of both northern and southern regions. The town of Cashmere, or the capital of the province, is situated on the river Thelum, over which there are three wooden bridges. All the houses in Cashmere are built with flat roofs, covered over with a thick bed of mould, and planted with flowers, which, in the summer season, present a most lively appearance.

IV.

No scenery can be more romantic and sublime than the general aspect of Nepaul. The snowy regions or Himalaya seem to hang over it. All the country is extremely mountainous, and intersected with numerous rivers. The roads are cut in the sides of the mountains, and often seem literally to hang over the deep wide precipices that yawn beneath. Here and there, villages are to be seen perched on their lofty sides; and low down in the valleys are fishermen's huts scattered along the banks of the streams. In some parts the sides of the mountains are covered with tall forests, chiefly composed of the pine tree, which here grows to a great size, and is so resinous that its branches serve for torches. Many of the common trees are serviceable to the natives not only for building, dyeing, and making cordage, but for food, the pith, in times of scarcity, supplying the poorer classes with an inferior kind of bread. It is surprising to see how cultivation has crept up these precipices. Corn-fields can be traced to the very summits of some of them; for industry will conquer even the most barren and stubborn land. The husbandman here builds a succession of strong walls, at different heights upon the declivity. He then fills up the intervals between every two with soil, so that a succession of levels is formed for the retention of water, and the nutrition of various crops. Thus they are imitating the Chinese.

V.

It appears that, notwithstanding the intricacy and difficulty of the Chinese language, the art of printing was known in that country at a very remote period. We can easily conceive, how an expert hand may put together the words of the English language, which are composed of twenty-five letters, from moveable types, arranged in compartments before him. But the Chinese language consists of 80,000 different characters. It would, therefore, be impossible to lay out such a number of letters before a printer; for he might require hundreds of each in printing one book. Our improved method being impracticable to the Chinese, they are far behind us in the art of printing. Their books are issued from the press in a very different way from ours.

Every work is first engraved on thin boards, each of which is the size of two pages. The board, when wet with the ink, is stamped down on the paper, and thus two pages are struck off at once, which are folded together, with the blank sides inwards. When sewed into a book, the fold forms the outer edge of the leaves, which are never cut. After the edition is worked off, the boards are carefully laid up, to reprint the work at any future time.

VI.

Assam is an extensive country to the north-east of Bengal, governed by an independent rajah. In length it is 700 miles by 70 the average breadth. The 25° and 28° of north latitude, and 94° and 99° of east longitude may be said to comprehend this mountainous region. It is watered by the Brahmapootra river. No country, perhaps, in the world of equal extent, has so many navigable rivers. Besides the great Brahmapootra, sixty streams have been ascertained to flow from the mountains through its valleys; thirty-four from the north, and twenty-six from the south; all of which are of sufficient depth, during the rains, for boats of the largest size; and a very great many of them admit a commercial intercourse, at all seasons, on shallow boats. Gold is found in the winding beds of these rivers, in great quantities.

In 1582, this country was described by Abul Fazel, as follows; "The dominions of Assam join to Camroop; he is a very powerful prince, lives in great state; and, when he dies, his principal attendants, both male and female, are voluntarily buried alive with his corpse."

The country is now thinly inhabited; for at the death of every rajah, bloody wars take place, before the succession is settled. These have desolated the fertile vales of Assam. Gergong is the capital; but the Swerga-rajah, or rajah of the heavens, which is his blasphemous title, resides at Rungpoor, a strong military post near Gergong. In 1793, a detachment of British troops assisted maha rajah Surgee Deo in regaining his throne, from which he had been expelled by an insurrection. Their services were requited by a commercial treaty with the Bengal government; since which time an intercourse has been kept up; but the climate of Gergong has been found fatal not only to Europeans but to the natives of Bengal.

VII.

Above the town of Rangoon, which is situated at the head of a bay, formed by the mouth of the river Irawaddy, stands a beautiful temple. It is built on a rising ground, which is ascended by a flight of 100 magnificent steps. Round the summit of the hill, terraces are cut and planted with rows of trees, whose rich foliage gives good effect to the lofty spires of the temple that rise above it. The centre and tallest of the spires is crowned at top with a sort of cup, in the form of an umbrella, which, as well as the spire that supports it, is richly gilt, and glitters beautifully in the sunshine. At Pegu the great temple has 100 tall spires, all richly gilt; and they seem, at a distance, like a forest of gold; whence the edifice is called the Golden Temple. The centre spire, with the cap or umbrella, is fifty-six feet in circumference. It is called the Tee; and round its rims are hung a multitude of small bells, which keep up such a continual sound, that the Tee is heard, night and day, at a considerable distance.

VIII.

The emperor's palace, in the city of Ummerapoor, is a spacious stone building with four gates. Its east entrance is called the golden gate; its west, the gate of favour; its south, the gate of justice; and its north, the gate of state. Our ambassadors entered at the golden gate, and passed through different superb apartments to the hall of audience, which was supported by seventy-seven pillars. At the end of it is a high gilded lattice, which conceals the throne. On his majesty's arrival, the folding doors of this lattice were thrown open. The throne is richly carved and gilded; and two tables stand near it, covered with large vessels and ornaments of gold. The emperor seemed scarcely able to ascend the flight of steps that lead to his seat, from the weight of his dress. He literally appeared to be cased in gold, with a wing of the same metal on each shoulder. His crown was a high cap, richly studded with precious stones; and his fingers were covered with rings. Four priests in long robes chaunted a song at the foot of the throne, and the numerous officers of state were dressed in rich silks.

IX.

The great wall of China is justly considered one of the wonders of the world. It is known to have been completed 300 years before the birth of Christ. It winds over a chain of mountains for an extent of 1200 miles. In the valleys it is full thirty feet high, and even on the ledges of rocks never less than twenty. Such is its thickness, that the top is flat, paved with stone, and so broad that a carriage might drive along it. There are towers along its entire length, at intervals of 100 yards; they vary from ten to forty feet in height. This great work is calculated to contain materials enough to build a wall six feet high and two feet thick, whose length, 50,000 miles, would twice go round the world.

X.

PEKIN, the capital of China, is considered to be at least twice the size of London. One large street, four miles in length, and 120 feet broad, runs through the central part of the town, and is crossed by another of equal length and breadth. Nearly all the other streets are narrow and dirty. The emperor's principal palace is situated within the walls of the city; and the pleasure grounds around it are laid out in a singular manner. This space is about a mile square; and it is surrounded by what is called the yellow wall, from the colour of the varnished tiles that compose it, and which glitter like burnished gold. The grounds are laid out in lakes and hills, formed entirely by artificial means. All these heights are richly planted, and a number of small pleasure houses have been built on them; while the lakes, being sprinkled with islands, cause the whole to have a most romantic effect. But his majesty has a great many other palaces, which are all spacious, strong buildings. The walls which surround Pekin, or a space of twenty-three square miles, are forty feet high, and twenty thick at bottom, rising like a pyramid to the breadth of twelve feet on the top. Along the wall stand high square towers, and outside of it there runs a deep fosse. These towers, the numerous triumphal arches which have been built in memory of remarkable men or great national events, the glittering temples, and innumerable flags and streamers hoisted by the shop-keepers and merchants, give the city, at a distance, a most singularly grand appearance to a stranger, who is for the first time approaching.

XI.

The cocoa nut tree is converted to no less than 360 uses by the natives of India, furnishing them with cordage, timber for building, arrack, vinegar, oil, sugar, milk, food, paint, and several kinds of domestic utensils.

XII.

Europeans were, for a long time, unsuccessful in raising our common table vegetables on the island of Ceylon. A colony of Chinese gardeners was introduced, for that purpose, by our government. They have not only succeeded in producing vegetables in great quantities, but also have some thriving sugar plantations under their management. Such is the effect of industry and perseverance. Their houses are very neat. At the upper end of the principal room, there is a high stand, over which hangs a tablet, written in Chinese characters, and containing the names of the forefathers of each family. A lamp is kept constantly burning before this to remind them of their native country.

XIII.

The great elephant craal or trap, on the island of Ceylon, is situated about sixteen miles from Negombo. It is in the shape of a funnel; composed of strong posts, made of whole trunks of trees, driven well in the ground, and lashed to others placed horizontally, with strong ropes. Fires are lighted near it on the outside, to intimidate the elephants when entrapped; for otherwise, they would easily break through it. When these animals are driven or decoyed into the trap, they are prevented from returning by men placed at the entrance with torches. At length the unfortunate elephant is driven down the funnel, till it becomes so narrow that he cannot turn. The hunters then close on their captive; two tame elephants, stationed on each side of the craal, put in their trunks, and seize that of the wild animal. He is then unable to move; and the hunters getting over the craal, fasten huge ropes round his legs and neck: after which, the stakes in front are removed, and he is forced forward by the two tame elephants, which press against him, to the tree or post where he is to be chained. For a long time he undergoes daily discipline, till at length he becomes quiet and resigned to his fate. Grief and indignation are strongly expressed by the eye of the elephant when he finds himself mastered. After trying every effort of his amazing strength for liberty, he sinks into deep melancholy, refuses food, and sometimes starves himself to death.

XIV.

Among the natural curiosities of Ceylon are swarms of red monkeys, whose gambols are truly diverting. Their great enemies are snakes *, which they kill by seizing them near the throat, and crushing the head of the snake on a stone or against the tree, till life is extinct. The monkeys are

* Vide LIV. of this Addenda.

dreaded by all kinds of birds, and it is most curious how ingeniously they form their nests, on the very trees inhabited by monkeys and snakes, so as to be secure from these devourers of their eggs and young ones. Some form them with a long opening like a purse, leave the entrance at the very bottom, and fix them hanging to the end of a slender branch. The tailor bird sews her little nest to a leaf at the tip of some branch, with some fine fibres which she picks up, making use of her bill for a needle. There are bird-catching spiders on the island of Ceylon, whose legs are four inches long, and their whole body covered with thick black hair. But, perhaps, nothing is more curious in that burning climate than the pitcher plant or nepenthes. It is an herbaceous plant, with thick roots and a simple stem, crowned with bunches of flowers. The leaves have no footstalks, but partly embrace the stem at the base, and are terminated by tendrils, each of which supports a hollow vessel of an oblong shape, which is covered with a top, like the lid of a box. These singular appendages contain each about a wine glass full of clear, wholesome, well tasted, and particularly refreshing water. In the morning the lid is closed, but it opens during the heat of the day, and a portion of the water evaporates; this is replenished in the night, and each morning the vessels are all full. It seems that these fountains are intended by Providence to cheer birds and other animals, for the little beauties of the woods are often seen dipping their parched bills into the cool goblets of the nepenthes.

XV.

The king of Candy's throne was removed to England, at the termination of the war, by which he was deposed, and now forms a splendid and highly valuable trophy belonging to the crown of the United Kingdom. It is covered with pure gold, studded with precious stones, and of beautiful workmanship. The two arms of the chair consist of golden lions, whose eyes are amethysts, as large as a musket ball. It is a curious circumstance, that the royal sceptre of the Candian monarch should have been a just emblem of cruel and despotic tyranny, being a rod of iron headed with gold.

XVI.

Among the natural curiosities of the Indian seas are the following wonderful fishes:

The whales which venture up the Bay of Bengal are seldom very large, and generally perish there in combats with the sword-fish, by which they are pursued from the Southern ocean. I have seen what I thought a large dead one, floating down the bay like a little mountain; and its stench was such, that though our vessel was a considerable way from it, we were obliged to shut our mouths, and hold our noses, while we gratified curiosity by looking at it. The sword-fish, which is often seen in the Indian seas, is of a large and most powerful description. Sir Joseph Banks, as president of the Royal Society, received from the captain of an East Indiaman part of the bottom of his vessel, with the sword of one of these fishes imbedded in it, which is now lodged in the British Museum. The fish had such force as to drive its sword completely through the bottom of the ship, but it was killed by the violence of the effort. Beautiful dolphins are sometimes caught in the Indian seas. They swim with such amazing rapidity, that they have been known to go round a vessel sailing at the rate of six miles an hour. A shoal of these fishes followed Sir Richard Hawkins upwards of a thousand leagues. The dying dolphin changes its colour several times, and excites the tear of sensibility, by a seemingly silent appeal to compassion, which has probably given rise to the classical fables respecting it.

Sharks are of enormous size in the Eastern seas. One was caught with a human corpse in his maw, that weighed 4000 pounds. The shark has 144 teeth, which he erects when darting towards his prey; and as his large goggle eyes shoot fire, I know of nothing more frightful than his appearance. A great many remora, or sucking-fishes, always attend the shark. Our sailors have called them pilots, because they are seen to precede him, and smell what he is approaching. Some naturalists have called them the shark's enemies, and asserted that they drain away his moisture by suction; for it seems they live on his body: but I am certain that he does not devour them; though I never saw him refuse any thing else, I have seen the pilot fish pass through his frightfully gaping mouth, when turning to swallow our baits.

I never saw the cuttle-fish in India, but I have heard that it grows to a great size there. It has eight arms, and possesses most extraordinary qualities, for which I refer the reader to its natural history. The young reader will also be amused by referring to the natural history of the remora, or sucking-fish, of which so much has been fabulously related by the ancients. The Indians of Jamaica and Cuba, in the West Indies, formerly used the sucking-fish in the catching of others, somewhat in the same manner as hawks are employed by a falconer in seizing birds.

The nautilus is another curiosity of the Indian sea. It has eight feet, web-toed like those of a duck, but exquisitely fine and transparent. By some unknown power it can screw its body out of a curious shell, and assume all the appearance of a little ship. Two feet are raised like masts and rigging, with a membrane that passes for a sail, and certainly catches the zephyr which floats on the waves when it is expanded. The other feet hang paddling on each side, and serve for oars to row with. Poets have given imaginary pleasures to the sailing excursions of this little beauty of the ocean. But it is probable, that when it swells the light sail to the breeze, and forsakes the shell, its swiftness is employed to escape from the crab, sea-scorpion, and trochus, not to amuse itself.

Another curious little fish is the fly-shooter, or beaked chætodon, which knocks down its prey by cautiously levelling a drop of water from its tubular snout, like a ball from a musket. M. Hommel, the governor of the hospital at Batavia, ascertained this extraordinary fact by ocular demonstration.

The flying-fish is of a beautiful shape, something like a herring. There are innumerable shoals of them in the Indian seas, which serve as food to the large fishes; when they are chased, they take to the air, and fly a considerable way like birds; but in this element also they have enemies; for the albatross, or tropic birds, are always on the wing, watching for them. Their wings soon dry; and I have seen flights of them fall on our ship, quite exhausted. While skimming along the ocean, they look very like swallows, having black backs, white bellies, and forked tails. Their wings glitter like silver in the sun.

Gold fishes are natives of China; and the most beautiful kinds are caught in a small lake in the province of Chekyang. Some are a fine orange red, sprinkled over with gold dust; others white like silver, spotted with red. When dead they lose all their lustre. The mangoe fish of the river Hooghly, near Calcutta, is, I think, the most beautiful in India; shaped like a small trout, it is charmingly speckled with bright yellow, or golden spots, on a dark ground. It has a fine beard, of long orange threads, which, when the fish is dead, lie close to its body; but in swimming they serve as fins, and give, when expanded, a stately and gay appearance to the fish.

XVII.

Of all insects, the white ant, or termes, is the most wonderful. Though a small creature, it is able to produce much mischief; and its instincts place it in a rank with animals of the largest size. In some parts of India, they form their settlements or cities, in the form of huge cones, with turrets and watch-towers. They form regular streets, nurseries, stores, habitations; work in divisions, under a seeming government, and take all the precautions for security and order that wisdom could suggest, even to animals possessed of intellect. But among them there is neither invention nor variety of taste. Every ant brings with it from the egg all its knowledge. They can undermine houses, destroy the supports and the wood work, make their way through the floors, consume clothes, furniture, books, and every article that is not made of stone or of metal. It is wonderful what they do sometimes in India: they have let excellent Madeira wine flow on the ground, by eating away the casks that contained it; and a military guard was once brought to a court martial, I am told, at Madras, for the loss of treasure. The defence was, that the white ants had eaten it; and, upon examination, it was found that they had really devoured the bottoms of the chests, so that the treasure sunk deeply into the sandy ground, and was not easily discovered. There are several species of these destructive creatures in India, some large, being nearly the size of a wasp, and others not larger than a small grain of rice. They have an insuperable antipathy to cow-dung, and will not approach any thing upon which it is smeared, till after it has lost smell and taste by exposure to the air; consequently, in many parts of India, the floors and walls of houses are washed every week with a solution of that substance in water.

The insects of India are very numerous. There are many varieties of the beetle tribe. The forests are sometimes illuminated with the glow-worm. At times the death-watch is heard, and the bombardier playing off his artillery. I have seen flights of locusts in Kattywar. The caterpillar tribes are, in some places, innumerable; and they hang from the branches of every little shrub in Guzerat, being concealed in little cases shaped like a barrel. These habitations are evidently made by the caterpillar of tender twigs, glued together, and lined with a substance like fine silk. I have seen these insects dragging their houses after them; for they can come out to feed, and travel from one shrub to another. The silk-worm is employed very extensively in Bengal. After each monsoon the ephemera break forth in countless numbers, and endless variety. I have seen thousands of them end their brief period of existence, by a flap of their variegated wings against our mess candle-shades, being attracted towards the light.

There are bees, wasps, gnats of a most mischievous description, called musquittoes, lice, fleas, prodigious spiders, bugs, innumerable centipes, or scolopendra, and leeches of a most voracious appetite, &c.

XVIII.

The bird of paradise is said to be the most elegant of all the feathered race. It is about the size of a thrush, with the most beautiful variety of colours that can be conceived, and a luxuriancy of plumage, which would require a long description. I therefore refer the young reader to its natural history. It is a native of Papua, or New Guinea; and though it has been seen in many parts of India, yet it is not known to breed there. It was long supposed that this bird had no feet, and that it never rested. The poets fable it as constantly floating in the atmosphere. But these, and many other stories respecting it, are set at rest. One of these beautiful creatures was brought in a living state to England; it had, however, entirely lost the fine floating side feathers, and did not long survive its arrival.

Among the remarkable birds of India may be mentioned the peacock, the vulture, the falcon, the owl, the tailor bird, the flamingo, the albatross, the bustard, and the parroquet tribe.

XIX.

The mangrove is always found in marshy places near the sea, where the tide can wash its stem. It is ten or twelve feet high, divided into a vast number of branches, and thickly covered with leaves. The trunk and lower branches send out several pliant shoots, which descend to the ground, and then take root; these become in time so interlaced as to form a thick grove, somewhat resembling the banyan tree. Nature conducts the seed of this tree to the earth in an exceedingly curious manner. Its fruit produces a single seed, enclosed in an oval case. This seed, when ripe, begins to sprout without falling from the tree, and proceeds in the form of a woody thread, till it reaches the ground, the seed being at the hanging end of it. The bark of the mangrove, which the Chinese employ to strike a black dye, gives out a strong smell of sulphur; and the wood has the same odour. It burns briskly, with a bright blaze.

XX.

For our only authentic account of the Javanese, I beg to refer the curious reader to Sir T. S. Raffles' History of Java. This accurate observer describes them as a very virtuous people, but debased by the vices of their rulers.

The anchar or poison tree of Java is one of the largest in the forests of that island. Its trunk rises often to the height of seventy feet, without pushing forth a branch. The bark, being wounded, yields plentifully the juice, from which the celebrated poison is prepared. Of the inner bark a coarse kind of linen is made; it has also been worked into ropes which are very strong, but it requires much bruising and washing before it can be used; for, if any of the poisonous gum remains in it, and touches the skin, a painful sore is the consequence. A cup full of poison may, in a short time, be collected from a large tree. The anchar, like the trees in its neighbourhood, is on all sides surrounded by shrubs and plants; and, in no instance, can it be observed injurious to vegetation. What could have induced the Dutch naturalist, Foersch, to assert such fables, nay, downright falsehoods, respecting this tree, it is impossible to conceive.

He begins his account of it with a flourish, that he would only relate simple unadorned facts, of which he had been an eye-witness. After this, he describes the country round the tree, for ten or twelve miles, as entirely barren. Not even grass would grow near it. For fifteen or eighteen miles round it, not only no human creature, he said, could exist, but also no living animal of any kind had even been discovered. Even birds flying over this tree, he assures us, fell down dead. The fact is, that he never was nearer an anchar tree than eighteen miles. He reported from the wild stories of some ignorant native, and misled all Europe for thirty years. Our naturalists found one of the largest of these trees so completely environed by the common shrubs of the forest in which it grew, that it was with difficulty approached; several vines and climbing plants, also, in perfect health, adhered to it, and ascended to nearly half its height. But that criminals alone were, for a long time, sent to fetch poison from the anchar tree, in the forests of Java, is well known; and that numbers of them perished, is also fact; some, perhaps, from contact with the poison, and others from the attacks of snakes and wild beasts. What Foersch relates respecting thirteen criminals, whose execution he witnessed, may be true. He says, they were sentenced to suffer death by a lancet, poisoned with upas. Being tied to stakes, their breasts were bared and lanced by the common executioner. In sixteen minutes, he says, by his watch, they were all dead. Their pain began in five minutes after the wound had been inflicted, and continued increasing till death released them from suffering.

Such has been the rapid effect of this poison in our experiments on animals.

The large boa is the greatest of all the serpent tribe. It is not only an inhabitant of Java, but also of America and Africa. Most likely it was an enormous specimen of the boa that stopped Regulus and the victorious Roman army. According to a letter printed in the German Ephemerides, a gentleman witnessed a combat, on the island of Java, between the boa and a large buffalo. When the serpent had mastered the buffalo, and twisted itself round his body, the bones of the dying animal were heard to crack almost as loud as the report of a gun. After all the buffalo's bones were smashed, the boa licked the whole body over, and thus covered it with a mucilaginous substance. It then began to swallow the whole; and in the act the throat suffered so great a dilatation, that it took in at once a body that was thrice its own thickness. In the Bombay Courier of August 31, 1799, there is an account of a man who was killed on the island of Celebes by an enormous snake. He had gone on shore from a vessel close to the island. His companions heard him, some time after, scream out for assistance. But on going ashore, they found him crushed to death. The attention of the serpent being entirely occupied by its prey, the people rushed upon him and cut off his head, just as he was going to swallow the dead man. The snake had seized him by the right wrist, where the marks of the fangs were very distinct; and the mangled corpse bore evident signs of having been crushed by the monster twisting itself round the head, neck, breast, and thigh.

XXI.

The Peloo Isles were probably first noticed by the Spaniards from the Philippines. They are situated between the 7th and 8th degrees of north latitude, and the 134th and 135th of east longitude. Their name seems to be derived from the tall palm trees with which they are covered. The chief islands are Carvora, Oroolong, Pelelew, and Angoor. These islands are well wooded. Ebony is found here, with the manchineel tree, and the cabbage, and bread fruit tree. Yams and cocoa nuts, betel nut, plantains, oranges, lemons, sugar canes, and bamboos also abound.

When the Antelope was wrecked here in 1783, the conduct of these islanders was so kind, that it commanded the gratitude of the crew. Yet the natives were engaged in incessant wars, and massacred their prisoners. They are rather above the middle stature; their complexions being deeper than the Indian copper colour, but not black. Their hair is long and flowing, and inclined to curl. The men go entirely naked; but the women wear little aprons, or fringes, made from the husk of the cocoa nut, and dyed yellow. When both sexes grow up, their teeth are blacked by means of a dye. They seem to have no religion. In return for the kindness shown by Abba Thulle, the prince of Peloo, to the crew of the Antelope, the East India Company sent him a present of live stock, besides seeds of several sorts, European swords, and hardware, with arms and ammunition. None of the islands first visited by the English had any kind of grain, nor any quadruped whatever, except some grey rats and a few cats. In 1791 the captain of the Panther, a Bombay cruizer, was so pleased with the manners of the natives, that he resigned his command, determined to spend the remainder of his life among them; but, after a residence of fifteen months, he grew tired, and sailed in a boat to Macao. The interesting history of Prince Lee Boo is well known. I need only add that, by late accounts, it appears the live stock left on the Peloo islands has wonderfully increased, and that the civilisation of the natives has been considerably improved by our accidental intercourse.

I am sensible that many other small islands in the Indian seas ought to have been noticed in this work; but, as I have nothing original to say respecting them, I prefer a reference to Hamilton's East Indian Gazetteer, which intelligent work comprises all I could say on the subject.

The Papuan Isles are certainly objects of curiosity, but we know very little respecting them from authentic sources. It appears that the natives are absolute savages. In 1791, when the Panther was off the coast of New Guinea, the natives decoyed the surgeon into their rude canoes and murdered him, after which they discharged a shower of arrows into the ship, and wounded four of the crew. For all we know respecting these islands, &c., I beg to refer the reader to Forrest, Leyden, Sonnerat, Keating, Maccluer, Zuniga, and Hamilton.

XXII.

I am aware that there are systems, which very learned men have advocated, quite opposed to my assumption. Man, according to my judgment, is a creature whose mind is formed by the institutions of his country. He stands high or low in the scale of mental improvement, just in proportion as these institutions are wise or foolish. That there are idiots from accidental malconformation, and that there are great differences in the capacities of men, perhaps also from accidental causes, do not unhinge my argument. But it has been asserted * that there are races of men whose organisation is such as to prevent the possibility of their advancement in civilisation, arts, and sciences, to any point near what we have attained. Whether this be true or not, it would be presumption in me to assert, because I do not know it, of my own knowledge; but, till it is proved, I will not believe that the Creator of man gave any region of the habitable earth properties which had power to destroy the intellect of man. I am aware that the Esquimaux, and many other savage races of men, exhibit so complete a torpor of intellect as not to be able to count thirty. But they are in fact in the state of children. My little girl of two years old bursts into passionate exclamations at what is new to her, dances in an excess of joy, or melts into a flood of sorrow: does not the uninformed mind, when matured by age, do the same? My child has not intellect to discover the common mode of getting what she feels and pants for out of my pocket; am I to suppose on this account that her intellect can never be improved to the state of mine? Those who advocate such systems as our holy religion cannot approve of, seem to argue like Dr. Spurzheim, who attributes crimes to nature, which are entirely the offspring of human laws for the security of property.

* Vide Mr. Lawrence on Physiology, Zoology, and the Natural History of Man, &c.

XXIII.

The tropical winds are three. First, the general trade winds, which extend to about 30° of latitude on each side of the equator, in the Atlantic, Ethiopic, and Pacific Oceans. Second, the monsoons, or shifting trade winds, which are in the Indian or Eastern Ocean, and do not reach above two hundred leagues from the land. Third, the land and sea breezes, which are periodical winds, and blow from the land, from night to about midday, and from the sea, from about noon to midnight. These winds do not extend above two or three leagues from the shore. In small islands the land and sea breezes seem to flow from, and to the centre of each, in the same way as rays of light come from the sun.

XXIV.

Most Hindoos will eat animal food of particular kinds. Even many of the Brahmans use it. In marching through India, we were never prevented from slaughtering goats, kids, sheep, and lambs: but in many places a general order was issued to the troops prohibiting the killing of oxen, cows, peacocks, monkeys, &c. Total abstinence from animal food is not at all general among the Hindoo sects. It is only a characteristic of a few of them. The Banyans and Jains never, if possible, destroy life. There is an hospital at Surat, endowed by the Banyans, for the use of old and helpless animals of every description, where they are fed and taken as much care of, as human beings are in our charitable institutions.

XXV.

There is a remarkable object of worship, mentioned by some authors, in Mysore, called Kala Bharaiva, which signifies the black dog. Kala and Bharaiva are names of Seeva. Though I resided some years in Mysore, I certainly never heard of the black dog; but the French missionary Abbé Dubois says in his late work, that there is an idol so called, and that women sacrifice their fingers to it, in the way described in the following passage of Hamilton's Gazeteer, p. 591. "About Silagutta, the principal object of worship with the Morasa tribe is an image called Kala Bharaiva; and occasionally at this temple, a singular sacrifice is made. When a woman is from fifteen to twenty years of age, and has borne some children, terrified lest the angry deity should deprive her of her infants, she goes to the temple, and, as an offering to appease his wrath, she cuts off one or two of the fingers of her right hand."

XXVI.

Among the natural productions of Bengal the angeah grass may be mentioned as a curiosity; for it grows to such a length and thickness, that a single stalk of it resembles a large rope. Another very great curiosity is the moving plant of Bengal. The stem is round, smooth, and branching; the leaves grow three together on the same leaf-stalk, and consist of two small ones, with a third of considerable size in the middle, which is long and tapering to a point; the flowers are of the same shape as those of the sweet pea, and grow in clusters at the end of the stalk. There is a constant motion kept up among the leaves of this plant. Some will move but little, while others are greatly agitated. This motion is not caused by the air, as in the aspen tree; nor by the touch, as in the sensitive plant. Repeated experiments have proved this. When the plant is in full bloom, its leaves shake the most, so that motion seems necessary to its healthful existence. Even a branch cut off, if kept in water, will continue to move in a close room for some days.

XXVII.

The Bengal royal tiger is sometimes fifteen feet long from the tip of the nose to the tip of the tail. His height has been known to be four feet; and such is his strength, that he can carry away a buffalo, of perhaps a thousand pounds weight. When impelled by hunger, he boldly attacks the human species. At other times he shrinks away from the sight of man. The son of Sir Hector Munro was killed by a Bengal tiger in 1792; and the following is the account given by an eye witness. "We went to shoot deer on Saugur island, of which we saw innumerable tracks, as well as of tigers: we continued our diversion till nearly three o'clock; when, sitting down by the side of a jungle to refresh ourselves, a roar like thunder was heard, and an immense tiger seized our unfortunate friend, poor Munro, and rushed again into the jungle, dragging him through the thickest bushes and trees, every thing giving way to its monstrous strength; a tigress accompanied his progress. The united agonies of horror, regret, and fear, rushed at once upon us. I fired on the tiger; he seemed agitated. My companion fired also; and in a few moments after this, our unfortunate friend came up to us, bathed in blood. Every medical assistance was vain; and he expired in the space of twenty-four hours, having received such deep wounds from the teeth and claws of the animal, as rendered his recovery hopeless. A large fire, consisting of ten or twelve whole trees, was blazing near us at the time this accident took place, and ten or more of the natives were with us. The human mind can scarcely form any idea of this scene of horror. We had but just pushed our boat from this hateful shore, when the tigress made her appearance, almost raging mad, and remained on the strand all the time we continued in sight."

XXVIII.

For much authentic and curious information, respecting central India, I beg to refer the reader to Sir John Malcolm's late work, on that part of Hindostan. No attentive officer, I think, can have served in India for several years without agreeing with me, that the instances of honour and valour, displayed by various classes of Hindoos, are numerous. Sir John Malcolm, in his evidence given to the house of commons on the affairs of India, states, that he has known innumerable instances of honour among the natives, particularly the military tribes, which would in England be considered more fit for the page of romance than of history. "There is," he observès, "a large class of menials, such as Gentoo palanquin boys, at Madras, who amount to twenty or thirty thousand, a great proportion of whom are employèd by the English government, or the individuals serving it, who, as a body, are remarkable for their industry and fidelity. During a period of nearly thirty years, I cannot call to mind one instance being proved of theft, in any one of this class of men, whose average wages are from three to eight rupees a month, or from seven shillings and sixpence to one pound. I remember hearing of one instance of extraordinary fidelity, where an officer died at the distance of nearly three hundred miles from the settlement of Fort St. George, with a sum of between two and three thousand pounds in his palanquin. Those honest men, alarmed at even suspicion attaching to them, salted him, brought him three hundred miles to Madras, and lodged him in the town major's office, with all the money sealed in bags."

XXIX.

NOTHING can exceed the rich and luxuriant appearance of the face of nature in many parts of Guzerat and Bengal. Whole plains are covered with fine fruit trees, and the most beautiful diversity of crops. The eye is not only pleased with the different shades of green, and the vast varieties of flowers that border the fields, but with the bright plumage of the feathered race, and the pranks of monkeys which occupy the trees. Under many a spacious banyan tree the religious devotees will be seen practising their austerities or sitting in a state of absorption in the cool shade.

The banyan tree, or Indian fig, has a stem, branching to a great height and vast extent, with heart-shaped entire leaves, ending in acute points. This tree is beautifully described by Milton :—

"Branching so broad and long, that in the ground
The bending twigs take root, and daughters grow
About the mother tree, a pillar'd shade
High over arched and echoing walks between."

Of all trees, it is the most charming of nature's productions, and contrary to most other things in animal and vegetable life, it seems to be exempt from decay. It is continually increasing. The Hindoos look upon the banyan tree as an emblem of the Deity; from its long duration, its outspreading arms, and overshadowing beneficence. I have reposed under the Cubbeer Burr, which is the name of a banyan tree in Guzerat of prodigious size. More than five regiments might be accommodated under the delightful shade of its canopy, impervious to the hottest beams of the sun. It is about 2000 feet in circumference, measured round the principal stems; the overhanging branches, not yet struck down, cover a much larger space. The chief trunks of this single tree (which in size greatly exceed our English elms and oaks) amount to 350; the smaller stems, formed into strong supporters, are more than 3000. It is filled with green wood pigeons, doves, peacocks, and feathered songsters; crowded with squirrels, and families of monkeys; and shaded by bats of large size, many of them measuring upwards of six feet from the extremity of one wing to the other. These hang to its upper branches in a torpid state, during the day. The tree affords shelter and sustenance to all its inhabitants; being covered amidst its bright foliage with small figs of a rich scarlet, which are exceedingly pleasant to the taste. Many animals in it live upon each other, and continual warfare and stratagem are kept up between snakes, birds, monkies, &c.

Among the various trees and plants of India the following may be mentioned: the sugar cane, the bamboo, the yam, the banana, the palm tree, the sugar tree, the betel tree, the cotton tree, the jack tree, which is a fine species of the bread fruit; the tobacco plant, the cashew apple tree, the palmetto tree, the white fig or plantain tree, the castor oil plant, the white poppy, the pine apple, the guava tree, the mango tree, the peach tree, the leechu tree, &c. with all the different spice trees and plants mentioned in other parts of this work, for nearly all the productions described in our notice of the common Indian islands are produced in Hindostan or round its sea coast.

Among the wild beasts * of India may be enumerated the lion, the tiger, elephant, rhinoceros, hog, buffalo, wolf, hyæna, leopard, and tiger cat, &c.

In the number of its reptiles are the tortoise, frog, alligator, guana, chameleon, lizard, &c. Among its serpents are the hooded or spectacle snake, called in Portuguese *cobra-de-capello*, the rat snake, black snake, common ringed snake, whip snake, and sea snake. There are scorpions of a most deadly nature. Among its worms is the Indian thread worm, which attacks the muscles of the legs of both Europeans and natives, and grows there, sometimes to the length of four yards. For some time after this monster has perforated the leg, no pain is felt, but as it grows and rolls itself round in a circle, inflammation takes place and considerable pain. The best way is to rub the part affected with mercurial ointment twice a day, till ulceration reveals the head of the worm, which must be carefully taken up and fastened to a small twig, that it may be drawn out very gradually and wound round it every day. For if it breaks, and any part remains in the leg, it will grow again to a great size in a short time.

* Vide LV. of this Addenda.

XXX.

Raynal may be tolerable authority in matters of commerce, but French writers are prone to give a partial account of European transactions in India, out of prejudice to their own nation. Mr. Hastings is particularly abused by them: on this subject, Mr. Mill has been, I think, too much of an imitator. The historian, who aims at informing posterity and instructing mankind, should consult his own judgment, before he joins in popular clamour, either of censure or praise. He should endeavour to place himself in the situation of him, whose character he describes; and surrounded by all the facts he can collect, he should, I think, ask his own heart—what would I have done under these circumstances? I perfectly agree with an intelligent gentleman, who has written to me, on this subject, thus:—"With Mr. Hastings the question was, are the English to remain in India? With England the question was, did he adopt the best means of enabling us to remain there? Let the result answer. No other man, then in India, could have preserved it to us. This may be safely asserted. That any one, who has since gone thither, could have preserved it, is more disputable."

XXXI.

Except in times of great famine, no one, however poor, stands in danger of starvation in India. Hospitality to strangers, and affording relief to mendicants of all descriptions, are duties prescribed to all Hindoos by their Sastras. Menu enforces hospitality with powerful arguments. The Sastra decrees "that if a family are unable through poverty to entertain a stranger or guest, they shall beg for his relief." A traveller, when he wishes to get rest for the night, is always sure of finding it, and every thing necessary, at the first village. Consequently, in every town and village, there is some public place for the reception of strangers. If they ask assistance, they are supplied with fire, a new earthen pot to cook in, rice, or split peas, oil, spices, &c. To plant fruit trees for travellers, to make wells and tanks for their use, and to build houses for the accommodation of strangers, are duties, which every Hindoo strives to perform. Vast sums are expended by the opulent in this way. A native of Burdwan, named Ramapalu, is mentioned, who in the course of his life made 100 tanks, each of which cost about 4000 rupees, or nearly 500*l.* each. There are several fine orchards in India, with care-takers; and every stranger may enter them and eat as much fruit as he pleases. A native of Serampore, who was formerly sircar to the Dutch East India Company, fed on an average 200 strangers, at and from his house, every day, for many years, spending annually on this kind of hospitality about 6000*l.*

XXXII.

I HAVE been a little particular in describing the reception of Vasco de Gama, at the Zamorin's court, because, in all the native courts of India, the same ceremonies are yet practised with very few exceptions.

XXXIII.

THERE are but few more affecting circumstances in history than the fate of those brave men, who were immured in the Black Hole of Calcutta, by Surajah-Dowla, in June 1756. Their sufferings are pathetically described by J. Z. Holwell, Esq. The following is a brief abstract of his interesting letter to William Davis, Esq.

Governor Drake, of Calcutta, had imprisoned an Indian merchant, and thereby drawn upon the English the resentment of the Soubah of Bengal, Surajah-Dowla, who attacked the fort and factory of Calcutta. Drake, on the approach of the Indian army, abandoned the place. But the fort was bravely defended by Mr. Holwell, the garrison, and the gentlemen of the factory, who at length, being overpowered, surrendered, on condition that their lives should be spared. Mr. Holwell says, that he believes the Soubah merely gave a general order for their security during the night, and that the tragedy which followed must be attributed to the cruel and revengeful spirit of some of the inferior officers. They were forced in the dusk of the evening, by the armed guards, into a room, commonly called the black-hole prison. This horrible place was a square of eighteen feet. Imagination can alone picture what a scene it became, when 146 persons were pressed into it, in the hottest season of a burning climate. The wounded and the dying were even forced into it; the female garb was no protection; the lady shared the fate of the soldier. Immediate suffocation was prevented by two small, strongly grated windows, but the circulation of air which they admitted was only sufficient to increase misery by prolonging torment.

When Mr. Holwell entered, he immediately saw the dreadful nature of their situation. From one of the windows, he endeavoured to prevail upon the guard by the promise of a large sum of money, to remove them from this grave, or, at least, to withdraw one half of their number to another prison. But the guard, after some inquiries, returned with this horrible answer, "I cannot, sir, no one dares to awake the general." Their bodies were soon drained of moisture, by profuse perspiration. A raging thirst ensued. Mighty struggles were made to force the door; it opened inwards, and their exertions were only serviceable by precipitating them sooner into the arms of death. The weak were trampled under the feet of the strong. All those situated at any distance from the windows began to grow outrageous, and many delirious; "water, water!" became the general cry. Some skins of water were brought; but they had no means of getting it into the prison, except by hats forced through the bars of the windows. The sight of it increased thirst to such a dreadful degree, that many sunk in struggles to be first served. So little could be conveyed through the bars, that it scarcely served to moisten the burning lips of the dying sufferers. The stench from the putrid bodies became intolerable. Respect was for a long time paid to the brave Mr. Holwell. At length all distinction was lost. Nearly crushed to death, he was forced from the window. He got to the farthest part of the prison, over the dead, and laid himself down to die on their reeking bodies. His pain increased to a maddening pitch. In phrenzy he again started up, and by an exertion of unnatural strength, once more gained the window, crying "water for God's sake!" His surviving companions had thought him dead. Respect for their beloved commander still remained alive. They cried out with one voice, "give him water! give him water!" Nor would one of them at the window attempt to touch it till he had drunk. Such is the effect that a generous and noble mind has over the affections of inferiors. The water only increased his thirst, as a sprinkling on fire increases flame. He kept his mouth moist by sucking the perspiration out of his shirt; and, O deplorable situation! he was even robbed of that liquid; for he detected one of his companions plundering him; their mouths and noses often met in the contest for that moisture, which his exhausted body still retained.

The survivors, finding that water only increased their misery, changed their cry to, "air, air!" till nearly every one expired with a heart rending sigh for, "air, air!" A vapour arose from their bodies, which Mr. Holwell compares to what is felt by holding the head over a bowl of strong spirit of hartshorn. From eleven o'clock till two in the morning Mr. Holwell sustained the weight of a Dutch serjeant on his back, and another soldier leaning with his whole weight against his head. He was at length forced from pressure to sink from the bars of the window, by which he had held. On getting behind the living, he found Mrs. Carey, an officers' wife, in the third rank, raving for air. His friend, the Rev. Mr. Bellamy, lay dead, with his son, the lieutenant, melancholy sight! hand in hand!

Mr. Holwell again resigned himself to fate. He lay down on the dead to die! Towards morning the survivors, recollecting that he might have influence to get them out of prison, caused search to be made for him. He was still warm, and upon being lifted to the window, recovered sensation and reason. About a quarter past six o'clock, A. M., after great delay and difficulty in opening the door, twenty-three persons were found alive out of 146! but in a condition which made it very doubtful whether they would see the morning of the next day. Mrs. Carey survived, but her youth and beauty caused her to be detained for the conqueror, or some officer of state. Her husband was no more. The others, after long suffering, were released. Poor Holwell, though in a burning fever, with his body covered with painful boils, was taken with the other prisoners, to the capital of Bengal, loaded with chains.

On the 25th of July they were conducted to the palace to have an audience, and to know their fate. Their release was hastened by the compassionate intercession of woman, who so often assuages the suffering of man. The Soubah's grandmother solicited their liberty at a feast, to which she was invited on his safe return. On seeing their condition, he looked at them with strong marks of compassion in his countenance, ordered two of his officers to see their irons instantly struck off, and to conduct them safely wherever they chose to go, giving them a strict charge, to see that they suffered no injury or insult by the way.

XXXIV.

Tippo Sultan was the inveterate foe of all Europeans, though he made use of the French, and told them that he only hated the English.

His throne was covered with plates of gold. Over it was a canopy of the same metal, supported by eight pillars. This canopy was fringed with large pearls, and crowned with the form of a bird of paradise, made entirely of precious stones. Underneath the throne lay the figure of a tiger in the act of devouring a white man, and this concealed a curious piece of mechanism, that produced sounds, resembling the cries of a person in distress, mixed with the roarings of a tiger. His cannon, in several instances, were ornamented with the head of a white man, and a tiger devouring it. He told the French that this represented an Englishman; to the Mahrattas he said the same; but to the Mohammedans he represented it as the head of an European, promising to destroy every Christian, and establish the Mohammedan creed. One of his palaces had a curious painting on its front, which represented the defeat of Colonel Baillie. The rare face of the palace was painted with fine representations of the trades of India, &c. When looking at these paintings in the great porches or virandas of the beautiful edifice at Seringapatam, to which I allude, I was reminded of Dido's palace, as described by Virgil. Tippo's wealth was immense. He had three magnificent palaces, 7000 elephants, 6000 camels, 11,000 horses, 400,000 bullocks, 100,000 buffaloes, and 600,000 sheep. His family consisted of twelve sons and eight daughters. There were 800 females in his seraglio. His treasure was immense.

XXXV.

Sir William Jones was born in London in 1746, and died at the premature age of 48. To his works I refer the reader for many beautiful effusions of the Persian muse, and for much of what I know respecting oriental science and literature. He was the founder of the Asiatic Society, to whose researches I am much indebted. In one of his last annual discourses to that society, he has done more to give validity to the Mosaic history of the Creation, than has been done by any contemporary writer. The following is his epitaph, written by and for himself. It is admired equally for its truth and elegance:

Here was deposited
the mortal part of a man
who feared God, but not death;
and maintained independence,
but sought not riches;
who thought none below him
but the base and unjust;
none above him but the wise and virtuous;
who loved his parents, kindred, friends,
and country:
and having devoted his life to their service,
and the improvement of his mind,
resigned it calmly,
giving glory to his Creator,
wishing peace on earth,
and good will to all his creatures,
on the 27th day of April,
in the year of Our Blessed Redeemer 1794

XXXVI.

On the morning of the 5th of November, 1817, Mr. Elphinstone, the resident at Poonah, received a most insolent letter from his highness the Peishwa, and observing an armed force approaching the Sungum, where he resided, he made his escape to camp. In a few minutes the British residency was in a blaze, and all his valuable property, manuscripts, and oriental curiosities, valued at 10,000*l.*, were either plundered or consumed. At the same time the European cantonments were set on fire, and entirely destroyed. Amidst the blaze, the Peishwa's army, estimated at 15,000 cavalry and 8000 infantry, approached the British position in battle array. A Portuguese named Pinto, who held the rank of major in the Peishwa's army, commanded a battalion of infantry organised in the European style, and his park of artillery, consisting of fourteen guns, were served by Portuguese. An officer present in this action, described the approach of this host, by comparing it to the waves of an angry sea. All the heights were covered with elephants, bearing the Peishwa and his great officers of state, who came out to witness the expected destruction of the force at Kirkee.

Colonel Burr had only, to oppose this army, 3000 fighting men. With these he bravely advanced to meet the shock. The attack began with a discharge of artillery on both sides, and an attempt by the enemy's infantry to make an impression on our line, which was soon followed by a charge of their cavalry. In a body they pushed directly for the Europeans; but receiving a cool and deliberate fire, turned, and forced their way through the 7th Bombay native infantry. These brave sepoys were for some time intermixed among them, and fought nobly with their bayonets. Large masses of the cavalry got into the rear, and the engagement became very critical, depending in a great measure on the steadiness of the Europeans in the right wing, who were quite unbroken. Just at the proper moment Major Ford, who commanded the Peishwa's brigade, arrived with his men from the cantonments at Dapore, and opening a well-directed fire upon the masses of the enemy that had got into the rear, struck a panic to their hearts, which was communicated to the whole, for they retreated in the utmost confusion, leaving vast numbers of dead on the field, and never after dared to hazard a renewal of the fight.

Mr. Elphinstone, now governor of Bombay, most gallantly exerted himself throughout the day, in setting a distinguished example of zeal and animation to the troops.

XXXVII.

General Smith (now Sir Lionel Smith, C. B.) encamped exactly before the Mahrattas, the river

Moota Moola running between, and the village of Yellara, which is situated near the bank, under a height, which was called Picket Hill, being on his side, with a fine plain extending for near a mile to the enemy's lines on the other bank. The river was, however, very rocky and difficult to pass, having deep banks, and being lined with Arabs. From the hill I had a full view of the position occupied by the Peishwa's army. The city of Poonah was on his left, whence his line extended to Harris's tope, having encamped on the ground where the British cantonments had stood. His forces were now estimated at 30,000 fighting men.

On the following morning, 14th of November, 1817, proper reconnoissances having been made, some guns were placed on Picket Hill, which swept the banks of the river with grape-shot; but the Arabs having good cover, rendered it impossible for us to examine the ford with accuracy. An attempt, therefore, made during the night to cross the river, was unsuccessful. During the whole of next day, there was constant skirmishing between the Arabs and riflemen, which produced a very great display of personal bravery; for the Arabs crossed the river, and several of them lost their lives in daring attacks upon Captain Clutterbuck, and part of the light company of the 65th regiment.

Next day Colonel Milnes crossed the river, as stated in the text, and, in fact, fought the Peishwa's army with one half of General Smith's force, retaining the field of battle on the enemy's side of the river, till joined before day-light on the ensuing morning by the other division.

What induced Sir Lionel Smith to fight the battle of Poonah with one-half of his forces, and when the victory was gained, not to push on and reap all the advantages of it, puzzled some of the old officers, who talked a good deal on the subject. Powerful motives, no doubt, suggested the line of conduct pursued by General Smith, who is undoubtedly an officer of talent and genius. He was anxious, perhaps, to save the effusion of blood, which might be the consequence of a rash attack upon an enemy so vastly superior in numbers. Moreover, it was the object of both Mr. Elphinstone and General Smith to preserve the city of Poonah from plunder and destruction, which a rash battle in its immediate vicinity might have occasioned.

XXXVIII.

The village of Ashtee is situated a few miles to the north of Punderpoor, a large town on the Bheema river. When the British squadrons gained sight of the plain of Ashtee, they heard the enemy's trumpets and drums loudly proclaiming surprise; and saw the Peishwa in rapid retreat, while Gockla with a great part of the cavalry was drawn up in line of battle across the main road; he having vowed to his highness that he would cover his retreat or lose his life.

General Smith hesitated not a moment. He dispatched his staff to the different commanding officers with orders, the substance of which was that the cavalry should move down in separate columns of attack, the 22d dragoons in the centre, the 2d Madras native cavalry on the left, and the 7th Madras native cavalry on the right, while the Bombay horse artillery were directed to take up the best position according to circumstances, and at the discretion of Captain Pierce. The rifle companies of the 65th regiment marched with such persevering spirit, that they kept up with the Bombay light battalion, though mounted on tats or little country horses, and were up to form a reserve. The cavalry dashed down the heights in fine style to charge Gockla. The ground was so rugged that the horse artillery could not get forward in time to form line with the cavalry, who made directly for the centre of the masses before them. It was an awful sight. A dead silence prevailed. Gockla had chosen his ground with great judgment behind a nullah, and other obstacles, which he justly calculated would keep back the artillery. His appearance was very formidable, the front ranks of his line having their spears couched, while the rear ranks seemed drawn up on a ridge higher than the front, armed with matchlocks. They opened a heavy fire upon the cavalry, when within 150 yards of their line, which was not returned till we arrived within a few paces of the Mahratta front.

The 22d dragoons commenced the action on our side, by discharging their pistols in the faces of the enemy, and charging their centre. For a few seconds it was a close and warm combat. General Smith, full of anxiety to see the cavalry close with the enemy, had galloped into the space between the right of the 7th and the left of the artillery, the guns having now come up. In this situation he was much exposed. Gockla knew that our artillery could not be used on account of the confused scene which a close combat presents. He had a chosen body in reserve behind his left wing, for the purpose of attacking our rear or flank; and, while the shock of the charge made by the 22d dragoons had forced his centre to give way, he wheeled with the greatest rapidity round his left, and passing between our guns and the right of the cavalry, attacked the 7th in rear with impetuosity. General Smith was cut down, and some confusion was produced; but Major Daw, with part of the 22d, charged Gockla, who was killed in this desperate but brave attempt. The whole of the Mahrattas immediately fled. General Smith had received the blow of a sabre on the back of his head, but fortunately the wound was not dangerous. The slaughter of the enemy was great, and they were pursued for many miles. All the plain was strewed with their dead and wounded. The main body was overtaken, but the Peishwa escaped on a fleet horse. A great many of his elephants and camels, some of them loaded with treasure, were taken, and the Sattara rajah, his mother, and his two brothers rescued, as I have related in the text. Our loss was only one officer, and thirty non-commissioned, rank and file killed and wounded, with some horses.

Gockla's body was found covered with wounds. It was burned in the evening, the ceremonial being accompanied with all due honours, according to the customs of his caste. His person was large, his features fine and manly, his complexion nearly fair. He had received several deep cuts on his face; but it could not be ascertained under whose hand he had fallen. Several inferior chiefs shared his fate around him. He wore on the morning of the action a rich dress of gold kinkob, a kind of thick satin finely flowered, with a pearl necklace, diamond earrings, and an ornament for the turban of great value, which became the plunder of some of the camp followers; for the bodies of all the officers were found nearly naked upon the return of the cavalry, our infantry with the camp equipage, &c. having in the meantime arrived.

It is impossible not to respect the spirit of Gockla. The judgment with which he prepared to receive General Smith, was only equalled by his valour and skill in bravely endeavouring to retrieve the day, upon finding that his centre could not withstand the charge of the 22d dragoons; and the muse of history will encircle his name with a laurel for fidelity and devotion in his country's cause.

XXXIX.

During the cool of each morning, the queen mother of Sattara and her two sons rode richly caparisoned Mahratta horses, and only mounted their elephants in the heat of the day. The queen managed her horse with great dexterity, and rode, according to the custom of the ladies of her country, as gentlemen do with us. She bore the traces of great beauty, wore a rich dress of embroidered muslin, with but few ornaments; she did not conceal her face, and was both familiar and talkative with such officers as approached. I have conversed with her on the line of march in Hindostannee, which she spoke in a very sweet tone of voice. In person she was rather above the middle size, and her complexion was almost fair. She evinced an ardent desire to appropriate every thing that was captured to herself; for she claimed all the elephants and camels, with every fine horse and tent she saw, as her own. Her age seemed between forty and fifty. She had none of that timidity which one naturally supposes to belong to Hindoo ladies. Her sons were richly dressed in gold muslins and kinkobs, with pearl necklaces of three rows set in gold, and sparkling with precious stones; their turbans and earrings were very costly; they wore trowsers with feet like stockings, and slippers turned up at the toes, covered with precious gems. They had a long procession of elephants and camels, with flags, streamers, and various instruments of music. Upon approaching towns or villages the trumpets were sounded, and the musicians, who rode on camels, began to beat their great drums, when the inhabitants came out in crowds, and prostrated themselves before their legitimate sovereign.

XL.

UPON the deposition of Bajee-row, late Peishwa, the rajah of Sattara was invested with the ancient rights of his family, and a considerable tract of territory round the fortress of Sattara placed under his government. His restoration does not, however, give him much political power; but it places ample means at his disposal to make himself and others happy in private life, or in ostentatious display. His history forms a parallel to that of the ancient family of Mysore, and his political existence is precisely of the same nature.

Sattara, his capital, is forty-seven miles south of Poonah. The name signifies seventeen, being the number of walls, towers, and gates, the fortress originally possessed. It was taken from the sovereign of Bejapoor, by Sevajee in 1651. I have been in it. It stands on a hill belonging to a range which it completely commands. The height of the fort is about 300 yards above the plain, its length 1200, and its breadth varying from 300 to 80 on the western point. There is a table land formed by the hand of nature on the top, which is a huge rock of granite; it is cut perpendicularly all round, at an average of thirty feet. On this solid foundation the rampart is built of masonry, about eight feet high and as many broad. Numerous towers and bastions are erected round it; and there were twenty-seven guns mounted on the works, when we took it in 1818. There is only one gate, exceedingly strong, but a sally-port, defended by two towers, opens in an opposite direction. Four fine tanks contain an abundance of water; and in short there is a small town on the summit, with an excellent house, in which the rajah resided, when a prisoner. The petah, or city of Sattara, lies below in the plain under the north face of the fort; it is of great extent. The houses are built of stone and lime, with good streets. The top of the hill commands a most delightful view of the valleys of Sattara, through which the Krishna and Oomronly rivers meander and glitter to the eye with pleasing variety, sometimes hid beneath the rich foliage of fruit trees, and occasionally breaking forth in unexpected turns upon the sight. These lovely vales are decorated with numerous smiling villages, and curious pagodas, the whole appearing to the eye like an extensive garden from its high state of cultivation.

XLI.

The Countess of Loudon will also participate with her noble lord, the sweet reflection of having done every thing in her power, during a long residence in India, to benefit her fellow-creatures of all colours. Her ladyship was a munificent friend to all the institutions in the East for the alleviation of distress, or the diffusion of knowledge; the zealous patroness of the education of the poor; the kind supporter of the widow and orphan; the unsolicited benefactress of the friendless, and a transcendant example of tenderness, morality, and religion. Her benevolence was the theme of poetry as well as prose.

> "Soft as the silver moon's refreshing rays
> Thy dewy kindness on poor blacky plays,
> And cheers the drooping head that friendless lies,
> And gives the heart, just sinking, hope to rise."
>
> *The Farewell at Champaul Ghaut; a Poem, written in* 1814.

XLII.

The history of the East India Company's establishments in Bengal is interesting. In 1553 the Portuguese began to trade with the natives on the banks of the Ganges. They at length established factories at several places in Bengal. Their influence was such, that other Europeans had, for a long time, to trade through them. Soon after the embassy of Sir Thomas Roe, the English were permitted to establish a factory at Pipley, a small town situated on the Subunreeka river, twenty-two miles from Bulasore. In 1642 the chief seat of our trade in Bengal was fixed, by Mr. Day, at Bulasore; but owing to the extortions of the officers of the Great Mogul, all our factories were at length withdrawn. A decided preference was evinced by the native authorities for the French, Dutch, and Danes, who were permitted to establish themselves in the vicinity of the Portuguese chief settlement at Hooghly, situated twenty-six miles above Calcutta. In 1670, owing to the prudent conduct of Mr. Job Charnock, the English were re-established in Bengal, and re-occupied a factory at Hooghly, which they had been permitted to build in 1640, soon after a great rupture between the Moguls and Portuguese. The Moguls besieged the Portuguese settlement at Hooghly in 1632, and took the place by storm, after four months' hard fighting. Matters, however, were afterwards adjusted between the hostile powers. In 1686 the English came to blows with the Moguls, in consequence of a quarrel between some of our soldiers and the Nabob's collectors of revenue in the bazar. After this Hooghly was thought an unsafe station; and on the 20th of December, 1686, the agent and council of the presidency of Bengal removed the seat of government to a little village, called Chuttanhutty, now named Calcutta, from a small place near it. Mr. Boughton, an assistant surgeon of the Company's service, had cured the daughter of one of the Mogul emperors of a dangerous disease, and obtained for his employers, if my information be correct, a title to the villages of Chuttanhutty and Calcutta. In 1696, during the rebellion of Soubah Sing, the English, Dutch, and French were permitted to build forts at Calcutta, Chinsurah, and Chandernagor. In 1698 the fort of Calcutta was strengthened, and called Fort William in compliment to the king of England. Here the Company flourished till 1756, when it was taken. Next year it was recaptured by Admiral Watson and Colonel Clive, who, on the 20th of June, 1757, fought the battle of Plassey, and laid the foundation of British empire in Bengal.

XLIII.

Fort William is superior to any other fortress in India. It is constructed on the most scientific principles of military architecture. The barracks in it are superb. In this fortress the Company have an excellent arsenal, and a gun foundry. The new fort was commenced in 1758. When I viewed the curiosities of Fort William, Vizier Ally, once nabob of Oude, was confined in it, in a room made to resemble an iron cage, for the murder of Mr. Cherry, where he lingered out seventeen years of his life, and died at the age of thirty-six, in the year 1817. The vicissitudes of his life are worthy of a brief notice.

The mother of Vizier Ally was a menial servant of low caste. She attracted the notice of Asoph-ud-Dowlah, nabob of Oude, who was a very eccentric character. Having no children of his own, he was in the habit of sending pregnant women, whom he met, to his palace; and among others he sent the mother of Vizier Ally, whom he afterwards adopted according to the forms of Mohammedan law. The Nabob is said to have expended 200,000*l.* annually on English manufactures. He had 100 gardens, 20 palaces, 1200 elephants, 3000 fine saddle horses, 1500 double barrel guns, 1700 superb lustres, 30,000 table shades, and as many large mirrors, girandoles, and clocks, two of which cost him 30,000*l.* He often entertained his European friends with champaign dinners, in a carriage drawn by elephants. There were a thousand choice beauties in his harem. In his treasury were jewels to the amount of 8,000,000 sterling.

All these became the property of his adopted son, Vizier Ally, whose wedding cost the Nabob 300,000*l.* It is described in another part of this work. Vizier Ally, when he became nabob, having broken his faith in several instances with the Honourable Company, was deposed, and placed on a pension of 25,000*l.* per annum. Being of a turbulent and intriguing disposition, it was thought expedient that he should reside near the presidency, and he had reached Benares, for the purpose of proceeding thither, when he most treacherously murdered Mr. Cherry, the Company's resident, who had invited him to breakfast. Upon a signal given, his armed retinue rushed in and cut Mr. Cherry and his assistant, Mr. Graham, to pieces. They then departed with the determination of massacring all the Europeans at that station, but were fortunately delayed by a noble defence made by Mr. Davis with a hog spear. Hearing of their approach, he posted himself at the head of his stairs, and blocked up the passage with the dead bodies of his assailants. By this time a detachment arrived from the cantonments. Vizier Ally and his followers fled, and escaped into the territories of a native prince, who refused to give him up except on condition of his life being spared. This our government thought it expedient to promise, and he was accordingly confined in the manner described. When I saw him, he was a poor emaciated being.

XLIV.

The Armenian merchants of India are a public spirited set of men. When Sarkies Joannes of Calcutta heard of the recovery of George the Third in 1789, he paid the debts of all the prisoners at that time in gaol, which so much pleased His Majesty, that he sent him his picture in miniature through Lord Cornwallis. Their dress is very splendid. In show and equipage they are exceedingly ostentatious; their ladies are covered with jewels, and wear crowns sparkling with precious gems.

XLV.

In Calcutta a civilian's lady considers herself a superior being to the wife of a military officer; the latter looks down with contempt on the partner of a country captain, who, in her turn, despises the shopkeeper, and frets if neglected by the merchant's wife. "To hand a lady to table, or to her carriage," says Tennant, "is an affair which requires deep cogitation, if it be aspired to by a gentleman whose rank is unequal to the office, instead of paying a compliment he is guilty of rudeness, and commits an unpardonable offence. When the ladies take the floor to dance, the most perfect acquaintance with all that has ever been written upon heraldry would not enable you to make a satisfactory arrangement either of the ladies themselves or of their partners." The Countess of Loudon discountenanced this fastidiousness; it is to be hoped effectually.

XLV.*

The governor-general's palace in Calcutta, and his gardens at Barrackpore, are perhaps inferior to none in the world in magnificence and extent. In the streets of Calcutta may be seen Chinese and Frenchmen, Persians and Germans, Arabs and Spaniards, Americans and Portuguese, Mohammedans, Hindoos, and English, all thronging together. Coaches, phaetons, chaises, gigs, hackeries or country carriages, palanquins, camels, elephants, and horses, also vary the scene. At night the jackalls keep up a constant serenade for vast quantities of broken victuals thrown away from every house during the day. There are several kinds of boats on the Hooghly, but the most elegant and commodious are called budgerows. They vary in size. Some of them are sixty feet in length. They are generally furnished with from twelve to twenty oars, and have one mast in the centre. There is usually one large apartment with two sleeping rooms, and in travelling on the Ganges each budgerow is generally attended by one or two small boats, to carry kitchen utensils and luggage. The Moors build their budgerows long and narrow. Sometimes they are a hundred feet in length, and not eight feet wide, so that, instead of having rooms, like the English travelling boats, they erect an awning along the deck, supported by pillars, which are usually gilt and painted. The whole being gaily ornamented, and the rowers in fancy dresses, the sight is very pleasing to behold; and the fine weather, which continues with certainty in this climate for several months, enables them to live in the open air very comfortably, merely requiring a canvas screen round them at night.

XLVI.

Madras, like Calcutta, rose from an insignificant village in a few years, under the English. In 1639 Mr. Day was invited by the local governor to form a settlement on his coast, and a grant of five miles of territory around, where Madras now stands, was obtained from the king of Vijaya-nagar. Here Mr. Day laid the foundation of Fort St. George. Sir Edward Winter in 1665, upon being superseded in the government of it, by Mr. Foxcroft, seized and imprisoned him. He kept possession of the fort and government for three years, when he delivered them up to commissioners from England, on condition of receiving a full pardon for all offences. Madras has suffered from no external attacks since the French were repulsed in 1759, although approached very near by Hyder Alli in 1767 and 1781. Since the return of Sir George Hilario Barlow in 1814, it has been well governed by the Honourable Hugh Elliot.

The town of Madras is situated upon a flat sandy shore, where the surf runs with extreme violence. Externally the houses are like marble temples; the interior, however, does not correspond with the outside; the apartments presenting nothing but white walls; few of them have ceilings, from the impossibility of finding any material that shall resist the ravages of the white ant. To a stranger approaching Madras from the sea, the whole scene appears like enchantment. The clear blue sky, the polished white buildings, the bright sandy beach, and the dark green sea, combine to abstract the mind. All my faculties seemed bewildered when I was entering the roads. The catamarans were paddling towards us, with naked Indians, who looked for some time as if they were walking on the water; for the catamaran is merely a log of wood or two, laced together. In the distance were the Mossolah boats dashing through the surf, crowded with natives in long muslin gowns and turbans, their ears and noses decorated with large rings of gold and pearls. They climbed our ships' side and saluted us with almost superhuman grace. I gazed at their jet black faces, and delicately formed persons, reminding me more of elegantly tall females than men. On going ashore, the motley group, to be seen in the streets, is equally interesting. The stranger is instantly surrounded by dobashes, or natives, looking for service with Europeans. The surf roars in his ears; their clamorous appeals add to his distraction. Every thing he sees is new and extraordinary. He at length, lost in wonder, retires to rest; fantastic dreams follow him; he disturbs the economy of his bed; the musquittoes enter, and he awakes the next morning, bitten all over by these voracious devils, which may be compared to the infernal furies of cold climate.

XLVII.

Sir William Jones long ornamented the East of India, like the morning star; and Sir James Macintosh rose in the western hemisphere of Hindostan, like the planet of evening. He was mainly instrumental in founding the Bombay Literary Society, whose labours have shed considerable light on the history of western India. Sir James's address to Lieutenants Macguire and Cauty, who were tried before him at Bombay, for rioting at night, &c. should be copied into the common place book of every officer in the service.
Fifteen Years in India, p. 159.

XLVIII.

The following particulars respecting Bombay are deemed interesting.

Bombay is one of a cluster of six small islands, which form together one of the safest and most commodious harbours in the world. Near the southern extremity of the island stands the lighthouse, which rises to the height of 150 feet above the level of the sea, and shews its light at the distance of twenty-one miles. Nearly the whole of Bombay belong to opulent Parsees. Their wealth is only equalled by their industry. Some of the entertainments given by the late great Parsee, Pestengee, cost 12,000*l*. In the last famine which desolated India, a Parsee merchant fed 5000 poor persons daily, for three months. The Company's dock yard of Bombay is entirely under the control of the family of the celebrated Lowjee. He and his successors have built four seventy-four gun ships, two thirty-eight, two thirty-sixes, besides twenty-five merchantmen, from 1000 to 600 tons burden, &c., and some smaller craft. The Parsees assist each other, like the quakers; none of them have been convicted by a court of justice for any crime or immoral practice for many years. Their wives and daughters are remarkable for virtue and affection. The pamphlet and bambalo of the Bombay reef, two species of fish so called, are remarkably fine.

The island of Elephanta, in Bombay harbour, so famous on account of its caves is about three miles in circumference. It consists of two rocky mountains and some rice fields, in a small valley between them, with a few cocoa nut plantations. The great stone elephant at the bottom of the principal mountain, from which the island derives its name, is now broken down, and lying in scattered fragments. Upon clambering up to the caves, I found a serjeant's guard of sepoys in charge of them, and a snug house built on the summit. The great cave is a huge chamber hollowed out of the rock, so as to leave four rows of massive columns standing, which appear to support the roof. These form magnificent avenues. The cave is 220 feet long, and 150 broad. At the upper end of this great room is the immense three headed idol, representing Brahma, Vishnu, and Seeva, with their symbols, &c. reaching nearly from the floor to the roof, a height of fifteen feet. Each face alone is five feet in length. Many of the fables related in Hindoo mythology, are represented in this cave on the living rock. The whole is a wonderful specimen of art and labour.

I went also to see the caves of Kenneri on the

island of Salsette. The great one is hollowed out of the rock. It is ninety feet long and near forty wide, with a high fluted concave roof. Two rows of columns divide it into three aisles; at the extremity of the centre one is a huge circular figure, about nineteen feet high, and forty-eight in circumference, which is believed to have been worshipped by the Jains. There are figures on the tops of the pillars, executed in fine style, representing bulls, elephants, lions, and fanciful animals. Farther up the mountain are numerous other caves, but of a smaller description, which are supposed to have been the habitations of the priests belonging to the large cave or temple.

Bombay has been much improved by its present governor, Mr. Elphinstone, who has caused new barracks to be built on the island of Calabah, which will shortly be connected with Bombay by a vellard, or great causeway.

XLIX.

As I had an opportunity of inspecting the caves of Elora, during my service in the Deccan, I beg to present the reader with a slight sketch of what I saw.

I approached the mountain of Elora across a fine plain, on which our army was encamped. The mountain is of a semicircular form, and in extent about 2000 yards. After passing a walled town called Cassebeara, I came to the extensive ruins of the city of Elora. Here I was met by a Brahman, who undertook to conduct me up to the caves. The mountain is a solid mass of fine granite, about 400 feet above the level of the plain. There are eight principal caves, and about twenty small ones, along its face, some of which are not worth notice.

Among the large caves, one is like Elephanta, and another resembles the great cave on Salsette. There is a pagoda here cut out of the solid rock, 100 feet high. Thousands of colossean figures, fourteen feet high, ornament the walls. A miser is seen, in one of the caves, cut out of rock, ten feet high, with his children and wife, imploring charity, while a thief is stealing away bags of money from behind him. The largest cave is called Rhylas or Paradise. It is 245 feet long and 143 broad. Some of the caves are of three stories, communicating with each other by a flight of stairs. Each story has a grand viranda, supported by fine pillars running along its front. The great pagoda has thousands of figures, both within and without, in basso relievo, together with numerous separate statues, representing the conquest of Ceylon, &c. There is between the pagoda and the scarped rock a considerable space. Under the rock are a viranda and galleries, in which fifty giants stand as guards. The height of the scarp is ninety feet, and from the galleries the pagoda appears as if it had been placed on the backs of elephants, tigers, and lions, and as if its weight were crushing them to death; for only the heads, legs, and part of their bodies appear outside.

L.

I AM aware that a good account of Dwarka pagoda is much wanted. The following brief sketch comprises the particulars which I have been able to collect respecting it, and other places connected with it.

Dwarka means the gate; it is a town, and celebrated temple in the province of Guzerat, situated at the south-west extremity of the Peninsula, called Kattywar, the point of which is named Okamundel, or the wild district. This place is at present possessed by Mooloo Manick, who has twenty-one villages, containing a population of 12,000 souls under him. Chrishna, the favourite Hindoo deity, long resided here, both before and after his expulsion by Jarasandha from Mathura. It is, therefore, a celebrated place of pilgrimage. About 20,000 pilgrims arrive there annually, and the revenue derived to the temple, &c. amounts to 18,000*l.* on an average every year.

In performing this pilgrimage the following ceremonies take place. The pilgrim bathes, for which he pays a certain sum. He then visits the great idol and makes offerings in proportion to his circumstances. Then he goes with a certificate, to a pagoda at Aramra, only a few miles distant, where he is stamped with a hot iron instrument, on which are engraved the shell, the ring, and the lotos flower, the insignia of the gods. The impression is generally made on the arms. At Aramra, the pilgrim embarks for the island of Bate, which is in sight, where he makes other offerings at a sacred temple there, and receives the final benediction. The Brahmans of India use the chalk of Dwarka for marking their foreheads. It is, therefore, a principal article of exportation, being supposed to have been deposited there by Chrishna. Merchants carry it all over India; and the Brahmans have a secret by which they can distinguish it from all other chalk, though similar in appearance. They can, in like manner, at all the temples in India, distinguish water brought from the sources of the Ganges, from any other.

The Okamundel is separated from Kattywar by a run, or swamp, formed by the sea making a breach from the north-west shore, near Pindletaruk, and extending in a south-east direction, again almost connects itself with the sea at Muddee, which is about fourteen miles distant from Pindletaruk. The breadth of this channel gradually decreases; at Muddee it is not more than a mile, and is separated from the ocean by a low bank, about fifty yards wide. The highest spring tides flood the run to the depth of eighteen inches; at other times it is dry, incrusted with salt, and may be crossed with ease. From the earliest period of history, commerce and agriculture have been disregarded here by the inhabitants, who addicted themselves to piracy, and still persevere in the habits of their forefathers. They are of Wagur origin, having come, it is said, originally from Cutch. Their appearance is wild and barbarous. It may be said they live by plunder. In courage and enterprise they are not surpassed by any people of India. The reliance they place on their deities at Dwarka and Bate inspires them with confidence to undertake any thing. Runchor, the god of Dwarka, is supposed to protect them while at sea. His priests are the chief instigators of piracy. Many vessels are fitted out in his name, as sole owner, and actually belong to the temple, which receives the plunder they bring back; as well as a part from all private adventurers. Recently, these predatory expeditions have been greatly restrained by the British naval power; but the inhabitants retain all their ancient propensity to the practice. In 1809 we compelled the chiefs of Dwarka, Bate, &c., to enter into treaties to restrain their subjects from acts of piracy; but since that period expeditions have several times been sent against the pirates of Okamundel.

Bate signifies an island of any kind, but the proper name of this small one is Shunkudwar. It derives this name from a Hindoo demon who lived here in a large shunk, or conch shell. An incarnation of Vishnu, called Shunknarrayan, destroyed him, and established his own worship on the island, where it continued until the flight of Runchor from Dwarka, to escape a Mohammedan army. He is now supreme. Bate has one good harbour, and a fort so strong, that it resisted our naval attack in 1803, when the British lost a number of men before it. About 150 vessels of different sizes belong to the port of Bate. The town contains about 2000 houses, with a population of 10,000 souls; but besides the town of Bate, the government or chief of that island has Aramra, Positra, Bhurwalla, and some other places. The whole revenue does not exceed 30,000*l.* per annum, from the temple and all other sources.

In 1816 I belonged to the field-force sent against the pirates of Okamundel. After rooting out several nests, we invested Dwarka, and the chief of that place was forced to surrender it. The town is small. It is surrounded by a weak wall and towers. An arm of the sea runs up along one of its faces, and forms a fine bathing place. The charms of this delightful sheet of water, which flows over sand so sparkling, that the bottom can be seen at all times, perhaps suggested the idea to some artful Brahman of establishing his worship here, under an incarnation of Vishnu. When the temples were built is quite unknown. Where the materials were procured is doubtful. The natives say they were built in one night by the gods. I could not obtain any information whatever respecting their early history, except such fables as my judgment pronounced absurd. They are, however, works of unquestionable magnificence; prodigious expense and labour must have been incurred in their erection. It does not appear to me that the antiquity of these pagodas is near so great as some others I have seen in India. There is a freshness about them which the great pagodas in the south of India have not. Yet their antiquity is certainly great, and there is proof that they have existed nearly in their present state for upwards of 800 years. Bate was taken in 1462 by Sultan Mahmood Begra, of Ahmedabad, and at that time there were accounts of the Dwarka pagoda for 500 years back. The priests pretend that the original island of Dwarka sunk, when Chrishna was translated to heaven; and that their pagodas were built by the gods to keep up his worship, where they now are, but that they are not near so magnificent as the old pagodas. In their books it is pretended that they have accounts of the present pagodas for some thousands of years: in short, since the death of Chrishna. Krisnu was the eighth avater, or incarnation of Vishnu. His era is not exactly known. Budha was the ninth avater of Vishnu, and Sir William Jones was of opinion that he existed in the year 1014 before the birth of Christ.

On approaching Dwarka, I was struck with the magnificent external appearance of the temples. Within the wall which surrounds the town there are two very large ones, and four much smaller. They stand on very elevated ground. One is an immense pyramid, at least 140 feet high, crowned with glittering balls, having a flag near the top, with a sun and moon. It is curiously carved from bottom to top, like the pagodas in the south of India, and composed of prodigiously large stones. There are seven stories in the pyramid, and two in the base on which it rests. The other great pagoda is not so high, but it is broader; the roof is carried up curiously, by one retirement after another, till it ends in a circular form, surmounted by a ball and flag. Round the outside of that temple, both above and below, there are curious galleries or virandas, which were crowded with Brahmans, who live in the upper part of the temples. The four small pagodas are pyramids, with flags, and glittering tops, but they are not very striking objects, compared with the two large temples. All these are built in the ancient Egyptian style of architecture. A handsome dome is put over the entrance to one of the pagodas, but I conceive this to have been a modern addition.

You go from the bathing-place up to the temples by a long flight of stairs, and pass through a strong gate, when the whole at once breaks upon the sight with a wonderfully grand effect. Indeed the bathing-place is also an object of curiosity. It extends along the shore in front of the town for 400 yards, and there are noble flights of stone steps down to the water, which is so clear, that you can see the sacred fishes sporting about, quite tame, and feeding from the pilgrims' hands. Along the bank, below the walls of the town, there are hundreds of little temples in the Grecian and Egyptian styles, supported on pillars, to screen the pilgrims from the sun, and for the Brahmans, barbers, &c. to sit in, who prepare the devotees for visiting the idols.

Runchor, the supreme idol, is on a throne in the great temple, and I could only see that he was gorgeously dressed, and covered with gold brocade. His face was frightfully painted, and he looked horrible amidst the glare of lamps that surrounded him in his abode, from which the light of day is excluded. In the other temples there are idols called Trincongee, Cullangee, &c. &c., which relate to the exploits of Runchor, if my information be correct. I was nearly crushed to death by the pressure of the crowd. The great drums were beating; the trumpets were sounding; large conch shells were roaring; shrill instruments of music were heard in all directions; the Brahmans were praying aloud, and extorting offerings from the unwilling devotees, some of whom were most anxious to purchase their certificates at as cheap a rate as possible; the devotees were prostrating themselves, and muttering various dialects; and, in short, the whole was a scene of noise and confusion, which to be conceived must be experienced.

We went afterwards to Aramra and Bate; but the temples are not worth description after Dwarka. Game is very plentiful in Okamundel. Hares, partridges, quails, foxes, &c., are numerous, with a wild hog starting from every copse. The camel breeds here, and thrives well on the various shrubs that grow into almost impenetrable jungles in many parts of Okamundel. It is said that there are wild camels in the jungles of Okamundel.

It should be mentioned that the Dwarka pagodas are enclosed in a square, whose side is about 200 yards, by a wall fourteen feet high, and of considerable thickness. Besides the great gate from the sea face, there are other small ones, which communicate with the town. I think there are about 1000 houses within the walls of the town, well built of stone and lime, with tiled roofs; but there is a petah, or suburb, near the bathing-place, which contains a great many people, and I think the population does not fall short of 10,000 souls. The town of Dwarka was taken by escalade by our troops in 1820; upon which occasion the pirates and Arabs, in the service of Mooloo Manick, took post in the pagodas, where they might have defended themselves for a long time. Their priests, apprehensive for the safety of the temples, persuaded the garrison to evacuate the sacred precincts, when our men were getting over the wall, after sustaining some loss. The Arabs and pirates then took post in a swamp, where they were surrounded, and forced to surrender by discharges of grape shot, but not till they had killed and wounded several of our officers and soldiers. To prevent the pirates from re-forming their forces, I understand there is a British detachment now stationed in the Okamundel.

LI.

Ramisseram is an island situated in the straits between the island of Ceylon and the continent. It is eleven miles in length, by six the average breadth. There is a pagoda here of very great antiquity. The entrance to it is through a lofty gateway, 100 feet high, covered with carved work. Its door is forty feet high, composed of single stones, placed perpendicularly, with others crossing over. The square of the whole is about 600 feet, and it is certainly one of the finest pieces of architecture in India.

Seringham is a sacred island, formed by the rivers Cavery and Coleroon, near Trichinopoly. The pagoda is composed of seven square enclosures, one within the other, the walls of which are twenty-five feet high, and four thick. These enclosures are 350 feet distant from one another, and each has four large gates, with a high tower. The outward wall is four miles in circumference. Its gateways are ornamented with pillars, several of which are single stones, thirty-three feet long, and five in diameter. The idols are placed in magnificent chapels, in the inner enclosure.

Conjeveram is a town of considerable size in the Carnatic, forty-six miles south-west from Madras. The pagoda here is dedicated to Mahadeva, or the mother of the gods. It is a magnificent structure. There is an edifice near it for the accommodation of pilgrims, supported by one thousand stone pillars, carved with figures of Hindoo deities in a very masterly manner.

The Chillambaram pagodas are situated on the sea coast of the Carnatic, a little to the south of Porto Novo, 120 miles from Madras. You enter them by a stately gate, under a pyramid 122 feet high, built with large stones, above forty feet long, and more than five feet square, all covered with plates of copper, adorned with a variety of figures, neatly executed.

There are in the Carnatic, many other great monuments of the arts, demonstrative of the civilisation of that part of India at a very remote period. Many of them are now in ruins. Others have been repaired at a vast expense, by devout individuals. To describe them all would lead me beyond my limits.

LII.

When Dowlutabad was taken by Allah-ud-Deen, it was called Deoghur, or Tagara, which means the city of God. It belonged to a powerful Hindoo rajah, and from the immense treasure found in it, the Moguls changed its name to Dowlutabad, which means the rich city.

One of the greatest curiosities of the Deccan is the hill fort of Dowlutabad, in which the Nizam has a garrison. It is cut out of the solid rock, and apparently impregnable; for the perpendicular height of each face is about ninety feet, and it has a wet ditch, thirty feet broad, and twenty deep. From the capital of the scarp, the hill shelves up to a point, so gradually, that even if the besiegers could mount the first perpendicular, their labour would be little more than commenced. The hill itself may be about 350 feet high from the base, and it is cut nearly into a square. It is quite a shell, the fort being excavated out of it, with tanks for the retention of water, and winding passages that astonish those who have visited its interior. These excavations were made before the invention of gunpowder, and the immense body of solid stone cut away was transported from its original situation to various parts of the fort and city, by the tedious means of human labour.

LIII.

THERE is a letter on record from Jeswunt Sing, rajah of Judpore, to the emperor Aurengzebe, which places the universal charity of the Hindoos in a very amiable point of view.

"Your royal ancestor, Acber, whose throne is now in heaven, conducted the affairs of this empire in equity and firm security for the space of fifty-two years, preserving every tribe of men in ease and happiness; whether they were followers of Jesus or of David, of Moses or of Mohammed; were they Brahmans, were they of the sect of Dhariens, which denies the eternity of matter, or of that which ascribes the existence of the world to chance, they all equally enjoyed his countenance and favour; insomuch that his people, in gratitude for the indiscriminate protection which he afforded them, distinguished him by the appellation of Jugot Grow, guardian of mankind. If your majesty places any faith in those books, by distinction called divine, you will there be instructed, that God is the God of all mankind, not the God of Mohammedans alone. The Pagan and the Mussulman are equally in his presence. Distinctions of colours are of his ordination. It is he who gives existence. In your temples dedicated to his name, the voice is raised in prayer; in a house of images where the bell is shaken, still he is the object of adoration. To vilify the religion and customs of other men, is to set at nought the pleasure of the Almighty. When we deface a picture, we naturally incur the resentment of the painter; and justly has the poet said, 'Presume not to arraign, or to scrutinize the various works of power divine.'"

LIV.

Mr. Percival, in his account of Ceylon, mentions the Indian ichneumon as a great snake destroyer. It is a little creature like a mangoose. On seeing a snake it instantly darts upon it, seizes the snake by the throat, and kills it, however large, by repeated attacks. It is said, the ichneumon knows certain herbs, which are antidotes against the poison of every species of snake. Mr. Percival witnessed many experiments. The ichneumon never would attack a snake, but in an open place, where upon being bitten, he could run and eat of the herb which he knew to be an antidote against the poison. He always returned with redoubled vigour to the attack after tasting the antidote.

LV.

Among the field-sports of India, hunting the tiger with elephants, and the wild hog with spears on horseback, are the most noble and dangerous. No country has a greater variety of game than India. The cheeta or a small species of leopard is used in hunting the antelope. Hawks are also used by some of the natives in field-sports. The natives have many ingenious and curious ways of catching game and fish. One is by gluing the feathered race to a long rod with bird-lime. The rod consists of a great many different joints, which are put on as they are wanted by the sportsman, who pushes it gently towards his object, till it touches and makes a prisoner of the unsuspecting creature, which takes it for a small branch, or some harmless twig. Water fowl are caught by a decoy placed over the head of the sportsman. The birds, not being afraid, permit him to swim towards them, when he catches them by the legs, and pulls them under water, without alarming the other ducks, or whatever he may be after. Fish are hunted into nets by a great many boys and girls, who form a circle in a fish pond, and beat the water with their hands and feet, making a great noise at the same time. The frightened fishes fly from them towards the centre, and leap into a large net, held so as to catch them.

LVI.

For an alphabetical abstract of the act 53 Geo. 3. c. 155. dated the 21st July, 1813, I refer the reader to the East India register and directory to be found in nearly every coffee-room in the kingdom. By this act the Company's charter is extended to the 10th of April, 1831, but it is not to cease and be determined until the expiration of three years' notice by parliament after that period, and payment of what is due from the public to the Company.

I also refer the reader to the East India Register and Directory for regulations respecting military and other officers retiring from the Company's service; furlough regulations, &c., &c.; tables of pay and allowances; a catalogue of oriental publications, or works on India, comprising the general literature of that country; with many other useful heads, and the present state of the Company's civil and military service.

LVII.

There are not in the world more liberal or considerate masters than the East India Company. The members of this distinguished body both individually and collectively truly deserve the title of honourable. It is their wish that every man in their employment should be happy. Certain independence is placed before their servants. Every one of their officers both civil and military may command the smiles of fortune by honour and fidelity. Military officers have nearly three times the pay and allowances in India, they receive in England. The civil servants have salaries rising from 40*l.* to 1000*l.* a month, or from nearly 500*l.* to 12,000*l.* per annum. Officers belonging to His Majesty's regiments serving in India, have the same pay and allowances as the Company's officers of the same rank. They have not, however, the same prospect of independence. Nearly all local staff situations are held by Company's officers. Many of them could not be held by King's officers, who take no oath of fidelity to the Honourable Company. Commands, however, are given to King's officers according to seniority; and the situations of brigade-majors, brigade-quartermasters, aides-de-camp, with a few other small posts, are open to captains and subalterns, but all the departments under the local governments are filled with their own servants. To be just before we are liberal, is right. When we reflect, however, that many King's officers serve twenty years in India, their exclusion from lucrative posts is a great hardship. In twenty years a military man seldom gets above the rank of a captain. Though his pay be three times as much in India as in Europe, his expences are far greater. He returns home poor and discontented. It must be acknowledged that if the Company's officers were excluded, they would have more reason to complain.

India on the whole is a fine country for military men. The art of war can be no where studied with more success than in the long campaigns which every soldier there experiences. Europeans may preserve health, if they take care. It is now well known that removal to the northern parts of India renovates the constitution after being relaxed by residence in the southern quarter of Hindostan. My experience authorises me to state, that the best plan for government to adopt, when a regiment arrives in India, from either Europe, or the Cape of Good Hope, is to station it for some time on the sea coast, where the commanding officer should be directed to have bathing parades three mornings every week, and on the alternate days exercise marches of about ten miles, or useful drills. Soldiers should not be paraded sooner than an hour before sunrise, nor should they be kept out too long, under the increasing heat of the day. Yet I am persuaded, that exposure to the sun, when an European is climatized, is not injurious to health, provided the fluids of the body be left to their natural powers of preserving due temperature. If they be irritated by gross food or spirituous liquor, fever and liver complaints are the consequences. The night air on the sea coast is delightful to the senses. Our soldiers, if not prevented, will carry out their mats and sleep under its bewitching freshness, but it is dangerous unless the body and head are well covered. After climatization the night air in the interior seems to be as little injurious to health as the noon-day rays of the sun.

After a regiment has had this seasoning for a few months on the sea-coast, it should be sent into the Deccan, or Mysore, which regions, being elevated about 3000 feet above the level of the sea, are cool and healthful. The corps, in the course of a few years, might be marched to the northern stations to receive the benefit of streams of air flowing from mountains of snow. Thus Europeans would, in my humble opinion, preserve health for ten or twelve years, and return to their country with unbroken constitutions, even after twenty years' residence in the East.

The East India Company's army has lately in its formation been considerably improved. Instead of a regiment of two battalions being placed under one colonel, each battalion has now a general officer at its head. This arrangement not only provides for a great many veteran officers, but gives a spirit to each separate corps which it had not on the old system. In short, the aspect of affairs in India is at present most flourishing.

In future ages when the historian shall look back on the records of time, he will pause in unqualified admiration at the space which the Honourable East India Company of England fill in the annals of the world. What will he behold? A company of British merchants struggling with the greatest difficulties, and overcoming kings and principalities by the force of integrity, perseverance, enterprise, and industry. Unambitious of empire, yet forced by the ambition of their enemies to become sovereigns; placed upon thrones to which they never aspired, by the efforts of others to deprive them of their property, and to drive them out of a country in which they had been permitted to settle; inclined to spare the fallen and raise the oppressed; sometimes made unwilling parties to the grasping desires of their servants, but ever anxious to expose their villany to public execration. If national gratitude be due for great and signal services rendered to our country, every Briton owes a large sum to the East India Company. In short, Providence seems to have raised them up as one of the great supports of England in her long and mighty struggle for political existence.

INDEX.

THE END.